The Story of
America's
Musical Theater

The Story of America's Musical Theater

DAVID EWEN

CHILTON BOOK COMPANY

PHILADELPHIA   NEW YORK   LONDON

Copyright © 1961, 1968 by David Ewen

Revised Edition   *All Rights Reserved*

Published in Philadelphia by Chilton Book Company

Library of Congress Catalog Card Number 68-13261

Designed by William E. Lickfield

Manufactured in the United States of America
by Quinn & Boden Company, Inc., Rahway, N. J.

Contents

The Story of
America's
Musical Theater

OVERTURE:

More Lives than One

Our story begins in a courtroom. The city is Charleston, South Carolina; the time, evening of February 8, 1735. The people of Charleston have converged on their courthouse to attend, not a trial, but the performance of a musical play. Without stage, scenery, or costumes— without footlights or limelight—a group of entertainers are presenting *Flora*, an English ballad opera.

This was the first musical production given in the Colonies. For this reason, that evening in 1735 was when the American musical theater was born.

Yet, the American musical theater has had more births than one, since it has also had several lives. Each time reborn it reappeared in a new shape and form, with a new personality and identity. Each time reborn it inherited from earlier incarnations now one trait, now one feature, now others.

From *Flora* our musical theater inherited a spoken play with interpolated popular tunes and timely lyrics. Thus a frame had been created. More and more details of the picture would come in that frame each time our musical theater was reborn.

Take, for example, the year 1828, when John Poole starred in a burlesque treatment of Shakespeare's *Hamlet*. This, too, was a year of birth for our musical theater since a new form came into being—that of burlesque. Burlesque in 1828—and for some decades thereafter—did

1

not mean the same thing it did in the 1890's and the early 1900's. In the early 19th century, burlesques meant parodies or travesties: satires on famous plays, performers, dancers—in song, dance, pantomime, dialogue. *La Mosquita,* in or about 1838, made fun of the celebrated Viennese ballet dancer Fanny Elssler in her performance in *Tarantella.* E. E. Rice's *Evangeline,* in 1874, was an outlandish, rowdy take-off of Longfellow's poem of the same name. Similar parodies and satires flourished on the American stage for about half a century; and from them the musical theater of a later day took broad humor and caricatures.

Female pulchritude became an important element of this form of entertainment in 1869 when Lydia Thompson and her English blondes shocked New York by appearing in skin-colored tights in the burlesque *Ixion.* Before many years passed, girls in pink tights—and not satire and parody—would distinguish burlesque entertainment.

Say, if you will, that our musical theater was born on February 17, 1843, at the Chatham Square Theater, and you will surely find many to agree with you. A new kind of stage entertainment was introduced that evening by The Virginia Minstrels headed by Dan Emmett. That entertainment consisted of Negro songs accompanied by the banjo, and Negro dances; an exchange of light banter; other types of variety or vaudeville entertainment. The performers wore blue swallowtail coats, striped calico shirts, white pantaloons, and blackened their faces. Thus the minstrel show came into being—the first authentically American kind of musical production seen in the United States, one that dominated the American theater for about half a century. Dan Emmett today is perhaps best remembered as the composer of "Dixie," one of the most famous ballads to come out of the Civil War; also of such popular tunes as "Old Dan Tucker" and "The Blue Tail Fly," the latter sometimes known as "Jim Crack Corn." He was, to be sure, one of America's first impor-

2

tant popular composers. But beyond this he was also the creator of the minstrel show.

Necessity was the mother of this invention. During the depression of 1842 many theaters had to close down and thus threw numerous actors out of work. Dan Emmett, a popular blackface entertainer of that period, was one of those who suddenly found himself unemployed. Realizing that there were not enough bookings around for single acts, he and three of his friends joined up in a new act made up entirely of Negro-type entertainment. Baptizing themselves The Virginia Minstrels they tried out their material successfully in a New York billiard parlor, and then opened at the Chatham Square Theater.

The Virginia Minstrels was a sensation. Overnight the minstrel show became a favored form of stage entertainment and, as a result, troupes sprouted like mushrooms in all parts of the country. The most famous of these new groups was the one headed by Ed Christy, with whom the pattern of the minstrel became standardized. From this time on all minstrel shows were divided into three parts. The first, known as the "olio," consisted of variety, or vaudeville, entertainment. The performers sat in a single row on the stage; on either end sat Mr. Tambo and Mr. Bones, while Mr. Interlocutor was in the middle. Mr. Interlocutor asked questions; Mr. Tambo or Mr. Bones responded with puns and gags. Between this exchange, one or another of the company would step forth to sing a song or dance. Sometimes the entire group joined in a choral number.

The second section was called "fantasia." Individual members of the cast were given greater latitude in exhibiting their gifts as singers and dancers. The minstrel show ended with a burlesque section in which some of the earlier routines were parodied.

The minstrel show was the first form of American stage entertainment for which important popular music was written. Dan Emmett conceived all of his best-known songs for minstrel shows, including "Dixie."

3

"Dixie" started out as a "walk around," or finale, for one of his minstrel productions, introduced in New York on April 4, 1859. Only after the Civil War broke out did the Southland confiscate the melody for its most rousing battle hymn. Among other outstanding popular tunes to come out of minstrel shows, and which are still remembered, are "The Big Sunflower," "Lubly Fan," "Polly Wolly Doodle," and "The Buffalo Girls." Finally, it was for Ed Christy's minstrels that America's foremost popular composer of his generation, Stephen Foster, wrote his first classics, including "Old Folks at Home" (or "Swanee River"), "Massa's in De Cold, Cold Ground," and "My Old Kentucky Home," all three introduced by Ed Christy between 1851 and 1853.

But the minstrel show made an even greater contribution to show business than merely providing a showcase for some wonderful songs. It helped pave the way for several later forms of entertainment. The "olio" part was the embryo from which grew vaudeville. The "fantasia" section was the predecessor of the Broadway revue. And the burlesque finale was the prototype for travesties later put on so successfully by comedians like Harrigan and Hart and Weber and Fields.

There are many historians who say that the American musical theater was born on September 12, 1866, when *The Black Crook* opened at Niblo's Garden in New York.

Never before had America seen a stage spectacle such as this! For five and a half hours the audience was held captive to spellbinding sights: spectacular stage effects, lavish scenes, grandiose ballets, breathtaking production numbers. The confused plot by Charles M. Barras, which tied the whole thing together, involved a "black crook" who makes a pact with the Devil to deliver a human soul each year. The fact that the play itself made little sense bothered no one. What *was* important was the staggering succession of scenic marvels. Now the audience witnessed a hurricane in the Harz Mountains of Germany;

now, a ballet of gems; now, a ritual by demons; now, fairies ascending and descending on silver couches; now, angels transported in gilded chariots.

The Black Crook proved a sensation. Its run of more than 400 performances was the longest thus far achieved by any production; but in its numerous subsequent revivals this extravaganza rolled up more than 2000 performances. The initial production brought in the-then unprecedented profit of over a million dollars. Since success of such dimensions always inspired imitation, *The Black Crook* was directly responsible for making the extravaganza an extremely popular form of theater during the next few decades.

The emphasis which *The Black Crook* placed on elaborate staging, big ensembles, ballets, and ornate production numbers was one of several reasons why it is often described as America's first musical comedy. Another reason was that it is here chorus girls first became a salient, attractive, and indispensable feature of musicals. It is also here that slyly suggestive songs further injected sex interest—especially a number like "You Naughty, Naughty Men," in which Milly Cavendish came to the front of the stage and wagged her forefinger at the men in the first rows. Because of the chorus girls and suggestive songs, *The Black Crook* was denounced from pulpit and in the press as a scandalous show. Then as now this merely served to pique the curiosity of even respectable people, and sent a steady stream of customers to the box office. Some saw the show several times. Women (who at that time rarely went to theater) wore heavy veils to hide their identity as they made their way into the theater.

Yes, *The Black Crook* did suggest some of the ritual later characterizing musical comedy. But for all that it was not a musical comedy as we recognize that genre today. Still several rebirths had to take place before the personality and physiognomy of musical comedy could be crystallized.

In the year 1874, on July 27, our musical theater was

again reincarnated at Niblo's Garden—this time with the burlesque *Evangeline,* which we have already mentioned in passing. There were two significant developments passed on by *Evangeline* to its successors. One was the term "musical comedy," which was now used for the first time to describe this form of stage play: In publicizing *Evangeline,* E. E. Rice—author of text and music —said he hoped his production would "foster a taste for musical comedy." Another important development in *Evangeline* was that this was the first occasion when an *entire* original musical score was created directly for a specific production; up to now, musicals, while sometimes introducing a few new numbers, were made up mainly of adaptations and interpolations of familiar tunes.

The year 1879 provides two dates when the American musical theater returned in new guises. On May 12, *The Brook*—book and lyrics by Nate Salsbury, music consisting of adaptations—was a pioneer effort to achieve some kind of unity among plot, dialogue, and characters. This was a farce built around mishaps attending a picnic in the country. The plot was trivial, the humor obvious, the characterization nondescript. Nevertheless, the attempt to create a book musical for the first time—and bring to it both naturalism and Americanism—represented a milestone. *The Brook* was also the first American musical given in London.

Earlier that same year of 1879, on January 13, still another significant stage event took place, still another rebirth, if you will: *The Mulligan Guard,* a burlesque-extravaganza by Ed Harrigan and Tony Hart. For a half dozen years Harrigan and Hart offered their farces about the Mulligan family and its friends which made stage history. Harrigan wrote text and lyrics. Hart helped him in writing the text. And the music—always original rather than adaptations or interpolations—was the work of David Braham, the official composer for all these productions.

The Harrigan and Hart burlesques grew out of the

early parodies and travesties of the early 1800's and the burlesque routines in the minstrel show. But Harrigan and Hart created a stage world all their own. Theirs was a broad caricature of life in New York among such national and racial groups as the Irish, the Germans, and the Negroes. This, then, was one of the earliest examples of musical theater calling upon ordinary Americans as characters and placing them in everyday situations. The humor came not merely from the blundering way in which these people tried to solve their homespun problems, but also from their individual speech and behavior patterns, and their personal mannerisms. The Mulligans consisted of Dan (always portrayed by Harrigan), his wife, Cordelia, their son, Tom, and their colored maid, Rebecca. The Mulligans, and those closest to them in their neighborhood, were carried through all sorts of adventures and episodes—all of them true to life—in productions called *The Mulligan Guard's Picnic, The Mulligan Guard's Chowder, The Mulligan Guard's Christmas, The Mulligan Guard's Silver Wedding,* and so on. Songs and dances were liberally sprinkled throughout the play to add further spice to these gay proceedings. And the play was usually brought to a close with a variety show. Not the least of the assets of these vivacious, American musicals were Braham's songs. The best and the most popular of these were "The Babies on Our Block," "The Skidmores' Masquerade," "Paddy Duffy's Cart," and "My Dad's Dinner Pail."

Harrigan and Hart broke up their partnership in 1885. With that rupture the stage life of the Mulligans ended.

After the end of the Civil War European comic operas began to influence the American stage. The French variety—known as opéra-bouffe—became a vogue in New York after the première of Jacques Offenbach's *La Grand Duchesse de Gerolstein* on September 24, 1867, starring the vivacious French star, Lucille Tostée. Opéra-bouffes from France flooded the New York market for a decade:

Offenbach's *La Belle Hélène* came in 1868, *La Vie Parisienne* and *La Périchole* in 1869, *Barbe-bleue* in 1870; Lecocq's *Giroflé-Girofla* in 1875 and *Les Cloches de Corneville* in 1877.

As popular as opéra-bouffes were, they were thrown completely into a shade by a craze for English comic operas that followed—specifically the comic operas of Gilbert and Sullivan. This began with the American première of *Pinafore* at the Boston Museum on November 25, 1878—still another date on which our American musical theater may be said to have been reborn. Probably no foreign importation had the impact on American people as this delightful travesty on the British Admiralty. In its first season in this country 90 companies were performing it throughout the United States, 5 of these running simultaneously in New York. *Pinafore* was performed by religious organizations, children's groups, colored people. There was a Yiddish *Pinafore*, and the parodies were too numerous to mention. The *Pinafore* rage was intensified when Gilbert and Sullivan came to America to conduct an authorized version of their comic opera on December 1, 1879 (all the earlier ones had been pirated). On the stage, in the streets, in the nation's living rooms, Sullivan's melodies were hummed, whistled, sung. Sayings like "for he's an Englishman" or "What never? No, never!" became favorite catch phrases.

In rapid succession all the other popular Gilbert and Sullivan comic operas were heard in America. *The Pirates of Penzance* received its official world première in New York on December 31, 1879, under the personal supervision of Gilbert and Sullivan. The world première of *Iolanthe* took place simultaneously in London and New York on November 25, 1882. The American première of *Princess Ida* was shared by New York and Boston on February 11, 1884. The disease of Gilbert and Sullivan infected Americans in the same way it did Englishmen. Indeed, this very infection spread even to American librettists and composers. In short order there now appeared American-made comic operas—and with it arose a new genus in the musical theater.

In 1879, John Philip Sousa (later on America's march king, composer of such march classics as *The Stars and Stripes Forever*) completed writing the score for the first of the dozen or so comic operas, *The Smugglers*. It was a failure. Sousa's greatest success for the stage did not come until 1896 with *El Capitan* (out of which comes the well-known Sousa march of the same name). But before this happened, there was produced in Philadelphia in 1886 the first successful comic opera of American authorship: *The Little Tycoon*, book, lyrics, and music by Willard Spencer. After a run of 500 performances in Philadelphia, *The Little Tycoon* went on to New York for another extended engagement.

The Little Tycoon points up the way in which the comic operas of Gilbert and Sullivan stimulated Americans to imitation. For it is second cousin—if, indeed, not a brother—to *The Mikado* which had been introduced in New York on August 20, 1885. Spencer's text was a satire (with highly recognizable Gilbertian nuances and accents) on Japanese dress and behavior, though it specifically directed its laughter at the weakness of many Americans for foreign titles of nobility. One of its principal characters is General Knickerbocker, an American striving to see his daughter marry a lord, even though she is in love with an American boy. At the General's estate in Newport, Rhode Island, the boy comes disguised as "the great tycoon" of Japan. He is ceremoniously welcomed, as he disports himself with all the exotic mannerisms, behavior, and dress Americans ascribe to Orientals. Before long, the General is only too happy to consider so noble a character as a prospective son-in-law.

If the text brings up continual reminders of W. S. Gilbert, Spencer's music also echoes and re-echoes the sententious phrases on the one hand, and the tripping fig-

9

ures on the other, of Arthur Sullivan—particularly in numbers like "Doomed Am I to Marry a Lord" and "Sad Heart of Mine."

On the crest of the wave of foreign importations from Europe came operettas from Austria and Germany. Where the opéra-bouffe and the comic opera accented the absurd and the nonsensical, wit and satire, the operetta stressed sweetness and sentimentality, glamour and romance. From the 1870's on—and for about half a century after that—the American stage paid host to virtually all of Europe's best loved operettas. It was no coincidence then that when the Casino Theater opened in New York on October 22, 1882 as a home for musical productions its first attraction should be a European operetta, Johann Strauss's *The Queen's Lace Handkerchief*. Already the operetta form was as beloved in New York as it was in its own habitat abroad. Between 1882 and 1889, 35 European operettas were seen at the Casino Theater. Nor was its popularity confined to New York alone. In one year alone—that of 1894–1895—14 companies toured the United States with foreign operettas.

The operetta, like the comic opera, soon found American librettists and composers ready and willing to write works for the stage in that style. America's first significant operetta was *Robin Hood*, in 1890. America's first significant operetta composer was the one who created its music—Reginald de Koven. De Koven, born in Middletown, Connecticut, in 1859, was trained in Europe as a serious musician. His youthful ambition lay in the direction of symphonies, concertos, and operas. After returning from Europe in 1882 and settling in Chicago, he married into wealth and engaged in business and real-estate speculations. He finally decided to abandon commerce and return to music, having by this time accumulated a considerable fortune.

While visiting Minneapolis he met a young writer, Harry B. Smith, who was interested in doing librettos for the musical stage and lyrics for songs. De Koven was encouraged by Smith to try the lighter side of music; and though he subsequently wrote some serious operas, the lighter side proved De Koven's forte. In 1888, Smith and De Koven wrote their first comic opera, *The Begum.* A "begum" is an Indian princess, and in the comic opera she is allowed to have as many husbands as she desires. But before long she grows tired of one of them, who happens to be a general, and in order to get rid of him she is compelled to create a war. Once again it is not too difficult to see the influence of *The Mikado* on the authors of *The Begum,* but with none too happy results. *The Begum* was a dismal failure, and so was their second comic opera, *Don Quixote.* But in 1890 they turned from comic opera to operetta and wrote a work that is still occasionally revived, and one of whose musical numbers has kept the name of Reginald de Koven alive. The operetta was *Robin Hood,* and the song it introduced was "Oh, Promise Me" to whose sentimental strains young Americans everywhere have joined hands in matrimony for many years now.

Robin Hood is, of course, based on the exploits of the one-time Earl become outlaw who, during the rule of Richard I of England, robbed from the rich to give to the poor. In Smith's play he frustrates the nefarious efforts of his enemy, the Sheriff of Nottingham, to get Guy of Gisborne married to the lovely Maid Marian; Robin Hood engages the Sheriff in battle and defeats him; and in the end, by royal decree, he is pardoned for his escapades and his wealth, title, and confiscated lands are restored to him.

The song, "Oh, Promise Me" was not originally in the *Robin Hood* score, but was an independent number, with lyrics by Clement Scott, which De Koven had published before *Robin Hood* was written. When a sentimental number was needed during the rehearsals of *Robin Hood* for the character of Alan-a-Dale, De Koven, instead of writing one, tried to get his published song accepted.

11

Nobody seemed to think it would do, including Jessie Bartlett Davis who was appearing as Alan-a-Dale. But De Koven's melody, somehow, stuck in her mind. The next day, in her dressing room, she began singing it, but an octave lower than written. The producer shouted to her excitedly: "Oh, Jessie, if you ever sing that song as you're singing it now, on the lower octave, it will make your reputation!" Only then did she consent to do the number in the play, and it was inserted into the third act just before the impending marriage of Guy and Maid Marian. The song helped to make a stage celebrity of Jessie Bartlett Davis, as the producer had prophesied. But not even he could have guessed the part it would play in making *Robin Hood* a stage classic.

Now that the American musical theater had given birth to its first successful comic opera, and its first successful operetta, many other writers and composers were impelled to write in a similar vein. In 1891 came *Wang*, once again in imitation of *The Mikado;* in 1892, *The Isle of Champagne;* in 1894, *Prince Ananias.*

The première of *Prince Ananias* was a red-letter day in the American theater, for it introduced America's first significant composer for the stage—Victor Herbert. Herbert is the first composer for the American theater whose best songs are still as fresh, and still as much loved, as they were in their own day. (De Koven, while coming before Herbert, is remembered only for a single song and consequently cannot be put in Herbert's class.) Herbert's best operettas and comic operas are among the first in our theater still to be continually revived on stage and screen, still able to afford pleasure and nostalgia to American audiences. Consequently, it is with Victor Herbert that the story of the American musical theater as we know it today can really be said to have begun.

And so, perhaps if only one date must be picked out as that when our musical theater was born, it might be November 20, 1894, when *Prince Ananias* was produced.

A King of Storybook Realms

Whether placed in some make-believe world like Grau-stark or Ruritania—or in the actual world, but with a picturesque or exotic setting—the operetta occupied story-book realms. Princes and princesses, saber-rattling officers, fine-plumed ladies, elegant gentlemen became enmeshed in intrigues from which the virtuous always emerged tri-umphant; the evildoers always met their just punishment; and the hero always won the heroine. Sentimentality fil-tered through the fiber of the operetta like a spray of perfume, and glamour endowed it with radiant colors. Romance was the silken thread on which to bead the pearls of ear-caressing tunes, colorful dances, and eye-arresting production numbers.

The operetta had the single function of entertaining. It did not matter if the plot was so confused that it often failed to make sense, or so unbelievable that it was im-possible to identify these goings-on with the world outside the theater. It did not matter if the long arm of coincidence was continually recruited to unravel the plot entangle-ments. It did not matter if a song, a dance, or a funny epi-sode had little or no relevance to the over-all story but was grafted onto the body of the operetta like foreign tissue just because it happened to suit the talent of some particu-lar star or because it had audience appeal. Nor did it matter that the characters were made from the same cardboard and papier-mâché as the scenery. But what did matter—

and matter a great deal—was that the scenes and costumes were nice to look at, the tunes delightful to listen to, and the performers pleasant to watch. The senses had to be catered to, never the intellect.

Such was the formula to which the operetta composers of Europe remained faithful: the Franz von Suppés, the Johann Strausses, the Karl Millöckers, the Franz Lehárs, and the Oscar Strauses. And such was the formula with which Victor Herbert was willing to operate. Herbert was of Irish birth and German training. Though all his operettas were written in America for American consumption he remained basically a European composer. Before coming to the United States he had been steeped in the musical and stage traditions of Europe. He was quite happy to conform to the conventions of the European operetta which he had loved from his childhood on. The music he wrote for his American operettas remained European in identity: essentially Irish in the sentiment and sweetness of melody, essentially German in harmonic idiom and orchestration.

Herbert, then, was no innovator. He did not inaugurate a new epoch for the stage, no more than he initiated a new musical style. He was the point of culmination for an era that had preceded him and in which De Koven and Willard Spencer had emerged. In his attitudes toward the stage, and in all his music, Herbert preferred to look not forward but backward. He was the summation of what had been happening on our stage for several years, not the starting point for new directions. Yet, being a genius, he managed to bring to our theater music a freshness, a charm, a loveliness, and a spontaneity it had thus far not known. His operetta songs are still very much with us, still a part of us, still capable of wooing and winning ear and heart. "My idea of heaven," once said Andrew W. Carnegie, "is to be able to sit and listen to the music of Victor Herbert all I want to."

For all his pronounced musical gifts—and, make no mistake about it, they *were* pronounced—Victor Herbert had a serious fault as a workman within the theater. The text and the lyric for which he wrote his music never concerned him particularly. He rarely rejected anything as being either too stilted, too stylized, too dull, or too naive. The trite situations and the stock plots which his librettists so often provided him satisfied him, and he never questioned their validity. The cliché-ridden lyrics for which he fashioned such wonderful melodies bothered him not at all. Like Franz Schubert, Victor Herbert could have set a menu to unforgettable music if he had a mind to do so. Music came so easily to him that his head was always swimming with the most radiant tunes. He had no difficulty ever in lifting as many musical ideas as he might need at any given moment for whatever libretto or lyric demanded a setting.

His incomparable facility and spontaneity made it possible for him to work on as many as four scores simultaneously. Each would lie on a separate table in his study. He would progress from one to the next like a wine sampler tasting vintages. Now he would write a song for one operetta, now an instrumental interlude for another, now complete some orchestration for the third, and now sketch a humorous ditty for the fourth. The fact that each of the four operettas had a different time, setting, or mood did not impede the flow of his music, nor, for that matter, did it influence the character of his writing.

He could in a month's time, even while engrossed with sundry other assignments, finish a complete score down to its orchestration—for, unlike most of our present-day popular composers for the stage, Herbert did his own orchestrations. "He would come in and work out a scene in my office," once recalled Florenz Ziegfeld, "and the next morning appear with the full orchestration." In less than 40 years he completed the scores for about 50 operettas, not to mention many independent numbers for various revues and musical comedies. At the same time he produced a library of serious music for concert hall and opera house.

It has been said that Herbert's songs sound better outside the theater than in it. Such is the nondescript personality of Herbert's melodies that they have very little connection either with the characters who deliver them or the stage business that surrounds them. Consequently, the impact of these melodies on the listener is often increased when one of them is no longer burdened by the stage nonsense that envelops them. It can also be said that Herbert's songs also sound better without their lyrics, and for the same reason that they improve away from the textual content. The lyric rarely adds anything, and often it detracts from, the musical interest.

These two observations point up Herbert's weaknesses as a creative force in the theater. His sole aim as a composer was to write beautiful, easy-flowing tunes—and few in America have accomplished this more successfully. That these tunes were written for the stage—or for a particular situation on the stage—was just a necessary coincidence. Herbert might just as easily have been a song composer working in Tin Pan Alley and producing songs solely for sheet-music publication. I doubt seriously if he would have been any less the song genius for all that, or if his place in American music would have been less secure.

Victor Herbert was born in Dublin, Ireland, on February 1, 1859. When his father died, Victor (age three) went with his mother to live in his grandfather's country house outside London, England. The grandfather was Samuel Lover, a famous writer of ballads and novels (among the latter was *Handy Andy*). As cultured as he was famous, Samuel Lover attracted to his home some of England's foremost writers, musicians, and artists. Victor spent his impressionable childhood in a highly sophisticated environment.

When he was seven, Victor started taking piano lessons from his mother. His gift was so pronounced that the grandfather insisted that the boy be taken to Germany for comprehensive musical training. Consequently, in his eighth year, Victor and his mother went to live in the German village of Lungengaren, fronting Lake Constance. There the mother married Carl Schmid, a physician. The Schmid family now settled in Stuttgart, Germany, at whose Conservatory Victor received a thorough background in the theoretical aspects of music as well as in playing the cello. His training as cellist was completed in Baden-Baden with Bernard Cossman.

At that time Herbert aspired to be a concert cellist and serious composer. For four years he played the cello in German and Austrian symphony orchestras conducted by such world-famous musicians as Liszt, Brahms, and Saint-Saëns. Associations with the great of the music world, and playing the foremost music of all time as a member of a symphony orchestra, inspired Herbert to write two ambitious works for cello and orchestra, a concerto and a suite, which were performed in Stuttgart between 1883 and 1885.

In 1886, Herbert fell in love with Theresa Foerster, a distinguished German prima donna who had hired him to give her some coaching. They were married on August 14 of that year. A few weeks later they both set sail for the United States where Mme Foerster had been engaged to make her American debut at the Metropolitan Opera. At the same time Herbert had been hired to play the cello in that opera-house orchestra.

Except for a brief visit to England, Herbert never again left America after 1886. He became an American in deed as well as spirit, by acquiring citizenship. And as a musician he identified himself in every way he could with American music. He played in, and he conducted, American symphony orchestras; he appeared at major American music festivals. In 1893 he succeeded Patrick S. Gilmore as conductor of the renowned 22nd Regiment Band. From 1898 to 1904 he was the principal conductor of the Pittsburgh Symphony, and in 1904 he organized an orchestra of his own for the performance of salon music.

As a serious composer, he began writing *American* music—music with a strong national identity. In time he completed compositions like the *American Fantasia* which was based on American national anthems and culminated with a rousing adaptation of "The Star-Spangled Banner," and the opera *Natoma,* on an American–Indian subject, introduced in Philadelphia in 1911. In 1916 he became the first American composer writing an original score for a motion picture, *The Fall of a Nation.*

All such achievements were impressive; they would have won for Herbert a place of honor in the musical life of our country. Yet all this is now obscured by his greatest contribution of all to American culture, his music for our popular theater.

Herbert's first attempt to write music for the stage came during the Chicago World Fair when he was asked to write some numbers for a pageant. As it turned out, the pageant was never produced, and Herbert's music never performed. Soon after that, Lillian Russell—one of the most glamorous singing stars of the New York stage —encouraged Herbert to write an operetta for her. *La Vivandière* as that operetta was named was never performed, as Lillian Russell soon lost heart in appearing in a musical by an unknown composer; and its manuscript has been lost.

Then an offer came to Herbert from a light-opera company in Boston which had been founded in 1879 to produce *Pinafore.* William MacDonald, its director, was encouraged by the then recent success of De Koven's *Robin Hood* to put on an American operetta, and he asked Victor Herbert to write the music for *Prince Ananias,* its libretto by Francis Neilson. The setting was 16th-century France, and the plot involved an outlaw, a nobleman's daughter, and the title character. *Prince Ananias* opened at the Broadway Theater in New York on November 20, 1894. Many critics did not like Neilson's text at all, but some of them had kind things to say about Herbert's music. What was particularly appealing in that score was the song "Amaryllis," whose "wistful melancholy . . .

18

delicate accompaniment and the interpolation of a dainty minuet make this a truly extraordinary selection," as Edward N. Waters has written.

Prince Ananias was no box-office triumph by any means, but it did well enough to encourage the light-opera company to take it on tour. To a novice like Herbert, this was all the encouragement he needed to make him go on writing operettas. And he did not stop until he had written over forty; and he was stopped only by death.

Many an operetta in the 1890's and 1900's came into existence only because some producer happened to have a star under contract for whom he needed a show. The producer would then call on a librettist and composer to manufacture such a vehicle. The librettist would create a character suiting the personality of this particular star and contrive incidents best calculated to set off his or her talent. After that it was not difficult for him to work out some convenient story, and to build up the machinery setting that story into motion. In the same way a composer would write his music, keeping in mind the range and the quality of a star's voice.

It was by such a synthetic process that Victor Herbert achieved his first successful operettas. Kirke La Shelle, manager of the Boston light-opera company that had produced *Prince Ananias,* was starting a producing firm of his own. For his initial venture he wanted an operetta for Frank Daniels, a popular stage comedian he had under contract, but who up to that time had never been seen in a musical production. La Shelle consulted Harry B. Smith, librettist of *Robin Hood.* Smith was a highly competent hand in manufacturing plays to any given specifications and consequently became one of the most prolific and successful writers of operetta and comic-opera texts in his day. Smith had some ideas about a farce with an Oriental setting. It did not take him long to devise an important role for Frank Daniels and to write out a full-length libretto. La Shelle suggested that Herbert write the music, and that job also went quickly. *The Wizard of the Nile,* as the completed product was named, came to the Casino Theater in New York on November 4, 1895, after trying out in several cities. It scored decisively, and went on for another extended tour.

Frank Daniels played Kibosh, a fake Persian magician who had come to Egypt when that country was being stricken by a drought. Knowing that the Nile was about to overflow, Kibosh uses hocus-pocus to convince the Egyptian king that his talent with necromancy can relieve the country's plight. The Nile overflows—but overplentifully. Egypt now threatened by floods, the king demands that Kibosh use his magic to arrest the tides. When the magician fails, he is condemned to die in a sealed tomb. By one of those happy accidents that can occur only in the world of the operetta, the Egyptian king becomes imprisoned in that tomb with Kibosh. But both manage to escape doom, and the king—grateful for getting a new lease on life—magnanimously forgives Kibosh.

As Kibosh, Frank Daniels romped around the stage with exaggerated and absurd motions of the body; grimaced, accenting his remarks with a personal way of arching a trick eyebrow; and indulged in many of the other antics for which he had become famous on spoken stage. The audiences loved him, could not have enough of him. A phrase he used continually throughout the play—"Am I a wiz?"—soon became so popular that New Yorkers everywhere (and after that the whole country) were repeating it *ad nauseam.* His robust way of delivering a comic song helped make "That's One Thing a Wizard Can Do" a highlight of the show. But the best numbers in Herbert's score—a warning of his later mature powers—came with tender, sentimental moods expressed in the waltz, "Star Light, Star Bright" and in "My Angelina."

Several of Herbert's most popular operettas after that were specifically built as a pedestal on which some attractive star could stand. *The Fortune Teller* (1898) was written for Alice Nielsen, a Victor Herbert discovery. In 1897, Herbert had cast Hilda Clark for the leading female role in *The Serenade*. Soon after the signing of this contract, Herbert heard Nielsen sing at the Murray Hill Theater. Though she was at the time an inexperienced performer, and had never appeared on Broadway, Herbert knew that she was the one to play Yvonne in *The Serenade*. With Hilda Clark already signed for that role, a convenient arrangement was devised whereby the two women played the lead on alternate nights. But it was Alice Nielsen who became identified with *The Serenade*. And one year after that it was for Alice Nielsen, now a star, that Herbert and Harry B. Smith had to write a new operetta. The result was one of Herbert's classics, *The Fortune Teller,* in which Nielsen soared to still greater heights of popularity.

She was cast in a dual role: as Musette, a gypsy fortune teller, and Irma, a ballet student. As Musette, she was in love with Sandor, a gypsy violinist; as Irma, her sweetheart was a Hungarian Hussar, Ladislas. Since Musette and Irma look alike they can pass themselves off as each other. In this way, Irma eludes the unwelcome advances of Count Berezowsky. Both girls finally get the men they love.

In *The Fortune Teller* Herbert adapts his sentimental Irish lyricism and solid Germanic harmonies to music pulsing with the heartbeat, and throbbing with the pulse, of Hungarian gypsy music. The score overflows with sensuous gypsy melodies and stirring Hungarian choruses. One of the most languorous and passionate melodies Herbert ever wrote is in such a gypsy style: "Gypsy Love Song," sometimes also known as "Slumber On, My Little Gypsy Sweetheart," with which Sandor serenades his beloved Musette.

It Happened in Nordland (1904) was conceived for Marie Cahill, who was seen as an American Ambassadress to the court of the mythical kingdom of Nordland. This was half a century before Irving Berlin wrote *Call Me Madam,* also about a brash American Ambassadress in a fictitious realm. But if *It Happened in Nordland* is remembered it is not because it anticipates Irving Berlin, but because out of it came two sophisticated numbers: "Absinthe Frappé" and "Al Fresco." The latter was an instrumental episode serving as background music for a carnival scene with which the second act opens. Before he had written his score for *It Happened in Nordland,* Herbert had published *Al Fresco* as a piano piece under a pseudonym (that of "Frank Roland"), his purpose being to see if it could become popular even if it was the work of an unknown composer. When the sheet music sold remarkably well, Herbert became convinced of its merit and adapted it for his operetta.

Mlle. Modiste (1905) was also written for a female singing star—in this instance, Fritzi Scheff, formerly a member of the Metropolitan Opera Company. In 1903 Herbert had induced her to leave the Metropolitan to star in one of his operettas, *Babette.* Her conversion from grand opera to operetta appeared at first to be a mistake, for *Babette* was a failure. But Victor Herbert promised to make amends by writing a new operetta where she could be set off to greater advantage. As Fifi in *Mlle. Modiste* Fritzi Scheff proved such a triumph that henceforth she was remembered for this performance alone, and specifically for her unforgettable rendition of one of Herbert's best sentimental waltzes, "Kiss Me Again."

"Kiss Me Again" had a strange history. It was written neither for *Mlle. Modiste* nor for Fritzi Scheff, having been put down on paper two years before the operetta went into production. The story goes—it is undoubtedly apocryphal—that on the opening night of *Babette,* Herbert went backstage to kiss his star. "Kiss me again," Fritzi Scheff whispered to him coquettishly—a chance remark said to have then given Herbert an idea for a waltz. In any event he did write this waltz in 1903, the year

22

of *Babette*. Unable to find a place for it at the time he put it aside for future use.

Our story of "Kiss Me Again" now becomes stranger still. As first heard in *Mlle. Modiste* it was not a sentimental waltz but a satirical number. In the first act, Fifi tries to show off her talent as a singer by performing a number called "If I Were on the Stage" in which several song styles were parodied. As a country maid she sings a gavotte; as a highborn French lady, a polonaise. Both were caricatures of their respective musical forms, and so was the waltz that followed. For his waltz parody Herbert reached into his trunk and pulled out the sentimental melody he had written two years earlier. When Fritzi Scheff stopped the show with it, Herbert wisely decided to revamp his melody into the main love song of the operetta and to present it as a dreamy tune instead of a parody.

The setting of *Mlle. Modiste* is Paris, where Fifi is employed as a salesgirl in a fashionable shop. She is in love with Captain Etienne de Bouvray, but his proud family can never consider his marrying a shopgirl. A wealthy American now becomes interested in her and finances her career in music. Under the stage name of Mme Bellini she becomes a famous prima donna who comes to perform at a party given at the De Bouvray estate. She completely wins the hearts of her audience with her singing. Once she reveals to the De Bouvrays who she really is, they are no longer reluctant to sanction her marriage with Etienne.

If *Mlle. Modiste* was Fritzi Scheff's operetta, then *Naughty Marietta* (1910) was Emma Trentini's. Like Scheff, Trentini had come from grand opera, and like Scheff again she was to become most famous in operetta. *Naughty Marietta* was tailor-made to fit her personality and voice: her personality with the title role, a fetching 18th-century lady of noble birth who had fled from Naples to New Orleans to avoid an undesirable marriage;

her voice with a song that finds Herbert at the peak of his lyric powers, "Ah, Sweet Mystery of Life," the composer's greatest success from the point of view of sheet-music sales. "Ah, Sweet Mystery of Life" plays an important part in the story. The heroine, Marietta, has heard a fragment of this melody in a dream. She promises to marry anybody who can finish the song for her. The hero, Captain Dick Warrington, is the one who completes the melody and wins her hand. But Herbert's remarkable score for *Naughty Marietta* had other winners besides this one. With "I'm Falling in Love with Someone," "Italian Street Song," and the virile "Tramp, Tramp, Tramp," Herbert's winning hand here boasted four aces.

It was not for a female singing star but for a pair of male comedians that *The Red Mill* (1906) was contrived. The comedians were Fred Stone and David Montgomery, who three years earlier had scored in the Broadway extravaganza, *The Wizard of Oz*. In *The Red Mill* the part of Con Kidder was devised for Fred Stone, and that of Kid Conner, for David Montgomery. They are two footloose, penniless Americans, stranded in a small Dutch town where they help to promote and bring to a happy resolution the uneasy romance of Gretchen and Captain Doris van Damm. One scene in particular was worked out to permit these comedians to go to town in their brand of tomfoolery. Gretchen is being forced to marry the Governor of Zeeland. The two Americans try to prevent this marriage from taking place by continually bursting into the wedding festivities in sundry disguises: as Italian organ grinders; as Sherlock Holmes and Dr. Watson; and so forth. In this scene, as the Italian organ grinders, they present one of the show's best comedy songs, "Good-a-bye, John." The romantic numbers—"The Isle of Our Dreams" and "Moonbeams"—are, of course, assigned to the hero and heroine for other scenes.

Since operettas liked nothing better than exotic, glamorous settings, Victor Herbert's more than 40 operettas roamed freely in far-off places and at times to spots that exist only in the imagination. Hungary, Paris, Holland, Nordland, and New Orleans were the locales of Herbert's operettas already discussed. Others went off to even stranger and more distant points on the actual or imaginary map. *The Idol's Eye* (1897) went to India; *The Ameer* (1899), to Afghanistan; *The Singing Girl* (1899), to Linz, Austria; *The Viceroy* (1900), to Palermo; *The Tattooed Man* (1907), to Persia; *Algeria* (1908), to that colorful French Moroccan city in North Africa; *The Enchantress* (1911), to the mythical kingdom of Zergovia; *Sweethearts* (1913), to old Bruges; and *Eileen* (1917), to the west coast of Ireland.

Perhaps the most unusual setting and characters of any Victor Herbert operetta can be found in *Babes in Toyland* (1903). This was an undisguised, unashamed attempt by Glen MacDonough, the librettist, to imitate—and thus capitalize on the fame of—*The Wizard of Oz,* the sensational Broadway extravaganza that had been produced one year earlier and about which we shall speak in a later chapter. The plan was to make *Babes in Toyland* a childhood fantasy-extravaganza in the same way *The Wizard of Oz* had been. Oz was changed to Toyland, where characters from children's stories and fairy tales came to life. Little Jane and Alan flee from their miserly uncle to find refuge in the land of stories and toys. The plot was loosely constructed and at times confusing as one arresting scene and spectacle followed the other: a Christmas fiesta, a butterfly ballet, an elaborate production number called "The Legend of the Castle." Toys come to life and overthrow the tyranny of the Toymakers. Tom Thumb, Jack and Jill, Bo-Peep, Red Riding Hood become actual characters. All the elements of childhood fancy are combined to make what the New York *Dramatic Mirror* reported was "a perfect dream of delight to the children [that] will recall the happy days of childhood to those who are facing the stern realities of life." The charm of a child's make-believe world was cap-

25

tured not only in the imaginative sets, costumes, and the big scenes, but also in Herbert's enchanting music—and with particularly telling effect in the still popular "March of the Toys," the haunting song "Toyland," and in a little number, "I Can't Do That Sum" which the children sing while beating out the rhythm with chalk on slates.

Herbert remained prolific up to the end of his life. He wrote not only complete scores for operettas and musical comedies, but also special numbers for revues and for the musical comedies of other composers. He never lost his gift at completing assignments efficiently, and at times he did not even lose his talent for expressive melodies. "Thine Alone" from *Eileen*—second only to "Ah, Sweet Mystery of Life" as his greatest commercial song success —and "A Kiss in the Dark" from *Orange Blossoms* (1922) are both unmistakably Herbert.

But if there was no diminution either in his capacity to work or in his melodic talent, there was a perceptible decline in his popularity in his closing years. *Sweethearts* (1913) was Herbert's last box-office success. *Eileen* (1913), which he regarded as his best score, lasted only 64 performances. Indeed, Herbert's reign as a king of operetta ended just before World War I. "My day is over," he told a friend sadly. "They are forgetting poor old Herbert." What Herbert did not know was that, far from being forgotten, he was destined to become a classic.

He was working on some special numbers for the *Ziegfeld Follies* when he suddenly suffered a fatal heart attack on May 26, 1924 and died in his physician's office. They had hardly buried Herbert when his music acquired a fresh lease on life through the then new medium of radio. No single composer of light music was played more often over the air between 1924 and 1930 than Herbert, and no American composer of light music sold so many phonograph records as he did in that time. Revivals of his operettas mushroomed in every part of the country year after year. *The Red Mill* had a remarkable run of over 500 performances when brought back to New York in 1945 with a modernized book; and in 1947, *Sweethearts* (once again with a revised libretto) reappeared successfully on Broadway with Bobby Clark as its star. In the winter of 1960, *Babes in Toyland* was ambitiously produced for television. In all these instances critics agreed that it was Herbert's music—and that alone —which kept these operettas appealing. No amount of surgery could revive the heartbeat of texts that in the first place had little life to them.

In addition, virtually all of Herbert's operetta classics have been made into motion pictures, some of them more than once, particularly after the screen had acquired a voice. And Victor Herbert's life story was dramatized for films in 1939 in *The Great Victor Herbert.*

"He is not dead, of course," said Deems Taylor in a eulogy in 1924, and his words still hold true today. "The composer of *Babes in Toyland, The Fortune Teller, The Red Mill,* and *Mlle. Modiste* cannot be held dead by a world so heavily in his debt."

There Were Other Kings— *2* and Princes, Too

On October 21, 1907, one of the most beloved and successful European operettas ever written was introduced to New York: Franz Lehár's *The Merry Widow*. Before coming, it had had a spectacular history in Europe. In Vienna, where it had received its world première, it had one of the longest engagements in the 100-year history of the Theater-an-der-Wien. It ran for almost 800 performances in London, while in Buenos Aires it was given in five different languages, in five theaters.

Nobody seemed immune to the allure of this romance of Prince Danilo and Sonia, the heiress from Marsovia —set against the exciting background of Paris. Nobody seemed able to resist the spell of the "Merry Widow Waltz." And America proved no exception. The New York engagement, which lasted well over a year, grossed over a million dollars. Donald Brian became a matinee idol in the part of Prince Danilo. Women's fashions of that day were influenced by the wasp-waisted gown and the huge ostrich-feathered hat Sonia wore in the play. Merry Widow shoes, Merry Widow gloves, Merry Widow fans, Merry Widow undergarments were on the market. The town, in short, went *Merry Widow* crazy.

The Merry Widow helped make the European operetta even more popular in America than it had been before 1907 with the inevitable consequence that more and more Americans were writing stage works in a similar style.

Victor Herbert was in his heyday, but his were not the only American operettas delighting New York audiences. There were, for example, *Madame Sherry* in 1910, and *The Pink Lady* in 1911, each a stage success of the first magnitude. *Madame Sherry*—music by Karl Hoschna, book and lyrics by Otto Hauerbach (who later changed his name to Harbach and became one of the most prolific writers of operetta and musical-comedy texts)—played to capacity houses for almost a year. The story, exploiting the popular device of mistaken identity, passed off an Irish landlady as the socially prominent Madame Sherry. Hoschna's music included a provocative little number which set the year humming (and whose title was continually quoted by the gay blades in 1910 with sly innuendoes): "Every Little Movement Has a Meaning All Its Own."

The Pink Lady had book and lyrics by Harry Morton while the music was by Ivan Caryll, an Englishman, who had just come to make America his permanent home. Hazel Dawn, as the heroine, sang the infectious "My Beautiful Lady" while appearing to accompany herself on the violin; also "The Kiss Waltz" as she offers her beau a lesson in osculation. *The Pink Lady* smashed attendance records for the New Amsterdam Theater, and had the most successful road tour of any company in 1911. It was also responsible for making pink the stylish color in female fashions that year.

Two composers stood head and shoulders above all the others writing American operettas after 1910. They were the kings to whom Victor Herbert turned over the reign when he himself had to abdicate rule. One was Rudolf Friml, the other, Sigmund Romberg. They helped keep American operetta popular on Broadway up to 1930. With them, the American operetta reached its zenith; after them, it went into discard.

It was through Victor Herbert that Rudolf Friml became an operetta composer. Born in Prague, Czechoslovakia, on December 7, 1879—son of a humble, music-loving baker—Friml spent his boyhood getting a thorough training as concert pianist in the Prague Conservatory. After he toured Europe and America with the noted concert violinist, Jan Kubelik, late in 1906, Friml decided to remain in the United States for good. He taught piano, made concert appearances, wrote concert songs and piano pieces. His career was neither eventful nor successful when, without warning, he was lifted by his bootstraps out of his obscurity and mediocrity to wealth and fame. Chance, not design, was responsible for this dramatic change in his fortunes.

What had happened was that, in 1911, Victor Herbert was planning a new operetta for Emma Trentini, after her personal triumph in *Naughty Marietta*. When *Naughty Marietta* was on tour, Mme Trentini let her eccentricities and temperament get out of hand. If she felt like it she refused to appear at a performance. She was given to tantrums. She dictated when encores should be given and when whole numbers should be deleted. One evening, after receiving an ovation for the "Italian Street Song," she was given a signal by Victor Herbert (conducting that evening) to repeat the refrain. Haughtily she ignored him and walked off the stage. Sorely tried by his star's caprices, Herbert lost his temper. He swore never again to conduct a performance in which Mme Trentini appeared, and he announced that under no circumstances would he write a new operetta for her.

Since Arthur Hammerstein (producer of *Naughty Marietta*) had counted on that new operetta for Mme Trentini for 1912, this dramatic turn of events left him without a composer. In searching for somebody to take Herbert's place he consulted two New York music publishers, Max Dreyfus of Harms and Rudolph Schirmer of Schirmer's. Their suggestion to Hammerstein was that he gamble on a new man. They both knew a competent musician named Rudolf Friml whose published songs and piano pieces revealed a pleasing melodic style and a sound technique. While it was true that this Friml had never done any writing for the theater, both Dreyfus and Schirmer felt that he had the necessary equipment and talent for such an assignment. Hammerstein signed Friml to a contract. That stroke of the pen added a rich chapter to our stage history.

The operetta for which the unexperienced, the untested, and the unknown Rudolf Friml was hired to write music was *The Firefly*. It opened at the Lyric Theater on December 2, 1912 and stayed on for a long, profitable run before embarking on an outstandingly successful road tour. The text was the work of Otto Hauerbach (or Otto Harbach as he was later known)—neatly sculptured to Mme Trentini's histrionic gifts. As Nina, she appeared first as a street singer who disguises herself as a boy and stows away aboard a Bermuda-bound ship. One of the passengers is a playboy millionaire, Jack, with whom Nina falls in love. Years later Nina becomes a famous prima donna invited to sing at a party where Jack is one of the guests. Nina is still in love with him, and it is Jack's turn now to be smitten. Now that she is a famous singer and not just a homeless waif, nothing stands in the way of their happy union.

Harbach's libretto carried more than a faint reminder of the one written by Henry Blossom in 1905 for Herbert's *Mlle. Modiste*. But Friml's music was his own. Its strong, expressive lyricism had a personal stamp. Nobody, not even Herbert, wrote so gracefully for the voice. It was for his heroine (and for Mme Trentini's voice) that Friml wrote some of the loveliest melodies in his score —indeed some of the most endurable melodies of his entire career: "Giannina Mia," "The Dawn of Love," "When a Maid Comes Knocking at Your Heart," and "Love Is Like a Firefly." Other members in the cast also had unforgettable tunes, one of which, "Sympathy," is still popular. But "The Donkey Serenade" (without which, it seems, no revival of *The Firefly* is today conceivable) was not heard in 1912. When *The Firefly* was made into a motion picture in 1937, Friml collaborated with Herbert Stothart in adapting his own piano piece, *Chansonette,* into a popular song (lyrics by Bob White and Chet Forrest). Interpolated into the screen production it became such a formidable hit that it almost threw the other wonderful musical numbers into a shade.

The success of *The Firefly* in 1912 meant that Broadway producers would now make frequent demands for Friml's services. During the next two decades, Friml wrote scores for about 20 operettas and musical comedies. But three—in which Friml adhered most faithfully to the customs and traditions of *The Merry Widow*—are the ones by which he will always be remembered. "When I write music for the theater," Friml once told an interviewer, "I like books with charm to them, and charm suggests old things, the finest things that were done long ago. I like a full-blooded libretto with a luscious melody, rousing choruses, and romantic passion." Stimulated by the romance, sentimentality, glamour, and excitement of operetta's make-believe world, Friml was a king of the stature of Herbert.

Rose-Marie (1924) carried its audience to a setting never before or since successfully exploited by operetta. In fact, this setting came before anything else. One day Arthur Hammerstein was reviewing in his mind all the strange and interesting places used by operettas for a background. It suddenly occurred to him that the Canadian Rockies were still virgin territory for the American musical theater—and that the heroic figures of the Canadian Mounted Police could provide exciting characters. Hammerstein asked Otto Harbach to work out a text for Friml; and Harbach, in turn, enlisted the collaboration of Oscar Hammerstein II, with whom he had previously worked on several occasions. It did not take them long to weave a serviceable fabric. Rose-Marie and Jim Kenyon are in love. When Jim is falsely accused of murder, Rose-Marie stands ready to marry a man she does not love in order to save Jim's life. But the Canadian Mounted

Police, headed by Sergeant Malone, are able to clear Jim and make Rose-Marie's noble self-sacrifice unnecessary.

With a Broadway engagement exceeding 550 performances—and tours by four road companies—*Rose-Marie* became one of the strongest box-office attractions of its day. It is still revived often, and on two occasions it was adapted for motion pictures. But if this operetta still has the capacity to win hearts and arouse enthusiasm, surely it is not for its stilted story or stereotyped love interest and denouement—nor, for that matter, for its unusual Canadian Rockies setting. It is Friml's music that keeps *Rose-Marie* alive. The title number, "Indian Love Call," "The Door of My Dreams," and "Totem Tom-Tom" (the last effectively staged, sung by a group of girls costumed to resemble totem poles) have become classics in American popular music.

The Vagabond King (1925) and *The Three Musketeers* (1928) both presented France in a bygone era, and populated it with swashbuckling characters. Both joined the box-office leaders of their respective years. *The Vagabond King*, in addition, was transferred to the screen on three occasions. Its picturesque hero is François Villon, the celebrated 15th-century vagabond poet. In a text by Brian Hooker and W. H. Post adapted from J. H. McCarthy's romance, *If I Were King*, Villon becomes the French king for a day. He makes love to the beautiful Katherine de Vaucelles, and helps to save Paris, and the French throne, from the Burgundians. His peasant sweetheart, Huguette, remains true to him, nor does she hesitate to exchange her own life for that of the man she loves when called upon to do so. Friml's music passes nimbly from romantic and sentimental moods to belligerent and vigorous ones: sentimental and romantic in "Only a Rose," "Some Day," and "Huguette Waltz"; stirring and robust in "Song of the Vagabonds."

The Three Musketeers was Friml's last Broadway success, the last of his beloved operettas. Its source was the popular romance of Alexandre Dumas adapted by Wil-

33

liam Anthony McGuire, lyrics by P. G. Wodehouse and Clifford Grey. D'Artagnan comes to Paris, falls in love with Constance, and joins three other musketeers (Athos, Porthos, Aramis) in numerous heroics and escapades. They set forth on a royal mission to retrieve from the Duke of Buckingham jewels rightfully belonging to the French queen. Once again Friml's music sings out with a loud, ringing voice on the one hand ("All for One" and "With Red Wine") and with tender tones on the other ("Heart of Mine" and "Ma Belle").

Friml's last appearance on Broadway was with a dismal failure, *Anina* (1934). He then went on to Hollywood, where he supervised the screen adaptations of some of his successful Broadway operettas and occasionally wrote new songs. His day in the American theater —lustrous though it was—was over. Nobody realized this more forcefully than Friml himself.

Friml's *The Three Musketeers* had opened on Broadway on March 13, 1928. Later the same year—on September 19—there came to the Imperial Theater the last of Sigmund Romberg's operetta classics, *The New Moon.* This was the closing chord of American operetta. Thereafter the Broadway stage would belong primarily to musical comedies, revues, or musical plays—but operettas were a thing of the past.

Though all of Romberg's writing was done in America, his musical roots were in European soil. The European operetta was the stage medium he understood best and to which his artistic sensibilities responded most strongly. He did write a good deal of music for revues, extravaganzas, and musical comedies; and in one instance, toward the end of his career, he was even the participant in the writing of a highly successful musical comedy. But, for the most part, when he deserted the operetta for the other forms of the American musical theater, he was not in his element. And when he died in 1951 a dynasty in the musical theater that had ruled over operetta passed away with him.

Few knew better than Romberg where his real strength lay. In the fall of 1942 he told an audience come to hear him conduct a concert of operetta music: "I have been told that the music I have lived with for many years now belongs to the past. . . . They tell me today is the day of the radio, telephone, the airplane, fast cars, and that life has speeded up so fast that no one can slow down to a waltz. Perhaps this is so. If so, they are right and I am wrong. But if some of the lovely music you have listened to this evening, and will listen to again when I've finished this rambling talk, if this music has touched you and made you remember that life was livable once and that it will be again, then *I* am right, and they are wrong."

The world and the people of operetta were the kind Romberg had grown up with and to which all his life he looked back nostalgically. He was born in a small Hungarian border town on July 29, 1887. His father was a *bon vivant* and a talented musical amateur; his mother was a poetess and short-story writer. Sigmund began studying music when he was six. While attending public school in Hungary he played the organ at church services, was a member of the school orchestra, and wrote his first piece of music (a march). Since his parents wanted him to become an engineer, he was sent to Vienna to enroll in the Polytechnical High School. At the turn of the 20th century, Vienna was the capital of the music world, a mecca of waltz music and operettas. It had been the birthplace of Johann Strauss II, composer of *Die Fledermaus* and *Zigeuenerbaron,* two of the greatest operettas ever written. It was the scene of the world premières not only of these operettas but also of those by Franz Lehár, Oscar Straus, Emmerich Kálmán, and many others.

Romberg plunged into the invigorating musical and

theatrical life of this fabulous city with the zest and anticipation of an overheated youngster diving into a clear, cool pool. He studied harmony and counterpoint with Victor Heuberger. He became a habitué of some of the better known musical salons. He went to concerts and operettas whenever he could muster the price of a ticket. He even managed, through a friend, to gain access to the backstage of the Theater-an-der-Wien where, nightly, he could watch performances of operettas. Then, when threatened with the loss of this privilege, he applied for and got a job as assistant stage manager so that he might continue seeing these productions.

He began losing all interest in his studies, as more and more he dreamed of making music his career. Any final decision about his future, however, had to be delayed until he had fulfilled the military duty required of all young men in Austria and Hungary. For a year and a half he served with the 19th Hungarian Infantry stationed in Vienna. When that period ended he made an irrevocable decision: he would become a professional musician, and he would go to America.

He came to the United States in 1908, settled in New York, and worked in a pencil factory for $7.00 a week. Before long he was earning his living through music. At first he worked as pianist in a small café house in downtown New York; after that, as pianist in a restaurant on 125th Street; in 1912, as the conductor of salon and dance music in one of New York's most famous restaurants, Bustanoby's. While holding the last job he started writing American popular music—two one-steps and a waltz that were published in Tin Pan Alley.

In 1913, J. J. Shubert, the famous Broadway producer, hired Romberg as staff composer for the many and varied productions he was then putting on Broadway each season. Romberg's Broadway bow took place on January 10, 1914 with *The Whirl of the World*, a Shubert extravaganza at the Winter Garden starring Eugene and Willie Howard, Lillian Lorraine, and Rozsika Dolly. There was no mention in the program that he was the composer of its music, but this omission bothered him but little. What was important to him was that he had finally made a start on the Great White Way.

After that Romberg was kept busy supplying musical numbers for Shubert's productions with due program credit. Between 1914 and 1917 he wrote 275 compositions for 17 musicals: extravaganzas, revues, and musical comedies. Prolific and facile, never at a loss for a tune, and oblivious to long hours of hard work, Romberg had no problem meeting his many commitments. None of the songs he wrote during this period have survived, because none rose above the level of mediocrity then prevailing in most of our musical theaters.

If he was just a mediocrity writing for extravaganzas and revues, he was destined to become one of America's most seductive and most appealing melodists once he turned to the operetta. The first time this happened was with *The Blue Paradise* (1915), an American adaptation of a Viennese operetta. Here were setting, background, characters, moods, and a way of life Romberg knew from personal experience and to which he could react instinctively. "The Blue Paradise" is a Viennese garden restaurant where Mizzi works as a flower girl. She and Rudolph fall in love. But Rudolph is on the eve of leaving for America, an occasion that calls for a festival farewell party at this restaurant. When Rudolph again returns to Vienna a quarter of a century has passed, and he is now a man of means. Sentiment draws him back to "The Blue Paradise," which is no longer a restaurant but the home of one of his old comrades. Here he meets Gaby, Mizzi's daughter, who comes out attired exactly the way Mizzi had been when she had bid Rudolph good-by years before. The information that Mizzi has become a shrew makes it possible for Rudolph to leave Vienna permanently without regrets, and once and for all abandon his recollections of a poignant past.

That Vienna was a setting able to arouse and inflame

37

Romberg's musical imagination was eloquently proved by the leading song in *The Blue Paradise*, "Auf Wieder-sehen," Romberg's first waltz classic. This haunting, evocative melody—which even today is still magic—is first sung by Mizzi and Rudolph at "The Blue Paradise" just before he leaves for America for the first time; and it is sung again a quarter of a century later by Gaby when she appears in her mother's dress to welcome Rudolph back.

As Romberg's first successful operetta, and as the source of his first important song, *The Blue Paradise* has a place of honor in the history of our musical theater. But there is still a third reason for its historic importance. In this production there stepped from obscurity to prominence a star of the Broadway musical stage who would add luster to our theater for many years to come—Vivienne Segal. When he had been busy casting *The Blue Paradise*, Romberg had been searching desperately, and without success, for an actress to play Mizzi as his imagination had envisioned her. One day a scout told him of a young vocal student in Philadelphia who might fill the bill. When Romberg auditioned her he shouted: "You'll do, thank God!" With her first Broadway appearance, Vivienne Segal became a star in Broadway's firmament, and she remained bright and luminous for the next 30 years.

Although he knew that with the writing of his first operetta score he had suddenly tapped within himself new creative resources, Romberg did not abandon the other media of the stage. He was still Shubert's staff composer and as such he still had to write a good deal of functional music for Winter Garden extravaganzas, some of which starred Al Jolson in several of his great triumphs, and for star-studded revues. But in all these efforts he was merely an efficient workman able to meet any demands made upon him but rarely lifted above acceptable requirements.

But in the operetta world he, too, was a king. His second significant operetta was *Maytime* (1917), with book and lyrics by Rida Johnson Young. The setting here is not Europe or a mythical land but Washington Square, in

New York City. The characters were not princes, princesses, or officers—not European gentlemen, waitresses, or flower girls—but New Yorkers. Nevertheless both the story and the people could easily have been transferred to a European locale without any loss of authenticity. In the glamour and sentimentality of the plot, in the charm and grace of the music, *Maytime* was a European operetta. If Romberg had left Vienna, Vienna had not left Romberg.

The time element of this play was spread over half a century beginning with 1840. Though Ottilie and Richard are in love, Ottilie must marry a worthless gambler who dies leaving her penniless. Years later, Richard buys Ottilie's family home on Washington Square and has it deeded to her without revealing who the benefactor is. This house becomes a dress shop managed by Ottilie's granddaughter, who falls in love with and marries Richard's grandson.

Maytime was such a box-office triumph that for the first time in Broadway history a second New York company was formed within a year of the première to play at the nearby 44th Street Theater.

Once again operetta helped Romberg uncover a rich, sensitive vein of melody. The hit song of *Maytime* was a waltz, "Will You Remember?", which recurred throughout the play. It was the love song of Ottilie and Richard and, in a later generation, of their grandchildren as well. Memorable, too, were other songs with a Continental flavor, such as "The Road to Paradise" and "Dancing Will Keep You Young."

Two subsequent Romberg triumphs were adaptations of famous European operettas. Though in each instance text and lyrics were the work of American writers, adapted for American tastes, both operettas retained their respective national identities for which Romberg's essentially Viennese style of sentimental and romantic melody was so admirably suited. One was *Blossom Time* (1921), based on the life and music of Vienna's beloved 19th-century composer, Franz Schubert. The other was *The Student Prince in Heidelberg* (1924), its background the old German university town.

Blossom Time was the American version of *Das Dreimäderlhaus*, a Viennese operetta classic that as late as 1958 was made into a Viennese color motion picture. Neither *Das Dreimäderlhaus*, nor its American adaptation by Dorothy Donnelly, had much traffic with biographical truth. In *Blossom Time*, Franz Schubert, in love with Mitzi, has written a serenade to her. Being exceedingly shy he prevails on his best friend, Schober, to sing it to her. Schober and Mitzi fall in love, a development that proves so crushing to the composer that he loses his inspiration for writing music. Incapable of completing the symphony on which he had been at work, he decides to leave it unfinished. Sick with his last fatal illness, and heartbroken with unrequited love, Schubert writes a last immortal song, the "Ave Maria." Any similarity between all this and the facts of Schubert's life is purely coincidental.

For his score Romberg went to the storehouse of Schubert's melodic treasures and recast them into Tin Pan Alley molds. "Song of Love," one of the most successful numbers Romberg ever wrote, was a popular-song treatment of the beautiful main theme from the first movement of the *Unfinished Symphony*. "Tell Me Daisy" was concocted from the principal subject of the second movement. The ballet music from *Rosamunde* was borrowed for "Three Little Maids" and the immortal song, "*Ständchen*," for "Serenade." It is tragic no doubt to recall that all Schubert ever earned during his entire lifetime from the writing of hundreds upon hundreds of deathless masterworks was about $500. And it is surely ironic to note that, through the years, Romberg collected in royalties in the neighborhood of one million dollars from his songs borrowed from Schubert's melodies! For with its original Broadway run of almost 2 years, with its road tour by 4 companies, and with repeated revivals, *Blossom Time* became one of the supreme successes of our musical theater.

In *The Student Prince in Heidelberg,* the music was entirely Romberg's, and it was some of the best he ever wrote. No other Romberg operetta has so many songs to remember. There is "Deep in My Heart, Dear," the main love duet of the Prince and Kathie; the Prince's love song, "Serenade"; the stirring drinking song for an all-male chorus; and "Golden Days" with its eloquent reminder of forgotten times. The action takes place in the mid-19th century, in Heidelberg. Prince Karl Franz meets and falls in love with Kathie, a waitress at the "Golden Apple" inn. Despite the sincerity of his feelings, he can never hope to marry her. For reasons of state he must leave Heidelberg and take a princess as bride.

Great though the success of *Blossom Time* had been, *The Student Prince* was greater still. Its Broadway run of 608 performances exceeded that of *Blossom Time* by sixteen; instead of 4 road companies, there were 9. And the sheet music sale of its principal songs proved so profitable that its publisher, Witmark—in dire financial straits when *The Student Prince* opened—became a power again in Tin Pan Alley only one year later.

There were two more Romberg operetta masterpieces after *The Student Prince. The Desert Song* (1926) was filled with all the pomp and pageantry for which the operetta had long become famous, and with the kind of exotic settings and characters the operetta was so partial to. The librettists—Otto Harbach, Oscar Hammerstein II, and Frank Mandel—had read a newspaper account of a revolt among the Riffs in French Morocco. Alert for subjects for operettas they knew that here they had a bountiful source. They gathered a conglomeration of picturesquely costumed characters from bandits, Riffs, harem girls, and French officers and enmeshed them in exciting intrigues and adventures in French Morocco. A bandit chief who went under the name of "The Red Shadow" is secretly in love with Margot, but Margot favors Pierre, son of the local Governor. The bandit abducts her to the harem of Ali ben Ali where she at first rejects him but soon becomes a victim to his charm. The Governor and his troops arrive to rescue her. When the Governor rushes to attack the bandit, the latter offers no resistance—to the disgust of his men who renounce him as their leader. But the bandit is vindicated of cowardice when the discovery is made that he is really Pierre in disguise and would not engage his own father in combat. Nobody is more delighted at this revelation than Margot, who need no longer struggle with her conscience about being in love with a bandit.

The critics were none too happy with *The Desert Song*. The goings-on were so contrived that the machinery was visible to the naked eye; the plot was old-fashioned and hackneyed even for an operetta. "The question of how simple-minded the book of a musical . . . can be was debated last night," reported Richard Watts, Jr., "and the verdict arrived at was 'no end.'" At first, then, it appeared that *The Desert Song* would have to close, mortally victimized by the attacks of critics. But Romberg's music soon triumphed over a stilted libretto. As his melodies gained circulation, attendance began increasing at the theater until *The Desert Song* became a solid hit with a run of 465 performances. The title song—sometimes also known as "Blue Heaven"—is one of Romberg's deathless melodies. But an iridescent score included other jewels as well: "One Alone" and "Romance," and in a more dashing style, "Sabre Song" and "French Marching Song."

The New Moon (1928) was the last of Romberg's famous operettas. The history of *The Desert Song* is here repeated with variations, for what started out as a disaster was converted into a triumph. In fact, in its out-of-town tryouts *The New Moon* was such a dud that it was hurriedly withdrawn for complete revision and recasting. By the time it came to New York it was a far different show than when it had first been rehearsed there, and St. John Ervine, an eminent English critic writing in the

New York World, could now describe it as "the most charming and fragrant entertainment of its sort that I have seen in a long time." After that its success was so great that when the screen rights were sold in 1929 it commanded the highest price thus far paid to a Broadway musical.

The authors of the text (Oscar Hammerstein II, Frank Mandel, and Laurence Schwab) reached into the history books for their hero. He was Robert Mission, a late 18th-century French aristocrat, who had come to New Orleans and become the bondservant of Monsieur Beaunoir. There he falls in love with Beaunoir's daughter, Marianne. Since he is a political refugee he cannot reveal that he is of noble birth. Apprehended by the French police he is shipped back to France aboard *The New Moon* to face trial. During the voyage, a mutiny erupts among the bondservants who gain control of the ship; they then land on a small island off the coast of Florida. Since Marianne had stowed away aboard ship to be near the man she loves, the love interest does not lag during these stormy developments. The news finally arrives that France has become a republic. Robert is cleared of all political charges against him. He now helps to found a new government on the island, with Marianne at his side.

No Romberg operetta ever failed to rise to its love interest with an appropriately eloquent love song. *The New Moon* was no exception. "Lover Come Back to Me" is the high point of this operetta—Marianne's poignant avowal of her love for Robert. But the sentiment and compelling emotion found in this beautiful number are not lacking in other songs, the best of which are "Softly as in a Morning Sunrise," "One Kiss," and "Wanting You."

Romberg's last operetta was *May Wine* (1935). After that he settled in Beverly Hills, California, to work for the movies, for which he wrote one of his unforgettable love ballads, "When I Grow Too Old to Dream." During World War II Romberg went on tour conducting an orchestra in concerts of light music. Billed as "An Evening with Sigmund Romberg," these performances attracted such large audiences that a world tour was contemplated. It did not materialize because of Romberg's sudden death in New York on November 10, 1951.

Meanwhile Romberg had returned to the Broadway theater, not with an operetta this time (for there just was no interest in operettas any longer) but with an American musical comedy. *Up in Central Park* (1945) was an immense commercial success. It was set in New York of the 1870's during the infamous political control of that city by the Tweed Ring. *The Girl in Pink Tights* (1954)—its music completed by Romberg just before his death, but produced posthumously—was a failure. This was a period piece built around the first production of *The Black Crook* in New York in 1866.

Despite the long run enjoyed by *Up in Central Park*, Romberg simply was not at his best writing for American musical comedies. It had one or two good songs—such as "Close as Pages in a Book"—but little of that melodic magic we find in his operettas. And the score of *The Girl in Pink Tights*, as Brooks Atkinson said, was filled "with mechanical melodies out of a departed era." The phrase "departed era" is worth underlining—for to the last of his days Sigmund Romberg was living and working in the past.

Though still capable occasionally of shedding a wondrous light, the American operetta in the late 1920's was rapidly coming to the end of a long, rich career. Audiences and critics had by now grown weary of Graustark, Ruritania, and Monte Carlo, bored with storybook characters with fancy uniforms and dress, impatient with stock love affairs. What they now wanted in their theater was realism rather than magic illusion, the vibrant present instead of a rose-tinted past. A new tempo had quickened American life since the end of World War I. The staid, sedate portraits of a bygone era found in operetta were

44

out of joint with the new times. Excitement was in the air, and the public wanted excitement on the stage. By the same token, the new young writers on Broadway were incapable of writing librettos and lyrics in a style now as old-fashioned as gaslight and horse-drawn carriages. They had to seek out texts that were vital, contemporary, and American; lyrics that were smart and sophisticated. In the same way the younger Broadway composers could no longer think in terms of the sweet, sentimental tunes once dispensed by Herbert, Friml, and Romberg—beautiful though they are. Jazz had brought to American popular music a new dynamism and cogency. This was the musical speech of the 1920's, and this was the way the new Broadway composers had to write for the stage.

Nostalgia and sentiment might keep some of the old operettas alive through revivals. It was always good to hear the old, beautiful songs of a departed day, even if the plays themselves were silly! But *new* operettas by Americans after 1930 were rarities. When they did appear they usually played to empty theaters, and closed almost as soon as they opened; on Broadway, as elsewhere, it is futile to try turning the clock back.

Nevertheless, once in a long while there did come a new operetta with enough stage and musical charm to cast a spell. In 1944 there was *The Song of Norway,* an operetta about the famous Norwegian composer, Edvard Grieg, with Grieg's music adapted into popular numbers. In 1953 there was *Kismet,* an operetta about ancient Bagdad, whose music was derived from Alexander Borodin. Both operettas were the work of Robert Wright and George (Chet) Forrest, who collaborated on both the music and the lyrics.

But neither revivals nor an occasional new successful production could disguise the fact that after 1930 the operetta had become obsolete in the American theater. A new era creates its own forms and traditions, just as it displaces the old. The operetta was dead. Long live musical comedy!

Another World—Burlesque, / **3**
Extravaganza, Revue

For about 40 years, then—from *The Little Tycoon* in 1887 to *The New Moon* in 1928—operetta flourished on the American stage. But during that time there were several other types of musicals—far different in method and manner from the operetta—to provide New York with enchanted evenings.

The burlesque—entertainment based on travesty, satire, and slapstick—did not die out with the split of Harrigan and Hart in 1885. Eight years after that came *A Trip to Chinatown* which far surpassed the box-office appeal of any single Harrigan and Hart production. Indeed, *A Trip to Chinatown* enjoyed the longest run up to that time in the history of the New York theater (650 performances). With book and lyrics by Charlie Hoyt, and music by Percy Gaunt, *A Trip to Chinatown* was shaped in the image of a Harrigan and Hart burlesque. The setting is a big city, San Francisco; the main characters are familiar types; the main dish is satire, in this case directed toward such then topical subjects as woman suffrage and the temperance crusade. But *A Trip to Chinatown* differed from Harrigan and Hart in one important respect: it occasionally digressed from naturalism and travesty to glamour, as when that fetching dancer, Loie Fuller, performed a butterfly dance with her flowing skirt simulating wings.

A Trip to Chinatown added as significant a footnote to

American popular music as it did to the American theater. It was the first show to acquire a huge additional revenue through the sheet-music publication of its principal numbers. Three of Percy Gaunt's numbers sold several hundreds of thousands of copies each; and one of these songs, "The Bowery," is as familiar to most of us today as it was in its own time.

The traditions of burlesque were carried into the 20th century by two of the most lovable clowns our musical theater has known: Weber and Fields. Joe Weber was short, plump, stocky; Lew Fields, tall and thin. Both wore outlandish checked suits too large for their frame (or, when the occasion called for it, equally ill-fitting evening dress) and ludicrous derby hats. Both sported little tufts of hair on their chins, the merest suggestion of a beard. Both spoke in a thick German dialect. And both presented mirth-provoking caricatures of Dutchmen. For 8 years the burlesques of Weber and Fields were the talk of the town—a bountiful source of merriment accentuating the absurd and the ridiculous. For 8 years, these burlesques also served as steppingstones on which more than one great musical-stage star, and more than one popular song, passed on to the dazzling limelight of public acclaim.

Both Weber and Fields were veterans of the stage when they introduced their first burlesques. They were each only 10 years old when they joined forces in an Irish song-and-dance comedy act in saloons and variety theaters in the Bowery, and at Duffy's Pavilion in Coney Island. In 1884 they became members of a burlesque company headed by Ada Richmond at Miner's Theater in the Bowery. While working with this group they started devising some of the routines which, in their final crystallization, helped make their act famous.

With a capital of less than $2,000 (most of it borrowed) Weber and Fields acquired a theater on 29th Street off Broadway in 1895 which they named the Music Hall. For the next few years this was to be a shrine of burlesque entertainment. Their first production, *The Art of Maryland*, opened on September 5, 1896 and consisted of two parts. The first was a parody of *The Heart of Maryland*, a then recently produced stage play starring Mrs. Leslie Carter. In their outlandish costume and with their ridiculous accent, Weber and Fields, through their uninhibited horseplay and rowdy humor, reduced to shambles a play once touching and sentimental. The second part of their show consisted of variety entertainment (in the style of the "olio" of the minstrel show). Leading members of the cast here did specialty numbers, and various other novelties were introduced. Weber and Fields did a skit about a pool game which forthwith became one of their specialties; Lottie Gilson sang; and a "new kind of motion picture," identified as an "animatograph," was introduced.

The pattern thus set prevailed for the next few Weber and Fields burlesques. The first half always devoted itself to mocking some popular Broadway play with slapstick humor—for example, Barrie's *The Little Minister*, Rostand's *Cyrano de Bergerac*, Gillette's *Secret Service*. The second part was a vaudeville show. The buffoonery of Weber and Fields was always the principal attraction, and their concept of the ridiculous was usually carried over in bits of stage business. A canary's cage might be the home for a pig; a smoking cigar might be seen protruding from the lips of a bust.

Lustrous stars were featured in all these Weber and Fields burlesques. Some were already established favorites, others were unknown. One of the greatest of them all was Lillian Russell—nicknamed "the American beauty" —often called the most beautiful woman of her day. Wherever she went she was surrounded by rapturous admirers, of whom the most ardent was Diamond Jim Brady. They lavished on her flowers, furs, and jewels; they drank champagne from her slipper at Delmonico's. She did not have a large singing voice, her style was nondescript, and her acting ability was hardly better than average. Yet when she appeared on the stage it became flooded with the sunlight of her personality as if a huge beacon had suddenly been lit.

She was already the toast of New York when in 1899 she made her debut in the Weber and Fields burlesque, *Whirl-i-gig*. There each night she stopped the show singing "When Chloe Sings a Song." She remained a main Weber and Fields attraction for the next few years. Her greatest triumph came with singing "Come Down Ma' Evenin' Star," which she introduced in *Twirly-Whirly* in 1902 and which henceforth became her theme song.

Dazzling, flamboyant, magnetizing though she was, Lillian Russell was only one of many to brighten the stage of the Music Hall. Among others were David Warfield (later one of Broadway's most important serious actors, but in *Hurly Burly* in 1898 a Jewish comedian!), Fay Templeton, William Collier, Marie Dressler (the same who subsequently became one of the screen's leading character actresses), Bessie Clayton, Cecilia Loftus, De-Wolf Hopper, and the McCoy Sisters.

Great popular songs, as well as great performers, stepped out of these Weber and Fields shows. Two of these have already been mentioned in conjunction with Lillian Russell. All the music for Weber and Fields was the work of John Stromberg, born in 1853. He was working in Tin Pan Alley when, in 1895, he wrote and had published his first song hit ("My Best Girl's a Corker"). Thus his name came to the attention of Weber and Fields when they planned opening their own theater. Stromberg was hired both to write the music for the burlesques and to conduct the orchestra. The long string of his song successes in these burlesques included "Dinah" (sometimes also called "Kiss Me Honey, Do"), "Ma Blushin' Rose," "Come Back, My Honey Boy, to Me," and "How I Love My Lu."

"Come Down Ma Evenin' Star," which Lillian Russell made famous, was his swan song. In 1902 (just before *Twirly-Whirly* opened), the manuscript of this number was found in Stromberg's pocket when the composer was discovered dead in his apartment by suicide. Two months later, *Twirly-Whirly* opened with a new conductor-composer (William T. Francis), but several numbers Stromberg had completed before his death were used in that show. As Lillian Russell introduced "Come Down Ma Evenin' Star," on opening night, she broke down and wept, and could not finish it.

The last Weber and Fields burlesque came immediately thereafter, *Whoop-Dee-Doo* in 1903. After 1904 Weber and Fields went separate ways in the theater. Weber was often seen as an actor in various comedies while Fields succeeded both as a producer and an actor. Only once, in 1912, was an effort made to revive the one-time glory of the old Weber and Fields combination—with *Hokey Pokey*, a sentimental reminder of days gone by. Its overture consisted of Stromberg's leading hits. The cast included, besides Weber and Fields, such old-time Music Hall favorites as Lillian Russell, Fay Templeton, and Bessie Clayton. But *Hokey Pokey* was only a minor success, and this merely for sentimental reasons. Audiences were no longer interested in burlesques. After that Weber and Fields appeared together on the same stage only once: in 1932 when the golden jubilee of their partnership was celebrated in New York. Lew Fields died in 1941, and Weber a year after that.

Thus burlesque was dead even while Weber and Fields were still alive. But what had proved true with operetta also held for burlesque. Once or twice after the heyday of Weber and Fields, the medium of burlesque was revived successfully. Two particularly triumphant efforts to reintroduce old-time burlesque entertainment on Broadway were made by a pair of zany slapstick comedians named Olsen and Johnson. In 1938 they presented *Hellz-a-poppin'*, which they described as "a free-for-all vaudeville entertainment" but which actually was a carry-over from Weber and Fields. Like their predecessors, Olsen and Johnson ran riot with scatterbrained stunts, outlandish tomfoolery, and plain slapstick. They parodied

Walter Winchell, Kate Smith, and Rudy Vallee (reminders of the day when Weber and Fields used to give hilarious impersonations of *their* stage contemporaries). They offered skits about Wall Street, maternity wards, and English detectives with the same broad strokes of humor that Weber and Fields had made famous. They indulged freely in the Weber and Fields brand of incongruity and paradox. A faked newsreel had Hitler speaking with a Yiddish accent; Mussolini and President Roosevelt were shown making speeches, but with outlandish sounds instead of words emanating from their moving lips. Weber and Fields absurdity returned when a cyclist rode a vehicle with four square wheels; when a gentleman Godiva rode a horse in the balcony; when a stuffed gorilla dragged a lady from her seat in the boxes.

Hellz-a-poppin' was one of Broadway's hugest financial bonanzas, accumulating almost 1500 performances. Its successor, *Sons o' Fun* (1941)—once again with Olsen and Johnson—ran for more than 700 performances. But not even triumphs of such a dimension could permanently revive Broadway's interest in burlesque. Once the novelty of the antics of Olsen and Johnson had lost its shock appeal, burlesque in the grand tradition of John Poole, Harrigan and Hart, Charlie Hoyt, and Weber and Fields could no longer provide a full evening of stage entertainment.

The extravaganza (first popular in 1866 with *The Black Crook*) had somewhat more durability than the burlesque, surviving well into the 1920's.

One of the most successful extravaganzas after *The Black Crook* was *The Wizard of Oz* (1903). The text was by E. Frank Baum adapted from one of his novels while the music was principally by A. Baldwin Sloane and Paul Tiejens. Young and old fell under the spell of his lavish fantasy which was a lush parade of overdressed production numbers, colorful stage pictures, unusual stage effects, and attention-arresting specialties. Oz is a fairy garden inhabited by the Munchkins. A cyclone lifts Dorothy Dale and her pet cow, Imogene, off a Kansas farm and brings them to Oz. There a good witch presents Dorothy with a ring able to fulfill two wishes. Dorothy wastes the first on a trifle, but her second is to bring Scarecrow back to life. When this happens, Dorothy learns that Scarecrow has lost his brains, and that the only one able to restore it to him is the Wizard of Oz. Accompanied by Tim Woodman (in search for his heart lost when he fell in love) Dorothy and the Scarecrow go hunting for the Wizard, with whom they finally catch up after numerous trials and adventures. At long last, Scarecrow recovers his brain, and Tim, his heart.

Fred Stone as the Scarecrow and David Montgomery as Tim Woodman became a starring comedy team in this ravishing spectacle. With their acrobatic antics, stunts, and grimaces as they follow Dorothy in her search for the Wizard, they brought a welcome infusion of merriment and slapstick to a production designed otherwise mainly to please the eye. So popular did they become as comedy partners that in 1906 Victor Herbert and Henry Blossom wrote *The Red Mill* for them.

The Wizard of Oz has not been forgotten; it has remained a stage classic for the young in the class of *Babes in Toyland* and *Peter Pan*. Again and again it has been revived throughout the country, most recently as a television spectacular. In 1939 it was made into a motion picture starring Judy Garland. It was in this film that Judy sang "Over the Rainbow," the Academy Award winning song by Harold Arlen to E. Y. Harburg's lyrics with which she is now always identified.

Two years after *The Wizard of Oz*, extravaganza found a home of its own, near Broadway: the Hippodrome, on Sixth Avenue and 43rd Street. For many years the most ambitiously conceived and lavishly mounted shows in the world were there on view. Advertised at the time as "the largest, safest, and costliest playhouse"—and boasting the most advanced and complex stage machinery then available—the Hippodrome opened its doors on April 12, 1905 with a gala program including a circus show, a ballet, and a "spectacular drama" entitled *Andersonville*. After that, the Hippodrome concentrated on entertainment in which every effort was expended on startling stage tricks, overwhelming scenes with giant casts, and magnificent settings and costumes. Everything else was of minor consideration, even the star performers, or the functional music that for many seasons Manuel Klein wrote for each production.

For a decade and more visual miracles took place on Hippodrome's mammoth stage. *Pioneer Days* (1906) opened with a giant production number involving cowboys, Indians, Mexicans, and the United States Cavalry. A naval battle and the Vanderbilt Cup Race were simulated in *The Auto Race* (1907). An airplane battle and a bird ballet were two of many attractions in *Sporting Days* (1908). In *Around the World* (1909) the audience was transported to Egypt, the Sahara Desert, atop peaks in the Swiss mountains, and other far-off places. In 1912, in *Under Many Flags,* a tornado and an earthquake were reproduced with stunning realism; in *The Wars of the World* (1914) there could be seen enactments of episodes from the French Revolution, the Civil War, the Battle of Vera Cruz, and several other historic military engagements. These and other extravaganzas featured such unusual and highly varied attractions as the pounding of a herd of deer in Arizona, the march of an army of elephants, performing stallions, a New York City fire, a sandstorm, Sousa's Band, a skater's ballet, and rush hour in Grand Central Station in New York.

For many years the *tour de force* of the Hippodrome extravaganzas was a tank act first seen in *Pioneer Days*. Audiences were mystified by it production after production. Here is how this author described this spellbinding

53

stunt in the *Complete Book of the American Musical Theater:* * "Bespangled chorus girls marched down a flight of stairs into a forty-foot deep tank filled with water, never to reappear. During all the years the Hippodrome flourished, the secret was never disclosed how this trick worked. But when the answer was finally revealed it proved remarkably simple. Behind the scenes there was partly submerged in water an airproof "shed," a kind of diving bell, which because of the pressure of water from underneath retained the air originally in it. The girls had only to hold their breath for two or three seconds, duck under the edge of the bell, and emerge inside it above the water. Having got their breath, they then ducked under the further edge of the bell and walked up a second set of stairs to the safety of the back stage. A telephone operator, sitting at his switchboard, within the bell, reported to a central office the safe arrival and departure of each girl."

In the 1910's and early 1920's there was a second temple of extravaganzas in New York. It was the Winter Garden, on Broadway and 51st Street, erected by the Shuberts as a home for their more spectacular offerings. It opened on March 21, 1911 with a dual bill. One half consisted of an elaborately mounted "Chinese opera," *Bow Sing.* The other half was *La Belle Paree* which the program described as a "Cook's tour through vaudeville with a Parisian landscape." *La Belle Paree* is important for reasons other than that it was one of two opening features of the Winter Garden. Its music was by a recruit from Tin Pan Alley—a still unheralded genius of popular music named Jerome Kern, who would soon become a giant in the theater. A second reason for significance for *La Belle Paree* was that it was here that Al Jolson made his Broadway debut, cast as Erastus Sparkle, "a colored aristocrat of San Juan Hill." In later Winter Garden ex-

---

* *Complete Book of the American Musical Theater,* by David Ewen. New York: Holt, Rinehart and Winston, 1958.

travaganzas Al Jolson would become the foremost black-face singing star of his generation.

Before coming to Broadway, and from the time he was a boy, Jolson had appeared in vaudeville and burlesque theaters. Slowly he started to assume and perfect some of the mannerisms he later made so famous. In vaudeville, as a boy performer, he began to imitate the Southern accent of a little Negro boy whom he had befriended. Then, in Brooklyn, he blackened his face with burned cork in keeping with that accent. Later on still, he got into the habit of sinking on one knee while delivering an emotional song, and stretching out his hands to the audience at a climactic point in the number.

In 1909 Jolson became a member of Dockstader's Minstrels (the last of the famous minstrel-show troupes) where he was featured as a singing-dancing minstrel in blackface. Lee Shubert saw him there and hired him for *La Belle Paree* at a salary of $250 a week.

After that, the history of Al Jolson and that of the Winter Garden were inextricably intertwined for many years. A year after *La Belle Paree* Jolson was assigned his first starring role, in *Vera Violetta,* also a Winter Garden extravaganza. That show had many attractions. The piquant French star, Gaby Deslys, sang "The Gaby Glide" which Louis A. Hirsch wrote expressly for her. There was a good deal of attractive staging and costuming. But it was Jolson who stole the show—Jolson prancing about the stage in blackface, singing, dancing, miming, making impromptu asides to the audience, and in all magnetizing the theater with his electrifying personality. It did not take the Shuberts long to realize what a treasure they had in Jolson. In 1912 they inaugurated Sunday evening "concerts" at the Winter Garden so that Jolson might perform for show people. A year after that, the Shuberts paid him a bonus of $10,000 to sign an exclusive 7-year contract with them at a salary of $1,000 a week for a 35-week season. (The rest of each year Jolson could command $2,500 a week in vaudeville.)

Jolson held sway at the Winter Garden for over a decade. In 1916 he appeared in *Robinson Crusoe, Jr.,* music mainly by Sigmund Romberg. Here a formula was introduced that would serve Jolson at the Winter Garden for the next few years. The entire show was built to set off his varied gifts as singer and comedian. These productions were fantasies in which Jolson played various roles, but usually a character named Gus who was sent to far-off places and sometimes into the distant past. Wherever he went—however strange the setting or remote the time —Gus always remained Al Jolson.

In *Robinson Crusoe, Jr.,* an American millionaire dreams he is Robinson Crusoe. Within that dream, his chauffeur, Gus—enacted, to be sure, by Jolson—becomes Friday. They are transported to a Spanish castle, to a pirate ship, to a forest in which the trees come alive as beautiful girls. But before the final curtain the story is completely forgotten to allow Jolson to step to the front of the stage and strut his stuff in his inimitable way.

Subsequent Jolson triumphs at the Winter Garden included *Sinbad* (1918) and *Bombo* (1921). In the former, Jolson is a porter named Inbad who is brought back to ancient Bagdad to mingle with characters out of *The Arabian Nights.* In *Bombo,* Jolson is a deck hand on the ship carrying Columbus to the New World. On arrival, the deck hand engages the Indians in a heated deal for the purchase of Manhattan Island.

It was at the Winter Garden that Jolson introduced the songs which will always be recalled as Jolson's; songs which he revived in the first sound picture ever made, *The Jazz Singer,* in 1928; songs which helped make a triumph of the two screen biographies, *The Jolson Story* and *Jolson Sings Again,* in 1946 and 1949. Though Sigmund Romberg was the composer of the basic scores for the Jolson extravaganzas, none of these well-loved and well-remembered Jolson numbers were by him. In keeping with Jolson's habit of interpolating into his productions any song he liked, and any time during the course of its run, numbers by many composers were heard from time to time in these Jolson productions. In *Robinson Crusoe, Jr.*, Jolson introduced "Yacka Hula, Hickey Doola" by E. Ray Goetz, Joe Young, and Pete Wendling; in *Sinbad*, "Rock-a-bye Your Baby with a Dixie Melody" and "Hello, Central, Give Me No Man's Land" by Joe Young, Sam M. Lewis, and Walter Donaldson, "I'll Say She Does" by Buddy De Sylva, Gus Kahn, and Al Jolson, and George Gershwin's first song smash, "Swanee," lyrics by Irving Caesar. In *Bombo*, Jolson made popular "Toot, Toot, Tootsie" by Gus Kahn, Ernie Erdman, and Dan Russo, "California, Here I Come" by Buddy De Sylva, Joseph Meyer, and Al Jolson, and "April Showers" by Buddy De Sylva and Louis Silvers.

The 1920's sounded the death knell for extravaganza as well as for operetta. In the early 1920's the Hippodrome ceased presenting those spectacles for which it had so long served as a mecca. But in 1935, a passing attempt was made to recall the one-time grandeur of the Hippodrome with a characteristic extravaganza. It was called *Jumbo*, with music and lyrics by Rodgers and Hart, and the book by Ben Hecht and Charles MacArthur. Billy Rose, its producer, tried to combine circus, carnival, and spectacle into an old-type Hippodrome stew. Paul Whiteman, the famous orchestra leader, rode on a white steed, and Jimmy Durante made his first entrance clinging to the neck of an elephant. Acrobats did stunts dangling by their toes from a plane, and a pair of performers balanced themselves precariously over an open cage of lions. All this was in the best tradition of the Hippodrome. But extravaganzas no longer appealed to Broadway audiences. *Jumbo* did not do too well, even though it introduced thrills and engendered excitement; even though it presented some of the greatest songs Rodgers and Hart ever wrote, including "My Romance," "Little Girl Blue," and "The Most Beautiful Girl in the World." Three years later the Hippodrome was torn down to make room for a garage—and with that demolition, extravaganza passed into permanent limbo.

Meanwhile, in the middle 1920's, the Winter Garden began to house other types of musical entertainment besides extravaganzas—musical comedies and revues. Al Jolson went to Hollywood to help inaugurate the age of talking pictures and to become one of its first greats.

While it was still flourishing and prospering, the extravaganza found a formidable rival in the presentation of productions with lavish fittings and complex stage machinery. That rival was the revue, really nothing more than vaudeville in fancy dress.

Vaudeville grew out of the olio section of the minstrel show where members of the cast were starred in song and dance routines. As a separate branch of the theater, vaudeville became crystallized by Tony Pastor, a showman who had graduated from the minstrel show. He opened the first theater in America for variety entertainment in Paterson, New Jersey, on March 21, 1865. He then brought this type of entertainment to New York on lower Broadway, attracting a new clientele of women and children not only by promising "clean entertainment" but also by offering door prizes of pots, pans, dress patterns, and sewing materials. He finally came to Union Square in the early 1880's, where the Tony Pastor Music Hall became a shrine of vaudeville entertainment. It was on that stage that Lillian Russell first became popular (indeed, it was Pastor who had coined for her that stage name, since her real name was Helen Louise Leonard); that Weber and Fields appeared successfully before they opened their own burlesque theater; that the young, dapper, George M. Cohan was seen as a member of the Four Cohans before he branched out as a star performer in and writer of musical comedies; that Ben Harney introduced to New York a new type of popular music called piano rags. But if Tony Pastor was the father of vaudeville, the term "vaudeville" for variety entertainment was coined by somebody else. Its first known use in this country was in Louisville, Kentucky, on February 23, 1871 when a variety troupe billed itself as "Sargent's Great Vaudeville Company."

It did not take long for some astute Broadway producer to realize that vaudeville entertainment decked out with the splendor of extravaganza could command far higher admission prices than those at Tony Pastor's Music Hall. George W. Lederer was that producer. In 1894 he rented the Casino Theater to present *The Passing Show*. It differed from vaudeville in that its text, lyrics, and music were written expressly for that production: book and lyrics by Sydney Rosenberg and music by Ludwig Englander. But in other respects *The Passing Show* was vaudeville in coat tails, top hat, and white tie. The program was made up of sketches, acrobatics, beautiful girls posing in "living pictures," spectacles—all climaxed by a gorgeously mounted "divertissement" in the recognizable format of the extravaganza.

So well was *The Passing Show* received that forthwith similar productions were put on by other showmen. *The Merry Whirl* came in 1895; *In Gay New York,* in 1896; *All of the Town,* in 1897; *In Gay Paree,* in 1899. By the time a new century was at hand, the revue had become a permanent fixture on the Broadway scene. It was now awaiting the hand of a producer possessing imagination and genius as well as enterprise.

Florenz Ziegfeld was that man. His brain child, the *Ziegfeld Follies,* was the yardstick by which all other munificently mounted revues were measured for a quarter of a century, the standard toward which they reached, the achievements they aimed to surpass.

Though the son of a serious musician—father Ziegfeld was president of the Chicago Musical College—Florenz knew early that he could find fulfillment only in the more popular areas of American culture. He became the manager of Sandow the Great, the circus strong man, and made him one of the leading attractions of the Chicago World Fair of 1893. Then—as naturally as tide drifts to the shore—Ziegfeld made his way to Broadway. His first production was *A Parlor Match* in 1896 starring Anna Held—diminutive, jet-black eyed French singer and dancer who captured men's hearts in this musical by rolling her eyes and singing in a delightful foreign accent, "Won't You Come and Play With Me?" In 1897, Ziegfeld married her. For the next few years his musical productions were built around her personality. He used all the ballyhoo at his command to make her one of the most publicized stage figures of that day—such as revealing to the press that she took baths in milk. One of the best of these Ziegfeld musicals was *A Parisian Model* (1906) where in one scene alone Anna Held wore six different gowns, one more ravishing than the other, and where once again she made male hearts palpitate this time by singing "I Just Can't Make My Eyes Behave."

It is possible that it was from being married to Anna Held that Ziegfeld acquired his lifelong taste for grand living, for the best and the most exquisite in foods and wines. He made his home in luxurious estates or hotel suites; he traveled in private railway cars; he bought the most fabulous gifts. In short, he liked to surround himself with the opulence attending an Eastern potentate. He had his personal valet, butler, and a whole retinue of servants cater to his slightest whim. He never wrote letters or telephoned when he could send wires, even if the person he was contacting was near at hand. He was a man who not only could live big, but who could think big, act big, and gamble big. When he wanted the best talent for his shows he did not hesitate to offer staggering salaries. He was a producer ready to defray $1200 for a gown worn in a single scene, and just as able to discard a $25,000 set without a second thought because the finished product did not completely suit his taste.

The *Ziegfeld Follies* was his masterwork—even though through the years he did also produce such fabulous musical comedies as Jerome Kern's *Sally* and *Show Boat,* and *Kid Boots* starring Eddie Cantor. Ziegfeld intended his *Follies* to be the American counterpart of the fabled *Folies Bergère* of Paris, and with this aim in view he produced his first revue at the Jardin de Paris, the roof of the New York Theater, on July 8, 1907. This was a comparatively modest affair in the beginning. The whole production cost him $13,000 and the weekly budget was less than $4,000. (By contrast, only a decade later he spent ten times these figures on each of his *Follies.*) But Ziegfeld's penchant for beautiful girls and equally beautiful stage and costume designs was already evident. In later years there would step into the chorus line of the *Ziegfeld Follies* some of the most beautiful women in the world; and out of it would graduate many glamorous stars of stage and screen including Mae Murray, Marion Davies, Lilyan Tashman, Nita Naldi, and Harriet Hoctor. In the first edition, in 1907, one of the main attractions was the 50 "Anna Held Girls," an eye-filling decoration for the production numbers. Other delights in that edition included Helen Broderick in humorous skits; Mlle Dazie performing an exciting dance as Salome; and a spectacular scene in which show girls swam around in a swimming pool in a simulated motion-picture production. "Mr. Ziegfeld," wrote one unidentified New York critic, "has given New York the best melange of mirth, music, and pretty girls that has been seen here in many summers."

For twenty-three editions (up through 1931) Ziegfeld glorified the American girl, dressing her up in some of the most stunning costumes ever seen on the American stage and placing her against stage trappings no less magnificent. He always had the courage to do what others regarded as sheer recklessness. He ignored budgets and production costs with a majestic gesture of indifference in his insatiable desire to make each one of his *Follies* more fabulous than the preceding one.

In 1909 he created for Lillian Lorraine a sea of soap bubbles from which she sang "Nothing but a Bubble," and devised for her a flying machine soaring high above the audience from which she could drop flowers while chanting "Up, Up, in My Aeroplane." In 1914, his first-act finale vividly re-created an episode from the Revolutionary War, the soldiers marching downhill behind George Washington. In 1915 there was featured one scene underseas and another in Elysium. In 1917, the revue culminated in a stirring parade of World War I troops with President Wilson in the reviewing stand.

But Ziegfeld's greatness as a showman lay not so much in the wonderful spectacles he created, not even in the beautiful girls he continually glorified, but in his instinct and astuteness in recognizing latent stage and musical talent.

Nora Bayes was earning $75 a week in vaudeville before a momentous *Follies* debut in which she sang "Shine On, Harvest Moon" (which she wrote in collaboration with her husband, Jack Norworth). Fannie Brice was a humble burlesque queen when Ziegfeld signed her for the 1910 edition in which she sang "Goodbye, Becky Cohen." Some of her most brilliant successes on Broadway came after that in the *Follies* where she was seen as a comedienne with a spicy Yiddish accent and a gawky manner. But in 1921 she startled the *Follies* audience by stepping out of character and appearing as a chanteuse in a plangent French lament, "My Man." The impact of this song was particularly overpowering since the audience knew well that, like the character in the song, Fannie had troubles with her own man, the gangster Nick Arnstein, to whom she was then married.

Ann Pennington made her first appearance in New York in the 1913 *Follies*. She was a dancing sensation, and she remained a dancing sensation in later editions—the queen of the "shimmy." W. C. Fields was an obscure comic when Ziegfeld brought him to the *Follies* of 1915. There he brought down the house with a pantomime billiard game. His impersonations, pantomimes, and rasping ad-libs brightened many a later *Follies*. Eddie Cantor

62

was an obscure member of a musical in California when Ziegfeld found him in 1916. At first Cantor was seen in 1916 in a revue then being produced by Ziegfeld on the "Midnight Roof" of the New Amsterdam Theater. Running up and down the stage, clapping his hands, his eyes almost popping out of their sockets, he sang "Oh! How She Could Yacki, Hacki, Wicki, Wacki Woo." The year after that he was made a star of the *Follies* where, evening after evening, he had to give a dozen or more encores of "That's the Kind of a Baby for Me."

Before 1917, Will Rogers was an awkward cowboy comedian. But in the *Follies* of that year Ziegfeld let him make trenchant social and political comments while twirling a lariat. "Congress is so strange," he drawled. "A man gets up to speak and says nothing. Nobody listens. Then everybody disagrees." A homespun philosopher was born.

These were only a few of the many who helped make the *Follies* a nursery for some of the greatest stars the American musical theater has known. But others were performers of established repute when they were lured by Ziegfeld to the *Follies* with fabulous salary offers: Leon Errol, Sophie Tucker (already a "red-hot mamma" in 1909), Marilyn Miller, the Negro pantomimist Bert Williams, celebrated for his poker-game routine, and the "perfect fool" Ed Wynn, even then famous for his strange assortment of hats, screwy inventions, and oily high-pitched voice.

Ziegfeld employed staff composers and lyricists to write the bulk of the songs for each of the editions. For many years his main lyricist was Gene Buck, and his principal composers were Dave Stamper, Louis Hirsch, and Raymond Hubbell. But Ziegfeld did not hesitate to engage leading members of Broadway and Tin Pan Alley for special songs and numbers. Some of the most important names in American popular music are found on the credits of the various *Follies,* among them being Irving Berlin, Jerome Kern, Rudolf Friml, Victor Herbert, and Gus Edwards. It was in the *Follies* that songs like these were either introduced or were first made famous: Irving Berlin's "A Pretty Girl Is Like a Melody" and "You'd Be Surprised"; Victor Herbert's "A Kiss in the Dark"; Walter Donaldson's "My Blue Heaven"; Jimmie V. Monaco's "Row, Row, Row."

Ziegfeld's fabulous career reached its climax in 1927. In that year he realized a life's ambition by opening his own theater—the Ziegfeld, on Sixth Avenue, a veritable Taj Mahal of show business. Befitting such an occasion he produced for its opening *Rio Rita,* a phantasmagoria of ballets, spectacles and scenic designs with a Mexican setting. Later the same year—and in the same new theater—he put on a musical that made stage history, Jerome Kern's *Show Boat.* From such dizzy heights he could go nowhere but down—and his descent was precipitous. The approaching depression, his refusal to lower his standards, his sublime indifference to practical bookkeeping, his personal extravagance—all this spelled inevitable doom. He went deeper and deeper into debt until nobody could help him anymore. Besides, his once magic touch in creating box-office bonanzas failed him. His last *Follies,* in 1931, had a run of only 165 performances—which, in view of the formidable expenses involved, meant financial disaster. He was virtually penniless when he died a year later, and what assets he had left were seized by his many creditors.

Musical Comedy Is Born / 4

If there is one man who can be singled out as the father of musical comedy as we know it today he is George M. Cohan. Musicals like *Little Johnny Jones* (1904) and *Forty-Five Minutes from Broadway* (1906) were neither extravaganza nor burlesque, neither operetta nor revue. This was a completely new form, combining some of the elements of all these branches of our musical theater. From the extravaganza, musical comedy took attractive costuming, mountings, and production numbers; from burlesque—travesty, satire, and chorus girls; from operetta—romance and glamour, a world where good always triumphs over evil and the boy always gets the girl; from revue—the star system and the set routines for principal performers.

Yet musical comedy also brought something fresh and new and personal: a racy American identity. In George M. Cohan's musicals the characters were the kind Americans were familiar with personally or through newspapers and magazines (a jockey, an ex-boxer, a U.S. Senator, a super-patriot, a manufacturer, and so forth). The settings were also familiar—New Rochelle, Broadway, or Washington, D.C., for example. All this may have been true more or less with the burlesques of Harrigan and Hart and Charley Hoyt, but what was not true of them —and was of Cohan's musicals—was that the dialogue was also colloquial and native; the lyrics and the music had a light and jaunty air about them uniquely American; and the over-all spirit engendered by the Cohan productions were breezy, cocksure, energetic, chauvinistic in an unmistakably American kind of way. One of Cohan's pet routines was to drape an American flag around his body and run up and down the stage singing the praises of country and flag. Figuratively speaking, the American flag was also draped all around the body of his musical comedies.

George M. Cohan's musicals were only one of many expressions of national pride prevailing in the early 1900's. The birth of the 20th century had brought a new era to this country. America had just gone through a brief and victorious conflict with Spain, and was about to extend her influence further by leasing the Canal Zone in Panama for the construction of a canal. The country was prosperous. Everywhere were signs of growth and expansion: in the West through the application of science to agriculture and through the development of railroad transportation; in the South with the exploitation of natural resources and the rise of factories; in the East through the bulging of the modern city and through expanded trade with Europe. The new century thought in big terms. The trust had become a giant in industry: a survey in the early 1900's revealed that some 5000 organizations had been swallowed up into less than 300 trusts. Finance was controlled by giants like Rockefeller and Morgan. The first skyscraper (the Flatiron Building in New York in 1902) carried a similar concept of bigness to architecture. Sheet music, newspapers, magazines, novels achieved bigness through fabulous circulations.

The new century looked into the future with confidence as electricity, the telephone, and other inventions opened new vistas. The railroad, the trolley car, the subway, and the automobile were quickening the tempo of everyday movement and living.

Everyone seemed conscious of the promises held by the new century. Consequently there was a bulging of the national ego, and a wave of chauvinism began to sweep over the country. It found a voice in the rousing marches which John Philip Sousa was writing. It was reflected in the books of Jack London, Edith Wharton, and Frank Norris, who sought out American backgrounds, experiences, and characters for their stories. It was found in serious composers beginning to free themselves from European traditions and thinking by having them write *American* music: composers like Henry F. Gilbert, who based concert music on minstrel-show tunes and Negro spirituals, like Edward MacDowell, who wrote symphonic works with American-Indian melodies and rhythms, and Walter Damrosch, who created an American opera in *The Scarlet Letter*. Native American drama emerged in plays like *The Great Divide* by William Vaughan Moody. Ziegfeld was glorifying the *American* girl. And, completely in the spirit of the times, George M. Cohan was writing *American* musical comedies.

George M. Cohan established some of the rules that would govern musical comedy for many years. Any thread of a plot, however slender, served Cohan's purpose, just so long as it could tie together into a neat package the kind of songs he liked to write, the kind of dances he liked to perform, the kind of humor he liked to project, and the kind of characterizations, ideas, and routines he liked to present. It did not concern him overly that the coincidences dramatizing his story and carrying it to a denouement were far-fetched, that the situations into which he thrust his people were highly improbable, and that most of his material was sublimely irrelevant to the basic plot line. The only thing he was interested in was projecting his cogent, dynamic, irresistible personality across the footlights and through that means providing an audience with an evening's entertainment.

And the personality he projected over the footlights with such assurance and skill was his, and his alone. He wore his hat cockily over one eye; and in his hand swung a bamboo cane. He sang out of the corner of his mouth with a peculiar nasal twang. He would continually gesture to his audience with a forceful forefinger as he delivered a homey message. He liked to strut up and down the stage as if it were his entire world, and he its emperor. He liked best of all to sing the praises of his country dressed up in a flag.

He wrote his own plays, lyrics, and music. But that was not all. Often he was the star performer as well, and occasionally even part producer. He was, in an age of trusts, a one-man cartel of the theater. He was not equally gifted in every department, and he knew it. "I can write better plays than any living dancer," he once remarked facetiously, "and dance better than any living playwright." And again: "As a composer I could never find use for over four or five notes in any musical number . . . and as a playwright most of my plays have been presented in two acts for the simple reason I couldn't think of an idea for the third act." But for all his limitations—and they were many—he was a cyclone that helped fell old ideas, foreign approaches, decadent procedures. A showman to the tips of his fingers and his nimble toes, he carried into the theater a gust of fresh wind and a quickened heartbeat. He helped to lift musical productions out of the doldrums into which they were rapidly succumbing through such dying forms as the operetta, burlesque, and the extravaganza; he carried our musical theater to the threshhold of modernity.

He was literally born into the theater, in Providence, Rhode Island, on July 3, 1878. (Later on in his life he liked to tell people he was a Yankee Doodle boy born on the Fourth of July; but his birth certificate refuses to co-operate with him.) His parents—Jeremiah and Helen Cohan—were veteran vaudevillians. When children arrived (George Michael was the youngest of three) they were dragged by the parents around the country to live in broken-down boardinghouses, and wait in musty, drafty dressing rooms of decrepit theaters. Under such conditions, a formal education of any kind was out of the question for George. His training came not from the three R's but from grease paint, the buck and wing, and meticulous, split-second timing in delivering a joke or a song.

Even as an infant he made stage appearances, used as a prop in a vaudeville skit. He spoke his first lines on the stage when he was nine, and at ten he joined his sister Josephine as regular members of an act henceforth billed on the vaudeville circuit as "The Four Cohans." Little George did a specialty number as a bootblack, performed buck and wing steps, recited sentimental poems. But this did not satisfy him. By the time he was eleven he started writing material for the act, and two years after that he contributed some of its songs for which he wrote melody and lyrics. Before the end of the 19th century veteran vaudevillians like the dynamic May Irwin were singing his songs, one or two of which were numbered among Tin Pan Alley's leading hits ("I Guess I'll Have to Telegraph My Baby," for example).

By 1900, The Four Cohans was a vaudeville headline act earning $1000 a week, and was appearing in the country's foremost theaters including the Tony Pastor Music Hall in Union Square. Young George M. Cohan was the act's star performer now, as well as its writer, composer, lyricist, and business manager. And yet he needed more worlds to conquer! He was now thinking of the Broadway stage. With a caution that did not usually characterize him he first penetrated the legitimate Broadway theater by expanding his vaudeville sketches into full-length musicals. But this did not work out. *The Governor's Son* (1901) and *Running for Office* (1903) were failures. It was then that he decided to write an original full-length Broadway musical with new material.

One of the most famous American jockeys of that period was Tod Sloan, who had gone to England in 1903 to ride in the Derby for the King of England. Sloan provided Cohan with the main character for his new musical, *Little Johnny Jones*. A visit to England where Cohan had been impressed by the dock at Southampton and the courtyard of one of London's hotels, contributed two settings. With these as his start, Cohan dashed off libretto and songs within the space of a few weeks. Then he himself staged the show, and when it came to the Liberty Theater on November 7, 1904, he played the title role. The plot was a mixture of unbelievable episodes and developments. Johnny Jones, an American jockey come to London to ride in the Derby, is falsely accused of being in league with big-time gamblers and of having thrown the race. A detective, who throughout the play poses as a drunkard, is hot on the trail of evidence to clear Johnny. The jockey first learns that his innocence can be proved at Southampton, where he has come to bid bon voyage to some American friends sailing for home. "Give My Regards to Broadway" he sings to them nostalgically, in what has since become one of Cohan's most frequently heard numbers. A prearranged signal of fireworks, leaping from shipboard, is to inform Johnny if the detective has come upon the evidence necessary to clear him. As the boat glides off in the distance, the shooting flames leap skyward from the boat. The villain in the play is an American gambler who runs a Chinese gambling establishment in San Francisco. The heroine is Goldie Gates, with whom Johnny is in love and to whom he can now propose marriage, having been cleared of guilt.

"Give My Regards to Broadway" is one of two songs made famous and introduced by Cohan in *Little Johnny Jones;* the other was the first of his celebrated chauvinistic hymns, "Yankee Doodle Boy." Cohan also assumed in this musical some of the stage tricks and mannerisms henceforth to identify him: that kangaroo dance step, for example, and the rendition of homespun philosophy in a recitation entitled "Life's a Funny Proposition After All."

Before *Little Johnny Jones* came on the Broadway scene several productions had been labeled musical comedies. Some of them suggested a few of the approaches or techniques of a later-day musical comedy. But it is with *Little Johnny Jones* that American musical comedy appears with most of its recognizable physical features and stereotypes. Later on, musical comedy would become slicker, smarter, more sophisticated; but its basic style, format, spirit, and aesthetics were those crystallized by George M. Cohan in 1904.

Little Johnny Jones was not received favorably by the critics. At first it looked as if its life on Broadway would be seriously curtailed by public apathy. Cohan closed it down after only 52 performances and took it on tour where he rewrote some of the scenes and tightened the structure. Out of town the musical was received most enthusiastically, encouraging Cohan to bring it back to Broadway where it now had an eminently successful engagement.

Cohan's second full-length musical comedy proved even more successful, *Forty-Five Minutes from Broadway* (1906). Its setting is the prosperous suburb of New York, New Rochelle, and its complicated story had to do with a lost will which, when finally found in an old suit of clothes, brings an inheritance to a lovable housemaid, Mary Jane. But Mary Jane is in love with Kid Burns, a man of principle who refuses to marry a girl for her money. Since love means more to Mary Jane than wealth, she destroys the will.

Forty-Five Minutes from Broadway created a disturbance among the citizens of New Rochelle who felt that their community was being slandered by some of Cohan's wry comments about suburban life and its people. Even before the play opened, the Chamber of Commerce voted to boycott the play and denounce it as a libel. This, of course, did not keep the play from opening, nor, for that matter, from being successful from the first night on. When the Chamber of Commerce came to the realization that Cohan was rapidly making New Rochelle famous, rather than the reverse, it quietly dropped all charges.

The best Cohan songs were the title number and two tunes inspired by the heroine, "Mary's a Grand Old Name" and "So Long, Mary." Beyond these songs, the musical boasted performances by two eminent artists. One was Fay Templeton as Mary Jane in her first perform- ance in what was described at the time as "a clean play" after two decades in burlesque and at the Weber and Fields Music Hall. (Indeed, it was for her that this mu- sical was written.) The other was Victor Moore as Kid Burns, a charming no-good who likes playing the horses, loafing, and getting into trouble—a character inspired by a one-time pugilist, also named Kid Burns, whom Cohan had known personally. Victor Moore had come to the Broadway stage after rich experiences in vaudeville and stock companies, and it was here that he introduced the first of many characterizations as a sad-faced, broken- voiced comic.

Later the same year of 1906 a second outstanding George M. Cohan musical appeared on Broadway, *George Washington, Jr.* Cohan here starred himself as a super- patriot who assumes the name of the first President of the United States and who succeeds in arousing an equally ardent patriotic fire in his father, an Anglophile. The flag routine that was a Cohan invention and spe- cialty was a notable attraction in this show, for which Cohan wrote "You're a Grand Old Flag." Strange to say, a considerable stir of opposition was at first created among patriotic circles against this song before the mu- sical comedy opened. Cohan was inspired to write it when a G.A.R. veteran, colorbearer during Pickett's charge on Gettysburg, told him about his war experiences and re- marked "she's a grand old *rag*" while pointing to a nearby flag. In Cohan's first version of his song he used the word "rag" for "flag," much to the chagrin of numerous pa- triots who felt that "rag" was a slur. When Cohan re- vised his lyric to replace "flag" for "rag" all was forgiven and forgotten.

Hardly a season passed between 1906 and the end of World War I without at least one, and sometimes sev- eral, Cohan musicals on Broadway. The best were *The*

Talk of the Town (1907), *The Yankee Prince* (1908), *The Man Who Owns Broadway* (1909), *The Little Millionaire* (1911), and *Hello Broadway* (1914). He also wrote all the material for the *Cohan Revue* in 1916 and 1918, besides being the author of some outstandingly successful nonmusical plays including *Get Rich-Quick Wallingford* and *Seven Keys to Baldpate*. In addition to all this, during the period of World War I, he wrote a popular song with which that conflict will always be associated and which must always be included among the most famous American war songs of all time—"Over There." A quarter of a century after it was written, this song earned for Cohan a special gold medal at the hands of President Roosevelt.

Cohan, then, soared as high as anybody could on Broadway in the era preceding and during the First World War. He was Mr. Broadway—by virtue of his plays, musical comedies, songs, performances as actor, owner of theaters, and producer. Then came the first of several incidents to change him into a bitter man.

In 1919, the Actors Equity Association called a strike in an effort to gain recognition from theater managers as a bargaining agent for its members, and also to remedy some abuses. Cohan joined the producers and managers in an all-out fight against Equity, and, before long, became the spearhead in the attack. The fact that many of his friends, and others who had been recipients of his benefactions, were on Equity's side seemed to Cohan like an act of treachery. In his eyes this struggle was no longer one between employer and employee, management and labor, but one between Cohan and ungrateful friends. He was intransigent in his position that there was no place for unionism in the theater. He refused to compromise. When Equity won out, and other producers rushed to make peace, Cohan looked on this development as personal defeat. He turned away from former friends and business associates. He dropped his membership in actors' clubs and closed down his producing firm. He insisted for a while that he was through with the Broadway theater for good.

The sad part of this situation—and its crowning paradox—was the fact that it was not Cohan who was through with the Broadway theater but the Broadway theater that was through with him. When this truth dawned on him, it became the second blow to destroy his spirit. He did not stay long in retirement; the blood of the theater was still warm and restless within him. He soon started writing again—musicals as well as nonmusicals—and producing them on Broadway. Most were miserable failures, while only one or two were moderately successful. "I guess people don't understand me anymore," he confided sadly to a friend, "and I don't understand them. It's got so that an evening's entertainment just won't do. Give an audience an evening of what they call realism and you've got a hit. It's getting too much for me, kid."

What he could not realize was that the theater had grown, whereas he had stood still. Librettists, composers, lyricists with sharper and more original gifts than his—with greater imagination, inventiveness, and technical skill—were beginning to teach Broadway how naive were Cohan's simple homilies, how ingenuous were his sentimental lyrics and melodies, how absurd his manufactured plots and synthetic characters. The product Cohan was trying to dispense in the 1920's was just too old-fashioned for a knowledgeable and sophisticated audience because it was exactly the same kind of product he had sold in the early 1900's.

He was administered an additional bitter dose of medicine in Hollywood in 1932, where he had gone to star in *The Phantom President*. He expected the red-carpet treatment befitting one who had been a lord and master in the theater for a quarter of a century. What he found instead were producers and directors trying to teach him how to act and sing. When an attempt was even made to show him how best to perform a flag routine—which

74

he regarded as his personal property—he exploded. He finished the picture under duress and vowed never again to make another. "If I had my choice between Hollywood and Atlanta, I'd take Leavenworth," was the way he put it.

Nevertheless there were still some triumphs left for him to enjoy. In 1933 he starred on Broadway in Eugene O'Neill's comedy of American life at the turn of the century, *Ah, Wilderness!* His performance completely won the hearts of critics and audiences. In 1937 he again received accolades for his acting ability when he impersonated President Franklin D. Roosevelt in the Rodgers and Hart musical comedy, *I'd Rather Be Right*. And in 1942 his life story was dramatized in a magnificent motion picture called *Yankee Doodle Dandy* in which James Cagney's impersonation of Cohan won an Academy Award. The day on which this motion picture opened in New York was proclaimed by Mayor La Guardia as "George M. Cohan Day" and (since this was during World War II) a capacity audience had purchased about 6 million dollars of war bonds to gain admission to the premiere performance. And 2 years before this, in 1940, President Roosevelt had conferred on him a gold medal.

To anybody else, all this would have represented a personal victory of the first magnitude; for Cohan it all had a hollow ring. In *Ah, Wilderness!* he was appearing in somebody else's play and speaking somebody else's lines. In *I'd Rather Be Right* he was singing somebody else's songs. When he did manage to appear on Broadway with something of his own he was vigorously rejected. His last musical, *Billie* (1928) stayed on less than 4 months and lost money, and his last nonmusical play, *The Return of the Vagabond* (1940) had only 7 performances. "They don't want me no more," he remarked when the latter play closed. And he never again was seen on the Broadway stage.

He died a little over 2 years after that—in New York on November 5, 1942—with all the honors a grateful theater could bestow on one who had been a giant. It is not hard to attack the Cohan musicals from the critical standards of today. It was not even difficult to attack Cohan while he was still popular and successful, and many did. James S. Metcalf, for example, wrote in *Life* in the early 1900's that Cohan was a "vulgar, cheap, blatant, ill-mannered, flashily-dressed, insolent smart Alec who, for some reasons unexplainable on any basis of common sense, good taste, or ordinary decency, appeals to the imagination and approval of large American audiences." Yes!—Cohan was flashy, obvious, trite, naive, cocksure, and sentimental. But no historian of the American musical theater can underestimate his achievement in creating the musical comedy. "He put the symbols of American life into American music," said Mayor La Guardia when Cohan died; he might have gone farther and added that Cohan put the same symbols on our stage. "He was the greatest single figure the American theater ever produced," said Gene Buck. Cohan had been on the stage 58 years. In that time he wrote about 40 plays, collaborated on 40 others, helped to produce another 150, and published over 500 songs. But, most important of all, he was the first important creator of musical comedy—and for this reason, if for no other, his immortality is assured.

A Trio of Musical Fame / 5

Between 1915 and 1918 several musical comedies known as the "Princess Theater Shows" were produced. They brought into our musical theater a new air of sophistication, an adult style and intelligence, a fresh viewpoint, and a developed writing skill in all departments.

The composer was at that time one of the most gifted to appear on Broadway since Victor Herbert; later on he would become a creative figure second to none in our theater. He was Jerome Kern.

Kern had made his Broadway bow almost a year before *Little Johnny Jones* had opened, and it had taken place with *Mr. Wix of Wickham*, an English musical adapted for Americans. It was not much of a show to begin with, and it was even worse when it came to America, which rejected it in no uncertain terms. But some of the fresh and unusual harmonic and instrumental sounds arising from the orchestra pit made at least one critic sit up and take notice. "Who is this Jerome Kern," inquired Alan Dale, "whose music towers in an Eiffel way above the hurdy-gurdy accompaniment of the present-day musical comedy?"

There was good reason why Alan Dale had not heard of him. Kern was about 20 years old at the time, a poorly paid, humble employee in Tin Pan Alley. His only experience in the theater up to this time had been acquired not on Broadway but in and around Piccadilly Circus in London.

Jerome Kern was born in New York City on January

27, 1885 to a comparatively well-to-do family. His academic education took place in the New York public schools and at Barringer High School in Newark, New Jersey. He received his initial training in music at the piano from his mother after which, for about a year, he studied harmony, theory, as well as the piano, at the New York College of Music.

His father, a successful merchant, wanted him to go into business. Jerry's inclinations lay in the direction of music. Besides playing the piano all the time at home he used to perform at school assemblies and write songs for school productions; teachers at Barringer High School used to refer to him as "that musical genius." One incident convinced the father that this boy was no business tycoon. After being graduated from high school, Jerry worked one summer for his father, the owner of a merchandizing firm in Newark. One day that firm needed two pianos, which it did not have in stock. The father sent his musical son to a New York wholesale dealer to get them. The owner of that establishment invited young Kern to his house for an Italian dinner and filled him with heart-warming Chianti wine. After that, the wholesaler did not have much trouble convincing Kern that the price he asked for the pianos was such a bargain that it would be a business coup for him to buy out the whole stock—200 instruments. This deal might have ruined father Kern if he had not finally managed to devise a shrewd installment plan whereby all the pianos could be disposed of at a profit. But the deal did convince the father that Jerry, whether or not he was meant by fate to be a musician, most certainly was not intended for the world of commerce.

It was at this point that the father permitted the boy to continue his music study at the New York College of Music. About a year after that—in the early fall of 1903—the father footed the bills for a European trip where young Kern might continue his musical education. In Europe, Kern traveled about a good deal, listened to a considerable amount of good music, took some lessons in theory and composition from private teachers in Heidelberg. Then he settled for a while in London, where he found a job for $10 a week writing songs for productions then being put on the London stage by Charles Frohman, an American producer.

Toward the end of 1903 one of Kern's songs appeared for the first time on the stage: "My Little Canoe" in *The School Girl* at the Pavilion Music Hall. It was sung by Billie Burke, then in her first public appearance as a singer, but subsequently one of America's glamorous stars of stage and screen, and the second wife of Florenz Ziegfeld. Other Kern songs appeared in various musicals starring Seymour Hicks, a popular English performer of that time. One of these numbers, "Mr. Chamberlain," became quite a hit. This was a topical song with numerous verses about a famous politician—the "Chamberlain" in the piece being the leader of the Liberal Unionists and father of Neville, England's Prime Minister just before World War II.

"Mr. Chamberlain" is important in Kern's life not only because it was his first song hit but also because it was the first time he wrote music to the lyrics of P. G. Wodehouse. In 1904, P. G. Wodehouse was a bright young columnist on one of London's leading newspapers. Before long he would become famous for his whimsical novels and tales in which the main character is a butler named Jeeves. And in the history of the American musical theater his name would stand out prominently through his collaborations with Jerome Kern and other famous Broadway composers; but much more will be said of this later on.

Kern returned to the United States in 1904. Now determined to make his way in popular music, he sought employment in Tin Pan Alley. At first he worked in the billing department of the Lyceum Publishing Company —a firm which, in 1901, had issued Kern's first published composition, *At the Casino*, for piano solo. After that,

Kern worked as a song plugger for Shapiro-Remick, demonstrating songs in five-and-ten cent stores. It was while he was holding this job that he got an assignment to adapt the British score of *Mr. Wix of Wickham* for Broadway.

In 1905, Kern went to work for Harms Publishing Company, his salary $12 a week, his duties to sell sheet music to and demonstrate songs in department stores. His employer was Max Dreyfus, a keen judge of creative talent. It did not take Dreyfus long to realize that there was something in Kern well worth watching and encouraging. He saw to it that Kern found opportunities to supplement his salary by working as Marie Dressler's accompanist in vaudeville, and by working as a rehearsal pianist for Broadway shows. Kern was also encouraged by Dreyfus to write songs which Harms published, beginning a publisher-composer relationship that persisted until the end of Kern's life.

It did not take Kern long to justify the faith and hope Dreyfus had reposed in him. One of the first Kern songs published by Harms was "How'd You Like to Spoon with Me?" Georgia Caine and Victor Morley introduced it in *The Earl and the Girl* at the Casino Theater in 1905 and it became a hit. The New York *Dramatic Mirror* described the number as "the most successful . . . introduced here; it was demanded again and again."

"How'd You Like to Spoon with Me?" was interpolated into the score of another composer, for the basic music for *The Earl and the Girl* was by Ivan Caryll. Interpolating songs into musical shows was a practice widely prevalent on Broadway in the 1900's and 1910's—we have already seen how Al Jolson used to do this consistently at the Winter Garden. This was part of an over-all tradition which dictated that songs, dances, humor, and big scenes did not always have to be basic to the musical-comedy text; often they could be introduced without any concern whether they fit into the general design or not, and just as often even after the show had started its

Broadway engagement. Thus, if a producer happened to come across a song he thought had entertainment value he did not hesitate to drop it into some convenient slot into his musical.

Such a haphazard procedure might play havoc with the over-all pattern, unity, or balance of a musical production. But it also proved a boon to unknown composers. Producers preferred experienced hands—men with established reputations—to write the music for their shows. But they were not reluctant to try out a single song by an unknown if that number happened to strike their fancy. Thus many novices in Tin Pan Alley found innumerable opportunities to get their songs placed on Broadway, either in musicals about to be produced, or those already running.

In the case of Jerome Kern, for 8 years after *Mr. Wix of Wickham* he had over 100 songs interpolated into Broadway musicals—most of them foreign operettas adapted for New York. Thus, before he was engaged to write a complete score of his own, he acquired a valuable apprenticeship. Over a period of many years he could learn first hand what made musicals tick, what spelled success for a song within those shows. He could develop his technique, learn the ingredients that went into good showmanship, discover what audiences reacted to most strongly and why. When he was finally required to write a complete score of his own he had a rich backlog of experiences to draw upon.

In 1911 he contributed seven songs to *La Belle Paree* which opened the Winter Garden. A year and a half later he wrote the full score for *The Red Petticoat,* a failure. Kern's first successful musical comedy appeared in 1914, *The Girl from Utah.* It was with this production that Kern's eventful career on Broadway can be said to begin.

The Girl from Utah was an American adaptation of an English musical. Kern's contribution consisted of eight numbers. Julia Sanderson played the title role, a girl fleeing to London to avoid becoming one of several wives of a Mormon. Though this Mormon pursues her, she succeeds in eluding him permanently and in finding a man she loves and wants to marry. Kern's score had two appealing numbers, and a third that is a classic. The two were "Why Don't They Dance the Polka Anymore?" and "I'd Like to Wander with Alice in Wonderland." The classic is "They Didn't Believe Me," lyrics by Herbert Reynolds—a number so fresh in melodic design, so unusual in its modulations, so poignant in its sincere emotion, and so beautifully sculptured in its structure that it stands out from most of the other songs heard on the Broadway stage at that time with the vividness and brilliance of pure gold in the company of faded brass. When Victor Herbert heard "They Didn't Believe Me" he remarked simply: "This man will inherit my mantle."

After 1914, Kern became one of Broadway's most prolific and significant composers. Each season, two, three, and sometimes more productions carried his songs to the footlights. Each season there was at least one Jerome Kern musical that stood at the head of the successes. Each season there was at least one Kern song to make the nation hum.

It was with the Princess Theater Shows that Kern helped musical comedy make its most dramatic and eventful advance since George M. Cohan. Sheer accident, rather than calculation, led to the creation of these musicals. The Princess Theater was a small house able to accommodate only 300 or so patrons. There were not enough stage attractions on Broadway catering to so limited an audience, and consequently this theater was always in the red. One day, Elizabeth Marbury, a literary agent, came to the theater's owner, F. Ray Comstock, with a plan. Why not devise musical productions suitable to the intimacy of this theater? Since the box-office receipts at the Princess were necessarily far below those of a normal-sized house, Marbury had in mind produc-

82

tions that were economically conceived—with small casts, limited sets and costumes, no stars, and an orchestra comprising only a handful of musicians. And, since the auditorium was so small, Marbury also had in mind keeping these productions intimate in style and format. "Now is the time to do something about elevating musical comedy," she told Comstock, revealing she had an idealistic as well as a functional mission in mind. She was sure that such an elevation could come by dispensing with much of the meretricious nonsense that had been encumbering musical comedy at the time and concentrating instead on good texts, good music, and good all-around performances.

Elizabeth Marbury arranged for Jerome Kern to work with the librettist, Guy Bolton, on a new musical for the Princess Theater. Bolton later became a shining light among Broadway librettists and lyricists. But in 1915 he was still a novice. He was an Englishman come to the United States to pursue a career as architect. A natural bent for writing led him to create stories, sketches, and plays, some of which were published. His first attempt to write a musical-comedy text had taken place earlier that same year of 1915 when he collaborated with Clare Kummer on *Ninety in the Shade,* for which Kern had written music. *Ninety in the Shade* was a dud.

That initial Princess Theater Show which Elizabeth Marbury hired him to write was Bolton's second adventure on Broadway as well as his second collaboration with Kern. *Nobody Home,* which opened on April 20, 1915, was an adaptation of an English comedy. Its central character was an amusing Englishman, Mr. Popple of Ippleton, who comes to New York and gets involved with a chorus girl. In Bolton's hands the play held its interest for the audience mainly through witty lines, amusing situations, and fresh characterizations. All else was on a modest scale. There were only 8 girls in the chorus line, and 11 musicians in the orchestra. The sets and the costumes were the last word in functional simplicity. The humor developed naturally out of the situations within the play, and so did songs and dances.

The hundred and more performances of *Nobody Home* realized a modest profit for the producers, and thus proved a stimulus to continue along the same lines. The second Princess Theater Show, *Very Good Eddie* (1915) ran over a year and brought in a profit of over $100,000. *Oh, Boy!* (1917) was an even greater success.

Very Good Eddie was an amusing escapade involving two honeymoon couples about to board a Hudson River Day Line boat. A mix-up ensues in which the husband of one couple and the wife of the other set sail, while the other pair is left stranded on the pier. The fiction that the sailing pair is married to each other leads to innumerable embarrassments and harassments. The comedy thus evolved is sharpened by Guy Bolton's flashing lines of dialogue and by deft performances by Ernest Truex and Alice Dovey.

In *Oh, Boy!* the setting is an American college town, and its gaiety stems from having a strange young lady conceal herself in the hero's apartment to escape false arrest. To protect the honor of her host she must assume various disguises.

In the first two Princess Theater Shows the lyrics to Kern's songs were written respectively by Bolton himself and by Schuyler Greene. But in *Oh, Boy* the lyricist is P. G. Wodehouse. Since 1904, when he had first started writing for Kern, Wodehouse had become a famous story writer and novelist. He then settled temporarily in New York where he wrote drama reviews for *Vanity Fair*. In this capacity he attended the première of *Very Good Eddie*. After the show, Kern and Bolton suggested to Wodehouse that in the future he join up with them in writing the Princess Theater Shows.

The new union of Kern, Bolton, and Wodehouse was to prove a most happy arrangement. The same kind of wit and graceful style, the same kind of impatience with a cliché and stereotype, that had made *Very Good Eddie*

such delightful entertainment now were found in Wodehouse's lyrics. In the 1910's the song lyric—both in Tin
Pan Alley and on Broadway—was a sad and weary marriage of bromides, miserable prosody, and stilted sentiments. Wodehouse's verses were a radical departure from
such shallow processes. His touch was light and nimble;
his versification, neat and precise; his turn of a phrase,
graceful. And he could give voice to sentiment without
lapsing into bathos.

So harmoniously did Kern, Bolton, and Wodehouse
work together in the Princess Theater that one unidentified commentator expressed his enthusiasm in the following verse:

> *This is the trio of musical fame:*
> *Bolton and Wodehouse and Kern;*
> *Better than anyone else you can name.*
> *Bolton and Wodehouse and Kern.*
> *Nobody knows what on earth they've been bitten by,*
> *All I can say is I mean to get lit an' buy*
> *Orchestra seats for the next one that's written by*
> *Bolton and Wodehouse and Kern.*

Oh, Boy! was their first triumph. After that came *Oh,
Lady! Lady!* (1918), which soon needed a second company, in a nearby larger theater, to accommodate the
pressing demand for tickets. Here a Long Island playboy,
on the eve of getting married, meets his old girl friend.
The ensuing difficulties provide a good amount of not so
innocent merriment. A subsidiary plot compounds comedy
upon comedy through the antics of a valet, who had once
been a crook, and his wife, a chronic shoplifter.

Oh, Lady! Lady! was the last Princess Theater Show
written by Kern, Bolton, and Wodehouse. The very last
of these intimate productions was *Oh, My Dear!* (1918),
for which Louis Hirsch wrote the music for Bolton and
Wodehouse.

The influence of the Princess Theater Show was decisive and permanent. Its wit and adult intelligence, economical approaches and intimate designs, its pronounced Americanism and over-all integration of material was a pronounced forward step from the musical comedies of George M. Cohan. As Guy Bolton himself once explained:

"The Princess Theater Show was straight, consistent comedy with the addition of music. Every song and lyric contributed to the action. The humor was based on the situation, not interjected by comedians. . . . Realism and Americanism were other distinguishing traits."

And the music of Jerome Kern represented a brave new world of sound. Nobody on Broadway, not even Victor Herbert, could match the personal way in which Kern fashioned an unforgettable melodic line, or the original approaches he brought to harmony, modulation, and rhythm. For *Nobody Home* Kern wrote "The Magic Melody" which Carl Engel, one of America's most distinguished musicologists, described at that time as "the opening chorus of an epoch." For *Very Good Eddie* Kern created "Babes in the Wood" and "Nodding Roses." In *Oh, Boy!* we find "Till the Clouds Roll By," a title used many years later for Kern's screen biography. The best songs of *Oh, Lady! Lady!* were "Before I Met You" and "You Found Me and I Found You."

"As the composer of . . . the Princess Theater Shows," Richard Rodgers has written, "he was typical of what was and still is good in our general maturity in this country in that he had his musical roots in the fertile middle-European and English school of operetta writing and amalgamated it with everything that was fresh in the American scene to give us something wonderfully new and clear in music writing in the world. Actually, he was a giant with one foot in Europe and the other in America."

The Revue Becomes a Mirror / 6
to the Fabulous 1920's

The 1920's was a period of great prosperity. Business flourished, and the stock market was spiraling continually toward new heights. The era was one of lavish spending and luxurious living. In such a climate, the musical theater knew one of its most flourishing periods. There were as many as 40—sometimes even 50—musical productions a season on Broadway. The percentage of box-office successes was high. Because of the competition, the average run of a musical in the 1920's was far lower than that of a later period. But production costs were low and admission prices, by comparison, high. A run of 200 performances represented a commercial hit, while a run exceeding 300 performances a smash success. Though thousand-performance runs were unknown, more musicals made money in the 1920's than ever before or since.

The extravagance characterizing American life in the 1920's could also be found within the theater. Productions grew increasingly sumptuous. Casts were made more luminous with a greater number of stars than heretofore. Production costs and weekly budgets skyrocketed. Ziegfeld was now spending more than $20,000 a week in salaries for a *Follies*, while his production cost before the curtain rose on a première passed the $100,000 mark.

Through the 1920's the *Ziegfeld Follies* were more than ever the most opulent productions on Broadway. But while Ziegfeld was the king of such revues, he had plenty of imitators and rivals. The plush revue was one of the favored forms of stage entertainment during this decade.

Since 1912 the Shuberts had been putting out each year resplendent editions of *The Passing Show*—the name, but nothing else, borrowed from the 1894 production with which the revue came into existence. In *The Passing Show*, in the 1910's, many a star was born: Willie and Eugene Howard, the incomparable pair of clowns, in 1912; Marilyn Miller, after years in vaudeville, rising to the heights by singing "Omar Khayyam," dancing, and giving impersonations, in 1914; Fred and Adele Astaire, once child performers and later vaudeville headliners, but in 1918 the most suave and elegant dance team since Vernon and Irene Castle.

The Passing Show, like the *Follies*, outgrew the 1910's and became a part of the 1920's; there were five editions between 1920 and 1924. But this was not the only elaborately mounted revue put on by the Shuberts in the 1920's. Between 1919 and 1928 they also produced *The Greenwich Village Follies*, and between 1923 and 1930, *Artists and Models*. A rose by any other name. . . . *The Greenwich Village Follies* and *Artists and Models* were both flowers from the same seed—*The Passing Show*.

Another successful revue of the 1920's was the *Earl Carroll Vanities*. Earl Carroll had been writing songs for some time when, in 1922, he built his own Broadway theater as the home for the *Vanities*. For that first edition he wrote book, lyrics, and music, while sparing no expense in making his show as attractive to the eye as humanly possible. One critic said: "One lavish scene is succeeded by another with such prodigality that one is given to wondering idly just how much money Mr. Carroll may have sunk in the venture." The *Vanities* continued to decorate the Broadway scene until 1932, catering to the fetish of the times for spectacles and stunning costumes.

George White was one of those who came closest to matching strength with the great Ziegfeld, to become one

of his most formidable rivals. White had been a vaudeville hoofer, and after that he became a leading performer in many Broadway musicals and revues including
The Passing Show of 1914 and *Ziegfeld Follies of 1915.*
In 1919 he decided to set out for himself as a producer
of revues, offering the *George White Scandals* at the
Liberty Theater. His production was calculated to stun
the senses, and it did just that. Ziegfeld immediately
recognized the threat posed by George White to his own
supremacy. After the opening night of the *Scandals,* Ziegfeld wired White offering to pay him $3,000 a week to
appear in the *Follies* together with the *Scandals* dancing
star, Ann Pennington. White countered by wiring Ziegfeld an offer of $7,000 a week to star in the *Scandals* with
his wife, Billie Burke.

White produced the *Scandals* up until 1939. He scored
a major scoop in his second edition, in 1920, by hiring
a comparative novice to write all its music. George Gershwin was his name and at that time he was 23 years old,
his potential as a genius of popular music recognizable
only to a meager handful. Gershwin was born in Brooklyn, New York, on September 26, 1898. His childhood
and boyhood were spent in New York's East Side where
in his twelfth year, he started studying the piano. Two
years after that, he became a pupil of Charles Hambitzer,
a sensitive and cultured musician, whose influence on the
boy's musical development was far-reaching. Hambitzer
introduced Gershwin to the world of musical classics, to
which he responded at all times enthusiastically, and
often with an all-absorbing fascination. Nevertheless,
young George was crazy about popular music. He knew
that this was *his* language, and he was determined to
find his lifework in it. Between his fifteenth and seven-
teenth years he worked as a piano demonstrator at
Remick's publishing house in Tin Pan Alley. During this
period he also began writing popular tunes. When he
brought some of these to the attention of his boss at
Remick's he was told roughly: "You're paid to play the

piano and not to write songs. We've plenty of songwriters under contract." But others were much more sympathetic. Sigmund Romberg liked one of Gershwin's songs so well that he used it in *The Passing Show of 1916*, for which he had written the basic score. Sophie Tucker's recommendation brought about Gershwin's first song publication, "When You Want 'Em You Can't Get 'Em" issued by Harry von Tilzer in 1916.

When Gershwin left Tin Pan Alley it was to promote more actively his career as a songwriter. He applied to Irving Berlin for a job as his secretary and arranger. "You can have the job if you want it," Berlin told him, "but I hope you have the guts to turn it down. You're much too good to be working for anybody else but yourself." He next approached Max Dreyfus, the head of Harms, who knew at once that here was something worth nursing and developing. Dreyfus signed Gershwin to a unique contract by which the young man was paid $35 a week to write songs. The job entailed no other duties, and no office hours. Through Dreyfus, Gershwin received a contract to write music for *Half-Past Eight,* a revue which opened (and immediately thereafter closed) out of town; Gershwin was never even paid the $1,500 fee promised him. But other ventures proved more fruitful. Nora Bayes interpolated two of his songs in *Ladies First,* a musical comedy in which she was the star in 1918. In 1919, Gershwin wrote all the music for his first Broadway musical comedy, *La La Lucille,* which had a run of several months. Soon after that Gershwin was the proud author of a smash song hit, "Swanee," lyrics by Irving Caesar. "Swanee" was introduced at the Capitol Theater, in New York, when it first opened in 1919. The number did not attract much interest at the time. But Al Jolson liked it and sang it at one of his Sunday evening concerts at the Winter Garden. After that he interpolated it into his Winter Garden extravaganza, *Sinbad.* Jolson's magic helped sell over 2,000,000 phonograph records and 1,000,000 copies of sheet music, in less than a year.

A single musical comedy and a lonely song hit is generally not enough to bring a young composer an assignment so desirable as that of writing all the music for the *Scandals*. But George White had long known of Gershwin and had long since become convinced of his rare gifts. In 1917, Gershwin was a rehearsal pianist for *Miss 1917*, a revue in which White was a performer. When Gershwin was freed from his duties to accompany singers and dancers, he often entertained the company by playing the piano, holding them spellbound with his jazz improvisations. Jerome Kern, who had written some of the music for this revue, was so excited by Gershwin's piano playing that he dragged his wife, Eva, to one of the rehearsals to listen to "this remarkable musician." Kern insisted that "this young man is going places." George White was also excited by Gershwin's pianism. When he was looking for a composer for his *Scandals*, in 1920, he asked Gershwin to take on the job.

Gershwin wrote at least two songs for the *Scandals* in which could be detected the touch of genius. One was "I'll Build a Stairway to Paradise" (lyrics by Buddy De Sylva and Ira Gershwin), remarkable for its skillful shifting rhythms and unusual progressions. This was used as the background music for a big production number in the 1922 edition in which dancers, dressed in black, cavorted up and down a huge white staircase. The second was the first of his immortal ballads, "Somebody Loves Me" (lyrics by Buddy De Sylva and Ballard MacDonald). This was a song with the most unusual intervallic structure which Winnie Lightner introduced in 1924.

It was also for the *Scandals* that Gershwin made his first ambitious attempt to write music in a frame of greater dimension than the popular song. For the 1922 edition he prepared the music for a one-act Negro opera, libretto by Buddy De Sylva. It was originally called *Blue Monday*, and it had a run of only one evening (August 28). George White, feeling that the opera was too somber to be part of a revue program, removed it from his production the day after its première. Since 1922 this opera has been revived several times under its new title of *135th Street;* it was given over television on the "Omnibus" program in 1953. But *135th Street* is not a successful opera, though some of Gershwin's individual numbers are poignant and appealing. De Sylva's libretto is downright silly. But as Gershwin's first effort to write a serious musical work in a popular style, *135th Street* has no negligible importance, particularly since it can be regarded as the ancestor of Gershwin's masterwork, the Negro folk opera, *Porgy and Bess.*

Gershwin wrote all the music for five editions of the *Scandals,* from 1920 to 1924. These productions had varied attractions beyond Gershwin's songs: Ann Pennington's shimmy dancing; the comedy of Lou Holtz and W. C. Fields; and in 1923 a stunning curtain made up of chorus girls.

Gershwin left the *Scandals* in 1924 to devote himself to writing music for musical comedies (on the one hand) and compositions for the concert stage (on the other). To replace Gershwin, George White engaged the song-writing team of De Sylva, Brown, and Henderson. Buddy De Sylva and Lew Brown collaborated on the lyrics; Ray Henderson was the composer. But the partnership was so interlocked and harmonious—each contributing ideas and suggestions to the others—that their songs can be said to have been the accumulated effort of all three men.

All of them had made a mark in Tin Pan Alley by the time they joined forces for the *Scandals*—De Sylva, most of all. He had been discovered by Al Jolson, who had helped set some of his lyrics to music and then introduced them at the Winter Garden. De Sylva's first royalty check of $16,000 left him with no doubts that writing lyrics was a lucrative business. He deserted his native California to work in New York's Tin Pan Alley. While employed at Remick's, he was contracted to write lyrics for Gershwin's music for *La La Lucille.* After that his success as lyricist was solidly set with Kern's "Look for the Silver Lining,"

Herbert's "A Kiss in the Dark," Gershwin's "Do It Again," and Louis Silvers' "April Showers." De Sylva was also Gershwin's lyricist for many of the songs in the *Scandals*.

Lew Brown was also an experienced hand in writing song lyrics. A native of New York City, Brown abandoned high school for Tin Pan Alley. There he started writing lyrics to Albert von Tilzer's music in 1912. With Von Tilzer he wrote one of the leading ballads of World War I, "I May Be Gone for a Long, Long Time," as well as "Oh by Jingo" and "I Used to Love You." In 1922, he became acquainted with Ray Henderson, then a mere fledgling as a composer. With him he wrote some numbers that were published, and one of these, "Georgette," appeared that year in the *Greenwich Village Follies*.

Henderson was born in Buffalo, New York, on December 1, 1896. As a boy he played the organ and sang in the choir of the Episcopal church in his native city. After that he received a thorough musical training at the Chicago Conservatory. While there he played the piano in jazz bands and on several occasions appeared in vaudeville in an act including an Irish tenor and a Jewish comedian. Leaving the Conservatory, he found employment in Tin Pan Alley, first as a song plugger, and then as staff pianist and arranger. As a Tin Pan Alley employee he met and started working with Lew Brown. But his greatest success came with other lyricists, in 1925: with Buddy De Sylva and Bud Green in "Alabamy Bound"; with Sam M. Lewis and Joe Young in "Five Feet Two, Eyes of Blue."

Though De Sylva, Brown, and Henderson started writing songs for the *Scandals* in 1925, they did not hit their stride until one year later, with a remarkable score including "The Birth of the Blues," "Black Bottom," and "The Girl Is You." The first of these was used as background music for a sumptuously mounted first-act finale. The second was written for Ann Pennington, who here and now introduced the "black bottom," a dance craze that swept across the country. The third was sung by Harry Richman. There was no edition of the *Scandals* in

1927, and in 1928 the music of De Sylva, Brown, and Henderson did not live up to the high standards set in 1926. Meanwhile this trio had started writing musical comedies, and it was in this area, rather than the revue, that they proved most fruitful.

Another series of sumptuously mounted and ambitiously conceived revues in the 1920's deserves our attention. It was the *Music Box Revue*—lyrics, music, and text by Irving Berlin. There were four editions in all. The first, in 1921, opened the new Music Box Theater on 45th Street, with appropriate pomp and fanfare. That edition was produced with the same kind of lavishness and splendor which Ziegfeld and George White expended on their own shows—and at a cost of $200,000, a figure not yet equaled by either Ziegfeld or White for any of their revues. "Such ravishingly beautiful tableaux," wrote Arthur Hornblow in *Theater Magazine*, "such gorgeous costumes, such a wealth of comedy and spectacular freshness, such a piling of Pelion on Osa of everything that is decorative, dazzling, harmonious, intoxicatingly beautiful in the theater—all that and more was handed out in a program that seemed to have no ending." But spectacle was accompanied by delightful humor and satire: the comedy of Sam Bernard; a delightful travesty on the contemporary dance. Two outstanding Irving Berlin songs lent further distinction: "Say It with Music" and "Everybody Step."

In 1921 Irving Berlin already was a colossus in American popular music. As a boy he had come to New York's East Side from Russia (where he was born on May 11, 1888) to escape a pogrom which had annihilated most of the Jewish citizens of the little town of Temun. The Berlins spent their first years in the New World in a setting of extreme poverty and want. Impatient with school —and the disciplines which a religious household tried to impose on him—Berlin ran away from home when he was nine. He earned his living singing sentimental ballads in saloons and along the streets of the Bowery. Later on he was hired as a song plugger for the publishing house of Harry von Tilzer. In 1906, Berlin became a singing waiter at the Pelham Café. While thus employed he wrote his first song (only the lyrics this time, the music being the work of the café pianist, M. Nicholson). That song, "Marie from Sunny Italy" was published by Joseph W. Stern and brought Berlin a royalty of 37 cents.

Soon after that Berlin found a job as a singing waiter in Union Square. He kept on writing lyrics to other people's music and soon made such a name for himself that he was hired as staff lyricist by the publishing house of Ted Snyder. Meanwhile he had started writing music as well. A vaudevillian had asked him to write a lyric for his act. Berlin complied by scribbling out some verses about a marathon runner named Dorando then in the news. When the vaudevillian decided not to use it, Berlin tried selling it to Ted Snyder who offered him $25 on the condition that the lyric had a melody. Rather than lose the sale, Berlin improvised a tune—his first.

He had a modest hit on his hands in 1909 with "That Mesmerizing Mendelssohn Tune," a ragtime treatment of Mendelssohn's *Spring Song*. Two years after that he became one of America's best known and most widely performed popular composers with "Alexander's Ragtime Band," which helped make ragtime a national passion and established Berlin as a "ragtime king." He wrote other ragtime tunes (here, as always from this point on, to his own lyrics) with such singular success that the Broadway producer, Charles Dillingham, engaged him to write lyrics and music for a ragtime revue, *Watch Your Step*, (1914) starring the dancing sensation of that period, Vernon and Irene Castle. For this, his Broadway debut, Irving Berlin wrote a ragtime melody tailored for the Castles, "Syncopated Walk," and with it a homespun number that is still remembered, "Play a Simple Melody." But "Play a Simple Melody" was not Berlin's first ballad. Two years before this, in 1912, Berlin's wife died soon after their honeymoon. The impact of that tragedy led him to write "When I Lost You." It sold over 1,000,000 copies of sheet music and forthwith placed its composer among Tin Pan Alley's leading writers of sentimental ballads. He maintained this position through the years with an incomparable succession of some of the most poignant melodies produced in Tin Pan Alley.

During World War I, Berlin served in the Army at Camp Upton. To raise money for a sadly needed Service Center, he put on an all-soldier revue. His cast was recruited mainly from rank amateurs, and all the material was his own. Named *Yip, Yip, Yaphank*, the revue opened in New York in the summer of 1918 and was described by *Variety* as "one of the best and most novel entertainments Broadway has produced." Soldier life was satirized, romanticized, and sentimentalized. Perhaps the most unforgettable moment came with the appearance of Berlin himself, dressed in uniform. Dragged from his cot to stand reveille he whined that immortal lament of all World War I soldiers, "Oh, How I Hate to Get Up in the Morning."

By playing to capacity houses for 4 weeks on Broadway and then going on tour, *Yip, Yip, Yaphank* brought in $150,000 for the new Service Center, four times as much as had been hoped for.

Immediately after World War I the giant personality of Irving Berlin dominated every phase of the popular music business. He kept on writing some of the most successful songs of the time. In the *Ziegfeld Follies of 1919*, two of these were introduced: "A Pretty Girl Is Like a Melody," an eloquent background for a stunning parade of Ziegfeld's beauties, and from then on a kind of theme music for later editions of the *Follies;* and "You'd be Surprised," whose suggestive lyrics were made even more provocative by the rolling pop eyes of Eddie Cantor in his jaunty rendition.

Besides writing the nation's song hits, Berlin also became a powerful publisher with the opening of the Irving Berlin, Inc., in Tin Pan Alley. This occasion inspired the celebration of "Irving Berlin Week" throughout the country. Berlin was also active as a performer by touring the vaudeville circuit in presentations of his best-loved songs. And as if all this activity were not enough to engage his energies and talent, he became in 1921 a theater owner (the partner of Sam H. Harris in building the Music Box Theater) and the creator of one of Broadway's most ambitious revues, the annual *Music Box Revue*.

Spectacle and satire, inspired melody and exciting dances were the keynotes of that first edition; and these elements continued to make the next three editions spellbinding visual and aural experiences. For the 1922 edition Berlin wrote one of the last, and one of the best, of his ragtime tunes in "Pack Up Your Sins"; travesty was found in an annihilating take-off on grand opera starring Bobby Clark and William Gaxton; spectacle was offered through a grandiose number entitled "Satan's Palace." In 1923, "The Waltz of Long Ago" and "An Orange Grove in California" were sung by a young performer who, only a few years hence, would become one of opera's most glamorous prima donnas, Grace Moore. In 1924 two immortal Berlin ballads were heard, "What'll I Do?" and "All Alone," while the satirical element was most pronounced in one of the best sketches written by George S. Kaufman, "If Men Played Cards as Women Do."

After the last edition of *The Music Box Revue* in 1924, Berlin wrote songs for some of Broadway's leading revues and musical comedies, and some of these will be discussed in later chapters. Here and now we need touch only on his personal life which underwent a major crisis soon after the last *Music Box Revue* was produced. In 1925, Berlin met Ellin Mackay, and they fell in love virtually at first sight. She was a member of blue-ribbon society, the daughter of Clarence H. Mackay, head of Postal Telegraph, and herself an heiress to a fortune then estimated at some $30,000,000. They talked of marriage, but Ellin's father refused to consider a match involving a Broadway songwriter, however successful, and particularly a man who belonged to a religion different from his own. Mackay used all the resources at his command to keep the lovers apart, and to discredit Berlin in Ellin's eyes. He compelled Ellin to go on an extended European holiday so that she might forget the man she loved. But all of Mackay's carefully contrived strategy proved helpless in the face of two young people who would not stay apart. On January 4, 1926, Irving Berlin and Ellin Mackay were secretly married, after which they embarked on a European honeymoon. Not until several years had passed did Clarence Mackay forgive his daughter and consent to see her again; and in time he even came to like and admire his son-in-law and shower his love on the grandchildren Irving and Ellin brought him.

A romance like this that broke down social and religious barriers was, to be sure, grist for the journalistic mill. The papers were full of every phase of this love affair. It even inspired a popular song, "When a Kid Who Came from the East Side Found a Sweet Society Rose," by Al Dubin and Jimmy McHugh. But all such publicity belongs to the long-forgotten past. What is not forgotten, and never will be, are the love ballads which Berlin wrote for Ellin: "Always" (all rights to which he presented to Ellin as a wedding gift); "Remember"; "Because I Love You"; "How Deep Is the Ocean" (withheld from publication until 1932); and, when happiness was finally found in marriage, "Blue Skies." The little man who grew up in the streets of the East Side and the saloons of the Bowery; who never took a music lesson in his life; who could not read or write a note of music; who played the piano badly by ear and then only in the key of F-sharp major—this little man had here created such eloquent and inspired melodies that George Gershwin was led to describe him as "America's Franz Schubert" and Jerome Kern to say of him that "Irving Berlin has no place in American music, he *is* American music."

The all-Negro revue—a child of the 1920's—was also rich in performing talent and elaborate stage paraphernalia. *Shuffle Along* (1921) was the first of these racial revues to hit the bull's-eye. It opened first in Harlem, where it attracted so many customers that the producer decided to bring it downtown, to a theater on 63rd Street. It stayed there for more than 500 performances. Its stars were Noble Sissle and Florence Mills; its strong suit, spectacular dances and choral numbers; its hit song, "I'm Just Wild About Harry."

The leader of all the Negro revues was *The Blackbirds of 1928*. This was the first of seven *Blackbird* revues, the last of which, in 1939, survived only 9 performances. But the 1928 edition was a box-office triumph. "Bojangles" Bill Robinson here achieved recognition on the Broadway stage for the first time, with his agile tap dancing either across the stage, or up and down a double flight of stairs. "His feet," said *Time*, "were as quick as a snare drummer's hands." Adelaide Hall sang the blues and Tim Moore did some burlesque skits about a prize fighter and a poker game. While lyrics and music were by whites— lyrics by Dorothy Fields and music by Jimmy McHugh— they, too, had an ebony hue. Two numbers were prominent among the year's song hits: "Diga, Diga, Doo" and "I Can't Give You Anything but Love, Baby."

The 1920's was also a period of iconoclasm and disenchantment. The recent crusade of World War I "to make the world safe for democracy" left the bitter aftertastes of cynicism and disillusion. What followed was an irreverent age that thought it smart to denigrate morality, ethics, religions, country. Debunking became a favorite pasttime of intellectuals whose idols were H. L. Mencken and George Jean Nathan; whose favorite magazine was *The American Mercury*, which Mencken and Nathan edited; whose favorite novelists were Sinclair Lewis and F. Scott Fitzgerald. Convention was regarded as old hat. Women bobbed their hair, shortened their skirts above the knees, smoked cigarettes in public. The speakeasy and the hip flask (symbols of open defiance against the Volstead Act prohibiting the use of alcohol), corruption in high places, and the mob rule of gangsters brought law and government into disrepute.

Sophistication was the wisdom of the day, the wise-crack and satire its intellectual food. Sex consciousness was rampant. On the screen Clara Bow glorified "It"; in Atlantic City, the bathing beauty came into existence. Tabloids, the gossip columnists, the confession magazines fed on flourishing scandals. Young people petted in public, and a reputable judge advocated trial, or companionate, marriage without benefit of license or ceremony. Social dancing grew increasingly abandoned with the Charleston and the Black Bottom. Popular music—they now called it jazz—was more hyperthyroid than ever.

A new kind of revue emerged to reflect the times. It was intimate, smart, sophisticated, and unconventional. It mocked at existing institutions. It enjoyed its irreverence, and it liked to shock. Actually, this new kind of revue was in part a rebellion against the ornate, over-dressed kind put on by Ziegfeld, George White, Earl Carroll, and Irving Berlin. By accenting freshness and originality of material over extravagant production procedures, by sidestepping stars and concentrating instead on good songs, dances, and sketches, by making a virtue out of simplicity, economy, and modest resources, this new kind of revue was in the 1920's the counter part of the Princess Theater Show that had rebelled so successfully in the 1910's against plush musical comedies.

The intimate revue was born in downtown New York, in an unpretentious little auditorium called The Neighborhood Playhouse in the East Side. In 1922, a group of youngsters presented there *The Grand Street Follies*, described in the program facetiously as a "lowbrow entertainment for highgrade morons." But this was no lowbrow entertainment by any means, nor could it appeal to a clientele of morons, highgrade or otherwise. The show did not feature a beautiful row of dazzling females; the cast did not number a single performer known to the audience; the sets looked and were of the simple do-it-your-

100

self variety of lowly stock companies; the stage was poorly equipped. And yet *The Grand Street Follies* was a winner, for it had wit and malice, freshness and vitality, spark and drive. Its scalpel-edged satire dug deeply into the flesh of grand opera, poetry (with an excrutiatingly funny parody of Walt Whitman), and the ballet. Its songs were generously coated with cynicism. Its attitudes were those of mild defiance to the *status quo*. The "roaring" Twenties were here—and *The Grand Street Follies* was its voice.

The Grand Street Follies stayed on throughout the 1920's, produced within the vicinity of Broadway after 1927. With each new edition the satire grew sharper, keener, and more daring; the wit, more mordant and audacious; the youthful attitudes more impudent. Headed by two remarkable mimics and pantomimists—Albert Carroll and Dorothy Sands—the cast indulged in outlandish travesties of the plays of Henrik Ibsen, the megalomania of the *Ziegfeld Follies*, the narcissism of John Barrymore, and so on. The South Sea Islands was recreated in the image of a Broadway musical comedy; the siege of Troy was retold as David Belasco, the flamboyant Broadway producer, would have staged it; Caesar's invasion of Britain was set to melody and lyrics by Noel Coward, then a still unknown upstart in the theater. The young, eager, enthusiastic performers included a tap dancer someday destined to achieve glory in Hollywood in a far different capacity—James Cagney; among the singers was a young lady who would later become a radio luminary—Jessica Dragonette.

Even before *The Grand Street Follies* moved uptown another brilliant intimate revue captured Broadway with its youth, courage, and distinctively 1920 attitudes. In 1924, the Theater Guild of New York—producer of outstanding drama each season on a subscription basis—was building for itself a new theater, on 52nd Street. A group of youngsters, accustomed to hang around the Guild and sometimes play bit parts in its productions, hit upon the idea of raising money for tapestries for the new auditorium by putting on an informal show in the style of *The Grand Street Follies*. On May 17, 1925, the *Garrick Gaieties* was given a matinee and evening performance. It parodied some of the more successful or provocative productions of the Theater Guild, including Sidney Howard's Pulitzer Prize play, *They Knew What They Wanted*; it presented a one-act burlesque of grand opera, in a jazz style; it mocked at Ruth Draper, a famous diseuse, and at the New York police. Critics and audience were delighted. Alexander Woollcott described the show as "fresh and spirited and engaging . . . bright with the brightness of something new minted." Robert Benchley called it "the most civilized show in town." As a result, the Guild put on four more performances in June, all completely sold out. Finally, the revue was put on a regular run which lasted about 25 weeks. A second edition, produced in 1926, also received accolades from the critics.

The most successful, the most significant songwriting team in Broadway history realized its first success in *The Garrick Gaieties*—Rodgers and Hart. Richard Rodgers, the composer, was twenty-two when the first edition of *The Garrick Gaieties* opened; Lorenz Hart, the lyricist, was twenty-nine. Both at the time were lowly and unappreciated practitioners of their respective trades to whom recognition seemed to be a century away. Indeed, by 1925, Rodgers was so discouraged about getting ahead as a popular composer that, on the eve of *The Garrick Gaieties*, he had decided to give up music for good and take on a job as salesman for a children's underwear firm.

Both Rodgers and Hart had come from well-to-do families. Rodgers was the son of a physician; Hart, of a successful promoter. Neither, then, had known poverty—nor, for that matter, a lack of appreciation or encouragement at home. But each had experienced a healthy portion of discouragement and frustration by the time *The Garrick Gaieties* gave them status in their profession.

Rodgers—born in Hammels Station, near Arverne, Long Island, on June 28, 1902—had been writing melodies from early boyhood on. His first song came when he was fourteen, while he was spending the summer at a boys' camp, for which he wrote words and music of "Campfire Days." After that, he contributed some melodies to various amateur productions put on by a New York boys' club—lyrics sometimes provided by friends, sometimes by the immediate members of his family. While attending Columbia College he became the first freshman allowed to write the annual Varsity Show: *Fly with Me,* for which he wrote all the music, while Lorenz Hart provided text and lyrics.

Hart was an extremely cultured young man who had devoured great literature, could quote Shakespeare by the page, was a passionate theatergoer, and was a lover of good music and opera. Hart had high hopes of becoming a writer, and his favorite pasttime was to write brilliant verses. Since Rodgers was a composer without a permanent lyricist, and Hart a lyricist without a composer, a mutual friend decided to bring them together. They met for the first time at Hart's house, in 1918, and hit it off immediately. Hart loved the sprightly tunes Rodgers played for him on the piano. Rodgers, on his part, was profoundly impressed not only by the wide range of Hart's culture and immense fund of general information, but also by the skill and freshness of his verses and by Hart's trenchant ideas about song lyrics. Hart could not see why it was impossible to bring to a song lyric the same kind of solid technique, rich imagination, and creative force that a poet brings to serious verses. Hart was sure that theatergoers were capable of responding to lyrics in which the rhyming was more ingenious and nimble than "June" with "moon," "slush" with "mush," and "love" with "of." Why did a song lyric have to be filled with so many clichés and bromides; why did sentiments about love have to be so mawkish; why did the grammar have to be so inept and the prosody so clumsy? Why not introduce into the song lyric a healthy infusion of satire, irony, and adult wit—all so sadly lacking in the lyrics of the 1910's and the 1920's? (Hart knew and admired the lyrics of P. G. Wodehouse for the Princess Theater Shows; but Hart also felt that this was only the first step in the bold and still untraveled direction he had in mind.)

Rodgers and Hart immediately decided to work together along the lines Hart had outlined. "In one afternoon," Rodgers later recalled, "I acquired a career, a partner, a best friend."

Their first published song was "Any Old Place with You," whose rhyming and tongue-in-cheek humor already began to suggest new horizons for the lyric.

> I'll call each dude a pest, you like in Budapest
> Oh, for far Peru!
> I'll go to hell for ya, or Philadelphia
> Any old place with you! *

This was also their first song to be performed within the Broadway theater—placed into *A Lonely Romeo* at the Casino Theater on August 26, 1919.

After that, Rodgers and Hart worked on the Columbia Varsity Show already alluded to, produced in the grand ballroom of the Hotel Astor in 1920. Four months after that came their first Broadway show, *Poor Little Ritz Girl*, half of the score by the veteran, Sigmund Romberg, the other half by Rodgers and Hart.

But though they had begun auspiciously, their road to success was still a distance away. After the *Poor Little Ritz Girl* every effort to market their songs to producers and publishers met with failure. The only ones willing to use their stuff were social, educational, and religious groups putting on amateur shows. Since these productions paid little (if anything at all), and since no one of consequence attended these performances, such oppor-

---

* Copyright 1919 by Jerome H. Remick & Co. Reprinted by permission of Remick Music Corporation.

tunities provided little encouragement. During one period of depression, Rodgers summarily gave up trying to write and sell songs and returned for 2 years of music study at the Institute of Musical Art in New York. Later on, early in 1925, when he once again became convinced there was no place for him on Broadway or in Tin Pan Alley, he came to the decision to enter the business world.

It was immediately after he had made the arrangement to start working as a salesman that he and Hart were invited to contribute some songs for *The Garrick Gaieties*. No payment was involved, and the two solitary performances originally scheduled for the revue brought small hope for a change in their destiny as songwriters. Nevertheless they consented to take on the assignment, mainly because they felt instinctively that an association with the Theater Guild (however tenuous) was not to be scorned. As it turned out, *The Garrick Gaieties* made Rodgers and Hart famous; it finally gave them a foothold in the theater; it propelled them into an incomparable career. Their songs—lyrics as well as melodies—were bright-faced with youth, bubbling with vitality: "Manhattan" and "Sentimental Me" in the first edition; "Mountain Greenery" in the second. Hart's rhyming was as agile as a tap dancer's toes, his phrasing and figures of speech as tart and fresh as mint. The sophisticated allusions to people, places, and things slanted his lines for a mature and not a 10-year-old mentality.

> We like to serve a mild dish,
> Of folklore quaintly childish,
> Or something Oscar Wildeish,
> In pantomime or dance.*

So ran some of the lines in the song "Gilding the Guild." "Manhattan," for Hart, was "an isle of joy," and "Mountain Greenery" a hymn to country life, in accents no less tonic. And phrase for phrase, line for line, Rodgers

* Reprinted by permission of copyright owners, Edward B. Marks Music Corporation.

matched Hart with spontaneous, lighthearted tunes that coincided beautifully with his light touch and effervescent moods. No wonder, then, that *Variety* said of these songs: "They clicked like a colonel's heels at attention."

The Garrick Gaieties—together with the newer editions of *The Grand Street Follies* uptown—popularized the intimate revue. In *Americana* (1926) there appeared a sad-faced comedian with a lugubrious expression—Charles Butterworth; and a dark-haired and soulful-eyed singer of torch songs who sat on a piano—Helen Morgan. *Merry-Go-Round* (1927) introduced still another torch singer, Libby Holman. And Libby Holman was one of several shining lights in *The Little Show* (1929), one of the best —theatrically as well as commercially—of the intimate revues.

The Little Show grew out of Sunday evening vaudeville entertainment put on by Tom Weatherly and James Pond at the Selwyn Theater. "They were far more artistic than the Sunday night variety programs then being offered at the Winter Garden," Weatherly has explained. "They became so successful that I was convinced there would be an audience for a really smart and sophisticated revue." And so, in conjunction with William A. Brady, Weatherly created the first "Little Show." Book and lyrics were mainly by Howard Dietz, while most of the music was by Arthur Schwartz. *The Little Show* helped point a finger on several remarkable performers, all of them more or less unnoticed by the general public before this. One was Libby Holman, a singer of plangent songs in a broody, husky voice who brought down the house with "Moanin' Low," music by Ralph Rainger, and lyrics by Dietz. Another was a one-time vaudeville juggler-ventriloquist, Fred Allen. In *The Little Show* he emerged as an incomparable monologist delivering a homey *spiel* in a dry, rasping voice; later on in the 1930's he would become one of radio's supreme comedians.

The Little Show also brought to prominence for

the first time the songwriting combination of Arthur Schwartz, composer, and Howard Dietz, lyricist. Arthur Schwartz, who was born in Brooklyn, New York, on November 25, 1900, had been trained for law, and for 4 years he practiced in New York. But his heart belonged to writing popular tunes. He managed to get one of them published, "Baltimore, Md., You're the Only Doctor for Me" (total income from royalties, 8 dollars!), and to place it in *The Grand Street Follies of 1925.*

Meeting Howard Dietz—a former advertising executive employed as publicist by Metro-Goldwyn-Mayer—was an important milestone in his career. Dietz liked to write song lyrics. The first of these to invade the Broadway scene was "Alibi Baby" (music by Arthur Samuel) introduced by Luella Gear in *Poppy.* With Morrie Ryskind he contributed all the lyrics for *The Merry-Go-Round,* music principally by Jay Gorney. Schwartz saw this revue, listened with delight to Dietz's sparkling verses, and immediately knew he wanted Dietz as his collaborator. This was in 1928. Their first important venture together came only one year after that, and it was *The Little Show.* Just as *The Garrick Gaieties* had previously given Rodgers and Hart a permanent place in the theater, so now *The Little Show* did a similar service for Schwartz and Dietz.

There were two more editions of *The Little Show* (in 1930 and 1931), but neither was particularly attractive or profitable. Dietz wrote the lyrics for both productions while Schwartz wrote the music only for the first of these. But in 1930, Schwartz and Dietz again worked to maximum creative capacity in *Three's a Crowd,* which was in the image of the first *Little Show.* It had basically the same stars—Libby Holman, Fred Allen, and Clifton Webb—and the same sophisticated appeal. Libby Holman sang a poignant ballad, "Something to Remember You By" to a sailor whose back only was visible to the audience. (That audience could hardly have realized at the time they were seeing the back of one soon to become a Hollywood great, Fred MacMurray!) She also introduced a second number destined to become a popular-song classic, "Body and Soul," music by Johnny Green. Allen delivered some more of his wry monologues and Clifton Webb performed a few more of the slick, suave dances that had helped make the first *Little Show* so memorable.

Though *Three's a Crowd* was produced in 1930, and its Schwartz-Dietz successor *The Band Wagon* in 1931, both are the recognizable offspring of the 1920's. In *The Band Wagon*, Fred and Adele Astaire appeared for the last time as a team, Adele going into retirement, and Fred after that going it solo. George S. Kaufman wrote some trenchant sketches including a broad burlesque on the Southland in which Frank Morgan was starred as a Southern colonel. Three of the songs were among the best Schwartz-Dietz ever wrote. "I Love Louisa" was used for the first-act finale, a gay Bavarian scene dominated by a colorful merry-go-round. "New Sun in the Sky" was introduced by Fred Astaire. And the classic, "Dancing in the Dark," was sung by John Barker and danced to by Tilly Losch while a slanting mirror reflected ever-changing colored lights. One of the two motion-picture adaptations subsequently made of *The Band Wagon* was named after this song in deference to its immense and permanent popularity.

There Were Giants / 7
in Those Days

The 1920's saw a proliferation of creative talent in the American musical theater. The then rapidly declining prestige of foreign operettas resulted in few importations from abroad. Our theater, consequently, had to make greater demands than ever before on homegrown talent. Since the annual output of musical productions was so large, men of established reputations found it impossible to meet the ever-pressing need for material. New, young, talented writers were consequently given a welcome hearing by producers. The sophistication of the times and the spirit of revolt in the air permitted these newcomers to tap creative resources formerly considered far beyond the pale of public consumption. "A sense of gaiety predominated among songwriters," said Douglas Watts of some of these novices, "but there was also a sense of pride . . . pride in breaking away from European-influenced operettas, and most of all, pride in their own audacity, for almost all of them were young men." Responding to the public's call for new approaches, writers created productions in which, as Alan Dale remarked at the time, the heroine "no longer . . . is a lovely princess masquerading as the serving maid; no more is the scene Ruritania or Monte Carlo. Today is rationally American, and the musical show has taken a new lease on life."

In this new generation of writers and composers were men who combined courage with their talent, curiosity and inquisitiveness with their powers of invention, iconoclasm with their fund of imagination. This new generation included composers like George Gershwin, Richard Rodgers, Arthur Schwartz, Ray Henderson, and Vincent Youmans; and lyricists and librettists like Lorenz Hart, Oscar Hammerstein II, Howard Dietz, Ira Gershwin, De Sylva and Brown, George S. Kaufman, Morrie Ryskind, and Herbert Fields. With men such as these came the dawn of a new day—not only for the revue but also for the musical comedy.

In this new day, as in an older one, Jerome Kern was still a dominating influence. Unlike Victor Herbert and George M. Cohan he had the flexibility and the inner creative strength and resources to grow and change with the times.

Despite his preoccupation in the 1910's with the intimate and economical Princess Theater Shows, Kern had not abandoned the more expensive, the more ambitiously conceived musicals then flourishing in other theaters with other producers. Even while the Princess Theater Show was at the zenith of its popularity, Kern wrote a traditional musical comedy of uncommon merits in *Leave It to Jane* (1917). Here, as in the Princess Theater Shows, his collaborators were P. G. Wodehouse and Guy Bolton. This was an adaptation of a George Ade play satirizing life in a small Midwestern college town where an attractive widow uses the wiles and guiles of her sex to keep a champion fullback from joining the football team of a rival college. *Leave It to Jane* was revived in an off-Broadway production in 1959 and proved so popular that it stayed on for more than 750 performances! While it is quite true that most of its charm in 1959 lay in the nostalgia and amusement that an old-fashioned comedy can provide contemporary audiences, it was equally valid that Kern's songs remained an undiminished delight to the ear and senses—especially the title number, "The

Siren's Song" and a humorous travesty on Cleopatra, "Cleopatterer." "I have remembered the Kern score with delight," reported Richard Watts, Jr., in reviewing the revival, "recalling five of the songs in particular. And hearing them again last night I was happy to find that not only was the score as a whole as charming and freshly tuneful as memory has made it, but my quintet came off easily the best of a gloriously melodious lot. . . . *Leave It to Jane* must stand on its unforgettable melodies."

When the popularity of the Princess Theater Show waned, Kern concentrated mostly on musical comedies in the more formal style and patterns. One of the best was *Sally* (1920). One need only remark that it was produced by Florenz Ziegfeld to recognize that it did not lack for munificence of staging and costuming. One need only recall that the title role was played by Marilyn Miller to realize that this was a production in which a star was one of the strong suits. Marilyn Miller played a dishwashing waif who, posing as a Russian dancer, invades the Long Island garden party of a millionaire where she meets and falls in love with Blair. But before she wins him she becomes famous as a star of the *Follies*.

One of the more spectacular scenes staged by Ziegfeld was the Butterfly Ballet for which Victor Herbert prepared a special score. But *Sally*, for all of Ziegfeld's lavish hand in staging, was really Marilyn Miller's show from first to last. The musical was written expressly for her by Guy Bolton—her first book musical after triumphs in the *Ziegfeld Follies*. The musical was produced expressly for her by Ziegfeld, who regarded her as one of the most beautiful women in the world and one of the most talented performers on any stage. The musical was tailored to the measurements of her talents as singer and dancer. She sang "Look for the Silver Lining"—one of Kern's most beautiful ballads, lyrics by Buddy De Sylva—and she flooded the stage with radiance. She danced—and a spell

111

of enchantment was cast on the audience. *"Sally,"* said one critic, Louis R. Reid, "is Marilyn Miller—from her head to her toes."

The traditional musical comedy continued to engage Kern's interest and activity for a number of years, with productions like *Stepping Stones* (1923) and *Criss Cross* (1926), in both of which Fred Stone was starred together with his wife, Allene, and his daughter, Dorothy; and *Sunny* (1925), another musical comedy concocted for Marilyn Miller, in which she introduced Kern's immortal song, "Who?", lyrics by Oscar Hammerstein II.

Not the least of Kern's significance came from the influence he exerted on other stage composers—on George Gershwin, for example. To a youngster like Gershwin, with high ideals about the purpose of popular music, the songs of Kern proved a revelation. Gershwin was only sixteen when, in 1914, he attended his aunt's wedding where the band played a melody that made his heart skip a beat. He rushed over to the bandstand to discover the name of the song and the composer, and was told that it was "You're Here and I'm Here" from the then current Jerome Kern musical, *The Laughing Husband.* This was the first time that Gershwin had heard about Kern. When he asked the band to play some more Kern music it responded with "They Didn't Believe Me" from *The Girl from Utah.* Then and there Gershwin knew he had found the Northern Star by which to guide his own career. "I followed Kern's work and studied each song he composed," Gershwin later confessed. "I paid him the tribute of frank imitation, and many things I wrote at this period sounded as though Kern had written them himself."

As we have already described, the paths of Gershwin and Kern crossed when the younger man was rehearsal pianist for *Miss 1917.* It was because of Kern's enthusiasm for Gershwin's talent that he recommended Gershwin as rehearsal pianist for a 1918 Kern musical, *Rock-a-bye Baby*. During these rehearsals a bond developed between the two men which continued until Gershwin's untimely death in 1937. Kern became so convinced of Gershwin's remarkable capabilities that he stood ready to turn over to him some of his own Broadway assignments to help the young man along in his career. But by 1921 Gershwin was already too busily occupied with his duties for the *George White Scandals* to take on any of these commitments. After 1924, Gershwin's success on Broadway was of such proportions that his career no longer needed any outside sustenance.

When Gershwin left the *Scandals* in 1924, it was to engage more actively in musical comedy rather than revue. By 1924 he had become a composer of considerable consequence, whose genius was already highly acclaimed by many astute and discriminating musicians and critics. Beryl Rubinstein, famous concert pianist and teacher, had told a startled newspaper interviewer as early as 1922 that "this young fellow [Gershwin] has the spark of musical genius." Then Rubinstein went on to add prophetically: "I really believe that America will at no distant date honor [him] for his talent . . . and that when we speak of American composers, George Gershwin's name will be prominent on our list." This, you must remember, was said at a time when devotees of good music looked with condescension on Broadway and Tin Pan Alley, and when nobody would dare to consider a popular tunesmith in the same breath as a serious composer. Another pronounced Gershwin fan was Eva Gauthier, renowned concert singer. At one of her song recitals in Aeolian Hall, New York, in 1923 she presented a program including many of the foremost song composers of past and present. As her last group she had the courage to do something nobody had dared before her: present several American popular songs, including some by Gershwin. Gershwin himself served as her accompanist for these selections. "I consider this one of the very most important events in American musical history," said Carl van Vechten.

Then in 1924 Gershwin electrified the world with his first symphonic composition in a jazz idiom—the now historic *Rhapsody in Blue,* written for an all-American concert by Paul Whiteman and his orchestra at Aeolian Hall, New York, on February 12. The *Rhapsody in Blue* made Gershwin famous and wealthy. For the first time he was now universally considered a *serious* composer. On stage, screen, and records, over the radio, in the concert hall, in theater and ballets, the *Rhapsody in Blue* achieved a popularity equaled by few concert works of the 20th century. It is still the most often performed piece of serious music by an American.

Gershwin's first musical comedy after the *Scandals* was *Sweet Little Devil* which opened on Broadway about 3 weeks before the première of the *Rhapsody in Blue.* His first Broadway musical-comedy success, however, came 10 months after the *Rhapsody* with *Lady Be Good,* in which Fred and Adele Astaire were starred as Dick and Susie Trevors, a brother-sister dancing team. The Trevors were harassed by financial problems from which they tried to extricate themselves by various devious means. *Lady Be Good* was, as some of the critics at the time suggested, only a "typical musical comedy" with many of the contrivances, improbabilities, and coincidences that characterized typical musical comedies. But one thing placed it solidly in a class by itself—Gershwin's music. In *Lady Be Good,* Gershwin achieved maturity and mastery as a creator of popular tunes. His tricky meters and rhythms in "Fascinating Rhythm"; his personal brand of poignant lyricism in the title number and "So Am I"; his highly individual harmonic colors in "The Half of It Dearie Blues"—all this brought a new stature to popular music.

It was also for *Lady Be Good* that Gershwin wrote what many consider the greatest song of his entire career, and one of the greatest by an American—"The Man I Love." But during the out-of-town tryouts of *Lady Be Good*, this song slowed up the action in the opening scene, where it had been placed, and had to be dropped. Some years later Gershwin tried to find a place for the song in another of his musicals (*Strike Up the Band!*) and once again it had to be discarded. Meanwhile, "The Man I Love" was released as an individual number and as such was acclaimed first in London (thanks to the enthusiasm of Lady Mountbatten) and after that in New York.

Lady Be Good enjoyed the best box-office returns of any Gershwin musical production up to that time. This was also the first musical for which his brother, Ira, wrote all the lyrics. Henceforth Ira was to be George's collaborator, and to become one of the foremost lyricists of his generation. The brothers Gershwin developed immediately into the most fruitful words-and-music partnership our theater has known. It was in the company of brother Ira that George would realize his greatest triumphs on Broadway.

Ira was two years older than George. When his schooling ended after a single year at college, he fumbled about in various jobs. He was a cashier in a Turkish bath, worked with a traveling circus, was a photographer's assistant, was employed by a New York department store. All the while he contributed little squibs and verses to papers and magazines, some of which were published. Before long he began writing song lyrics, adopting the pen name of Arthur Francis so as not to capitalize on his younger brother's growing esteem in Tin Pan Alley. The first time George and Ira worked together was in 1918 in "The Real American Folk Song" which Nora Bayes introduced in *Ladies First*. Their first published song appeared in 1920, "Waiting for the Sun to Come Out," interpolated into the Broadway musical, *The Sweetheart Shop*.

In 1921 Ira was hired to write lyrics for *Two Little*

115

Girls in Blue, a musical comedy whose score was written collaboratively by Vincent Youmans and Paul Lannin. It had an 11-month run. Now a recognized lyricist credited with a highly successful Broadway musical, Ira could take off the disguise of "Arthur Francis" early in 1924 with *Be Yourself* and receive program credit for his lyrics under his own name. And it was under his own name that he worked with George on the songs for *Lady Be Good* later the same year.

After 1924, George Gershwin became, in Isaac Goldberg's picturesque description, a colossus of music with one foot in Tin Pan Alley and the other in Carnegie Hall. As a serious composer he completed within half a dozen years a piano concerto, several piano preludes, a second orchestral rhapsody, and the orchestral tone poem *An American in Paris*. Such formidable musical organizations as the New York Symphony Society, the Boston Symphony, and the New York Philharmonic were playing his compositions. He had truly become, as many now said of him, "the white hope of American music."

As a popular composer, he created some of the most original, brilliant, and freshly conceived songs with which the theater of the 1920's was acquainted. These songs were far ahead of their day in the variety of their harmonic and rhythmic idioms, their technical astuteness, the flexibility of their modulations, their untraditional structures. Their impact on Tin Pan Alley was like an atomic blast, reducing to sheer rubble all the pat formulas and convenient devices that had so long governed popular songwriting. A new generation of composers was now appearing in Tin Pan Alley and Broadway—solid musicians with sound musical values and consummate techniques—composers like Vernon Duke, Harold Arlen, Vincent Youmans, and Johnny Green. All these received their first stimulation from Gershwin, in much the same way Gershwin had once received his from Kern. All these spoke of their indebtedness to, as well as admiration for, Gershwin in no uncertain terms.

Not all of Gershwin's musicals were red-letter days in the American theater. Some, as a matter of cold fact, were dismal failures, and deserved this fate: *Rosalie* (1928) and *Show Girl* (1929), both produced by Florenz Ziegfeld; and *Song of the Flame* (1925) in which Gershwin made a pathetic effort to write an operetta in collaboration with Sigmund Romberg. The salient attraction of *Show Girl* was a song which Gershwin himself always looked upon with particular favor, "Liza," sung and danced to by petite Ruby Keeler. Since Ruby Keeler had then recently married Al Jolson, *Show Girl* boasted an attraction not listed in the program, and not paid for by Ziegfeld. During Keeler's rendition of "Liza," Jolson, whenever he was in the theater, would leave his seat and run up and down the aisle singing the song to his wife on the stage.

But if the bad Gershwin shows were pretty awful, the good ones were very good, indeed: musicals like *Oh, Kay!* (1926), *Funny Face* (1927), and *Girl Crazy* (1930).

In *Oh, Kay!*, Gertrude Lawrence, the glamorous and captivating English star—previously seen on Broadway in *Charlot's Revue* imported from London—appeared in her first American musical comedy. Several Broadway producers, Ziegfeld included, had been bidding for her services. The only reason Aarons and Freedley, producers of *Oh, Kay!*, won out was because Gertrude Lawrence wanted to appear in a show for which Gershwin wrote the music. To her singing and acting, Gertrude Lawrence brought that unique kind of iridescence and that personal magnetism which from then on would characterize her presence on the Broadway stage. As a welcome contrast to her charm and grace, *Oh, Kay!* provided the comedy of Victor Moore as a bootlegger—a little man with a broken, squealing voice and ineffably sad countenance, bewildered by the world around him, befuddled in a profession he was never intended by nature to follow. Bootlegging was the central theme of the text by Guy Bolton and P. G. Wodehouse. Kay is the sister of an English duke, both come to America to allow their yacht to be used for rumrunning activities since they have fallen into dire financial straits. Pursued by prohibition agents, they find refuge in the Long Island estate of Jimmy Winters. Its basement is secretly utilized to hide the illicit liquor; and Shorty McGee (the part enacted by Victor Moore) takes on the job of butler so that he can keep a watchful eye over the contraband stuff. Jimmy and Kay fall in love. Before they can get married, Kay must free herself from the false charge of smuggling, and Jimmy must extricate from the retinue of girls continually pursuing him.

Gershwin's music was, as Brooks Atkinson noted, "a marvel of its kind." Gertrude Lawrence introduced the immortal ballad, "Someone to Watch Over Me." The other distinguished Gershwin numbers included two with his characteristically agile and dexterous use of rhythms and changing meters ("Clap Yo' Hands" and "Fidgety Feet") and two with his most ingratiating melodic charm ("Do Do Do" and "Maybe").

Funny Face (1927) united Victor Moore and Fred Astaire in the two leading male roles. This time Moore was a thug come to steal the heroine's jewels from the safe of her guardian. The guardian was played by Astaire, and the heroine by his sister, Adele. With the incomparable dancing of Fred and Adele Astaire, Moore's comedy, and the equally inimitable songs of George and Ira Gershwin, *Funny Face* was a sure winner. The best of Gershwin's songs were " 'S Wonderful," "He Loves and She Loves" and "My One and Only."

Girl Crazy (1930) hurled a new satellite into the theatrical orbit, one of the greatest stars the American musical theater has known. As Ethel Zimmerman she had worked as a typist in Astoria, Long Island, with dreams of a stage career. Then, her name changed to Ethel Merman, she began to appear as a singer in small night clubs and at various weddings and parties. During an appearance at the Paramount Theater, in Brooklyn, New

118

York, she was heard by Vinton Freedley, then occupied with the business of casting *Girl Crazy*. Freedley, in turn, brought Merman to Gershwin's attention. Merman auditioned for Gershwin at his apartment on Riverside Drive. "Don't ever go near a teacher," Gershwin told her, "he'll only ruin you." Gershwin then played for her the numbers he had in mind for the role of Kate Fothergill in his new show—and Merman knew she was being hired.

Nobody knew much about her when she stepped on the stage for the first time on opening night of *Girl Crazy*. Dressed in a tight black satin skirt slit to the knees, and a low-cut red blouse, she sang her first number, "Sam and Delilah." Later on in the play, she delivered "I Got Rhythm" and "Boy! What Love Has Done to Me." Her shrill, trumpet-like tones flooded the theater with wonderful brass; her personality shot electric currents through the house. In the second chorus of "I Got Rhythm" she held a high C for 16 bars—as clear and unwavering and as metallic as a tone from Louis Armstrong's horn—while the orchestra continued with the melody. She brought down the house. And the house has been hers ever since.

There was a second momentous debut in *Girl Crazy*, that of Ginger Rogers playing her first Broadway starring role. As Molly Gray, the heroine, she was required to introduce two Gershwin song classics, "Embraceable You" and "But Not for Me." Comedy was injected by Willie Howard as a Jewish taxicab driver—who, with the disarming way musical comedies had of introducing incongruities, was required to give several sharp impersonations of show people including Maurice Chevalier and Rudy Vallee. There was also an amusing hillbilly quartet that kept drifting in and out between scene-changes to chant "Bidin' My Time." As if all this were not riches enough, the orchestra pit for *Girl Crazy* contained an ensemble embracing several all-time greats of jazz, including Benny Goodman, Glenn Miller, Red Nichols, and Gene Krupa. "A never-ending, bubbling of pure joyousness" as one critic described it, *Girl Crazy* was not only one of the triumphs of the theater season of 1930 but also of Gershwin's entire Broadway career.

For those interested in what *Girl Crazy* was all about it can be said that its central character is Danny, a Park Avenue playboy. His father—wishing to separate him from the wine, woman, and song of Broadway—sends him out to a dude ranch in Custerville, Arizona. To make this trip, Danny engages a taxi driven by Gieber Goldfarb. After arriving in Custerville, Danny proceeded to make another Broadway out of this one–horse Western town, and to convert the dude ranch into a hot spot with girls, hot music, liquor, and gambling. But when Danny falls in love with the local postmistress, Molly Gray, he finally sees the error of his way. Kate Fothergill, portrayed by Ethel Merman, is the wife of the man running the gambling concession.

All the above Gershwin musicals were, as we have indicated, more or less typical. They all willingly submitted to the rules of the game which dictated that the parts of any musical were more important than the whole. They were all beautifully packaged. They were all generously studded with performing stars. They all boasted delightful routines—terpsichorean, musical, and humorous. The only way in which these musicals was exceptional was that most of their integral material was exceptional. They never pretended to be anything more than wonderful entertainment.

But there were two other Gershwin musicals which did succeed in being more than entertainment, which did point out some new directions for the musical theater, which did rise above the low intelligence quotient then prevailing in Broadway musical comedy. About *Strike Up the Band!* (1930) and *Of Thee I Sing* (1931) we shall have much more to say in a later chapter.

Three of the brightest musical comedies of the 1920's came from the pens of De Sylva, Brown, and Henderson. Like Gershwin they had graduated into a book show

from the *George White Scandals*. All three musicals were
interested in sports. *Good News* (1927) concerned itself
with college football; also the way in which our hero is
kept from making a fatal fumble in Tait College's game-
of-the-year. The whole production was alive with a rousing rah-rah college spirit—from the overture on, in the
middle of which the musicians interpolated a loud college cheer. Songs like "Varsity Drag" and "The Girls of
Pi Beta Phi" had a pronounced Ivy College flavor. Other
numbers were of the hit-parade variety, the finest being
the title number and "The Best Things in Life Are Free,"
the latter used as the title for the screen biography of
De Sylva, Brown, and Henderson released in 1956.

Hold Everything (1928) turned to the boxing game.
In this musical Bert Lahr became a musical-comedy star
for the first time; before this he had appeared in vaudeville and burlesque, while his Broadway stage debut had
taken place in 1927 in a minor revue. As Gink Schiner,
a has-been pugilist, Lahr came fully into his own as a
Broadway comic: with his rough-and-ready brand of humor, and his amusing interjection of peculiar guttural
sounds ("gang, gang, gang") into his colorful colloquial
speech. His grimaces, shenanigans, and diction were well
suited to a text lampooning the fight game. The hero is
a welterweight champion who loses all interest in a forth-
coming bout because he has just lost his girl, Sue. His
fighting spirit, however, is revived in time for that all–
important match when he learns that his opponent has
made some snide remarks about Sue. "You're the Cream
in My Coffee," one of the all-time hits of De Sylva,
Brown, and Henderson, was a musical highlight.

Now golf, and coincidentally country-club life, comes
in for some gentle ribbing in *Follow Through* (1929),
with Jack Haley as a psycopathic son of a business tycoon. The heroine comes out on top in two distinctly
different contests: in a professional golf game, on which
the whole plot pivots; and in a love rivalry for the golf
champ, Jerry. Haley's comedy was seen to best advan-

tage in a hilarious burlesque of a golf game in which he is a duffer. He also helped present one of the show's two main songs, "Button Up Your Overcoat"; the other was the principal love song, "You Are My Lucky Star."

The last of the De Sylva, Brown, and Henderson Broadway successes came in 1930 with *Flying High*. Bert Lahr was here cast as a comedy air pilot, Rusty, who manages to break all existing records for keeping a plane in air because he does not know how to carry it down to earth again once he has managed to fly it. Rusty's girl friend, Pansy, was played by a new performer who forcefully demonstrated something of her future potential with a song in "Red Hot Chicago." She was Kate Smith. The other important numbers were "Wasn't It Beautiful While It Lasted" and "Thank Your Father."

As far as Broadway was concerned, De Sylva, Brown, and Henderson were essentially children of the 1920's. In the early 1930's they worked for Hollywood, and after that they separated, each going his own way either in Hollywood or on Broadway. De Sylva died in Hollywood in 1950, and Lew Brown in New York in 1958.

Wildflower (1923), *No, No, Nanette* (1925), and *Hit the Deck* (1927) rank with the best of 1920's musical comedies. In all three, Vincent Youmans wrote the music.

Youmans was born in New York City on September 27, 1898, the son of a successful hat merchant. A career in engineering being planned for him, he attended the Sheffield Scientific School and, for a short time, Yale University. Youmans then came to the conclusion that he was not interested in engineering at all. With some vague notions of going into finance, he found a job as clerk in a Wall Street brokerage house in 1916. In 1917 he enlisted in the Navy, where he was assigned to help produce Navy shows and write the music for some of them. One of his pieces was extensively played by army and navy bands; a decade later Youmans used the same melody for one of his greatest hit songs, "Hallelujah."

After the war, Youmans worked for a while as a staff pianist in Tin Pan Alley, and also on Broadway as rehearsal pianist, where he helped Victor Herbert coach the singers. Youmans was also busily engaged in writing popular tunes. "Who's Who with You" was the first to get heard inside a Broadway theater, in *From Piccadilly to Broadway* (1918); "The Country Cousin" (title inspired by a motion picture of the same name) was the first to be published, in 1920.

His first musical comedy came two years after that: *Two Little Girls in Blue*, for which Ira Gershwin wrote all the lyrics, and in which Youmans collaborated with Paul Lannin on the music. With a run of more than 100 performances, *Two Little Girls in Blue* helped put Youmans' songwriting career into high gear. His next show, *Wildflower*—for which Oscar Hammerstein II wrote both book and lyrics—was an even greater box-office attraction. This time working collaboratively with Herbert Stothart, Youmans created an exceptionally fine score "prepared with taste and understanding" as the critic of the *New York World* said, "a most essential part in the make-up of the whole." Two songs are still remembered: the title number and "Bambalina."

But the success of Youmans' next musical comedy was not confined exclusively to Broadway. After a successful tryout in Chicago in 1924, *No, No, Nanette* opened in London where it stayed on for 665 performances. Then, before opening it on Broadway, the producer shattered precedent by sending out three road companies to tour the United States. Only then did *No, No, Nanette* appear in New York, on September 16, 1925, where it stayed on for almost a year. After that about a dozen different companies toured Europe, South America, New Zealand, the Philippines, and the Orient.

One comic sequence followed another rapidly in a

briskly paced book by Otto Harbach and Frank Mandel. The main character is a wealthy publisher of Bibles who has a weakness for attractive girls. Three ravishing females cross his path. His efforts to take each under his protective wing complicate his life no end, particularly since he is a married man. When matters get out of hand, an ingenious lawyer helps to set things right between this sadly harassed publisher and his irate and jealous wife.

In *No, No, Nanette*, the music was exclusively Youmans', and stamped him now as a stage composer of first importance. Two of the songs are Youmans standards: "Tea for Two" and "I Want to Be Happy," lyrics by Irving Caesar.

Hit the Deck was Youmans' first musical in which he served in the dual capacity of producer and composer; and it was the last of his musicals to be a box-office success. The book was adapted by Herbert Fields from a popular stage play, *Shore Leave*. Loulou, proprietess of a coffee shop in Newport, Rhode Island, falls in love with Bilge, a sailor. Bilge is not indifferent to Loulou's charms, and is not unhappy to see her follow him around the world when he is forced to set sail. But the path of true love is obstructed when Loulou inherits a fortune; for Bilge is not the kind of fellow willing to marry a woman for her money and live on her assets. Loulou contrives a way out of this dilemma by sacrificing neither wealth nor love. She signs away her entire fortune to their first-born child, an arrangement that apparently satisfies Bilge's conscience.

It was Youmans' music that lent distinction to this ineffectual plot. At the time Alan Dale prophesied that the melodies from *Hit the Deck* would be "radioed, and gramaphoned, and whistled, and pianoed, and pianolad, and even jazzed until you'll cry for mercy"—and he was not wrong. "Hallelujah" (the tune Youmans had written during World War I, but which here appeared with lyrics by Leo Robin and Clifford Grey) and "Sometimes I'm

Happy" (lyrics by Irving Caesar) were at the head of the hit songs of 1927, and are still the songs by which Youmans is most often remembered. "Sometimes I'm Happy" had been used with other lyrics and another title in an earlier Youmans musical comedy that had been a total flop, and it made no impression whatsoever; its reincarnation in *Hit the Deck*, with new verses by Caesar, worked wonders; it clicked instantly. "If 'Sometimes I'm Happy' isn't sung all over the world until sometimes you'll be unhappy," Alan Dale went on to say, "I'll eat my chapeau."

After 1927, Youmans suffered a sustained losing streak on Broadway. All of his subsequent musicals lost money; only *Take a Chance* (1932), Youmans' last musical—and for which he collaborated with Richard A. Whiting and Herb Nacio Brown on the music—turned in a profit. Yet there was much in some of these commercial disasters to recommend them, particularly in the song department. In one or another of these failures there were introduced some of those songs which made Youmans one of the foremost popular-song composers of his day: "Drums in My Heart," "Through the Years," "More than You Know," "Without a Song," and "Time on My Hands."

In 1933, Youmans went to Hollywood to write the music for a screen musical, *Flying Down to Rio*, starring Fred Astaire and Ginger Rogers. His poor health laid him low after that. A victim of tuberculosis, Youmans had to be confined to a sanitarium for several years. With an improvement in his health, Youmans tried to make a comeback in the theater with an ambitiously conceived production, *The Vincent Youmans Ballet Revue*. But though it tried out in Baltimore and Boston, the revue never reached Broadway. After that Youmans' health broke down again. He spent the last months of his life in a Colorado sanitarium, where he died on April 5, 1946.

A Second, and Even / 8
Greater, Triumvirate

The greatest impact of all on the musical comedy of the 1920's was made by Rodgers and Hart, supplemented by Herbert Fields, who wrote the texts. As Frank Vreeland wrote with remarkable acumen in reviewing *Dearest Enemy,* the first produced musical comedy on which the three men collaborated: "We have a glimmering notion that some day they—Fields, Rodgers, and Hart—will form the counterpart of the once great triumvirate of Bolton, Wodehouse, and Kern." Actually, the musical comedies of Rodgers, Hart, and Fields far surpassed the Princess Theater Shows in daring, invention, and creative imagination. In an age when musical comedy still was a machine-made product, Rodgers, Hart, and Fields introduced the handmade creations of craftsmen who touched their work with an artistic and personal stamp.

How Rodgers and Hart first came into their own with *The Garrick Gaieties* in 1925 has already been described. Later the same year they were again represented on Broadway with *Dearest Enemy,* text by Herbert Fields. Herbert was the son of Lew Fields, the partner in the celebrated comedy team of Weber and Fields, and after that a distinguished Broadway star and producer. The Fields family was an uncommonly gifted one. Herbert's older brother, Joseph, became a fine playwright as well as an outstanding author of musical-comedy texts. Herbert's younger sister, Dorothy, acquired fame both on

126

Broadway and in Hollywood as the lyricist for such important composers as Jerome Kern, Cole Porter, Jimmy McHugh, and Sigmund Romberg. Herbert was born in New York City in 1897 and started out in the theater as an actor in minor roles. He was Lorenz Hart's friend from early boyhood on, and a friend of Rodgers since 1919. It was at the suggestion of both Rodgers and Hart that Fields decided to become a librettist. His first effort was a musical comedy, *Winkle Town*, for which Rodgers and Hart supplied the songs, but which was never produced. Then, under a single pseudonym, the three men wrote a Broadway stage comedy about Tin Pan Alley, *The Melody Man*, in which Lew Fields starred and which he produced. This was a failure. After that they sometimes joined forces in writing material for various amateur shows.

Just before the first edition of *The Garrick Gaieties* helped make Rodgers and Hart famous, the three young men were strolling along Madison Avenue in New York. Their interest was attracted to a plaque on a building on 37th Street. It explained that in that very house, during the Revolutionary War, Mrs. Robert Murray, on instructions from General George Washington, delayed several British officers long enough to permit the Continental Army to make a strategic withdrawal. Rodgers, Hart, and Fields said nothing as they read the inscription, but they exchanged meaningful glances. Each knew at once that they had been provided with the stuff for the makings of a musical comedy rich in historic color, dramatic interest, and sex appeal.

That musical comedy turned out to be *Dearest Enemy*, and it was written before the first *Garrick Gaieties* was produced. Since the three were unknowns, with no impressive credits behind them, nobody seemed interested in their musical comedy. Even Herbert's father, Lew Fields, was indifferent to it. "Who ever heard of a musical based on American history?" he inquired. But when *The Garrick Gaieties* finally made Rodgers and Hart prominent, producers suddenly became receptive to their ideas. They no longer had any trouble finding somebody willing to gamble on *Dearest Enemy*. Opening on September 18, 1925, it was done up in the grand style demanded by musical comedy in the 1920's. Picturesquely gowned men and ladies (each looking as if he or she had just stepped out of a painting by Joshua Reynolds) moved against beautiful Colonial sets. "This alone," said Alexander Woollcott about the costumes and sets, "is worth the price of admission." The visual attractions included a striking intermission curtain on which old New York was portrayed.

The program described *Dearest Enemy* as "a musical play," and not as a "musical comedy," one of the earliest usages of that term for a popular Broadway production. This was the clue that the authors were striving to create something more than superficial entertainment for eye and ear. Their aim was to re-create vividly a chapter from American history—in song and dance, laughter and romance. The gaiety—oftentimes a bit risqué—had youthful vivacity and impudence that proved infectious. The dances helped to cull forth 18th-century grace and stateliness—as in an old-world gavotte with which the second act opened. As for Rodgers' music, it was far more than a stringing together of Tin Pan Alley tunes. It consisted of duets, trios, choral numbers, and instrumental interludes, some evocative of the past, others (as in the hit song, "Here in My Arms") of the vibrant present. So important was music to the play that Percy Hammond was tempted to describe *Dearest Enemy* as a "baby grand opera."

It was a solid box-office success. Since it came so soon after the first *Garrick Gaieties* it further lifted Rodgers and Hart to a position of undisputed significance in the American theater. Their services were now eagerly sought after.

Dearest Enemy also helped to jell the partnership of Rodgers, Hart, and Fields. While each had his specific job, they worked as a team with remarkable harmony and unanimity of spirit. All three were young men of trenchant intellect, copious imagination, and a reckless spirit for creative adventure. Without minimizing Herbert Fields' talent as a writer of musical-comedy books—and in the 1920's and 1930's he was one of the best—we cannot underestimate the influence Rodgers and Hart had on him. If Fields was fired with the ambition of trying things in musical comedy which nobody before him had essayed on Broadway, he found stout support from his two collaborators; if Fields was occasionally tempted to descend to stereotypes (as he did in *Hit the Deck* when working with Vincent Youmans), Hart and Rodgers were there to restrain him. And always there was at work the restless intelligence of Rodgers and Hart to provide Fields with fresh, new ideas in seeking out subject matter for musicals, or in developing that subject matter within musical-theater terms.

Rodgers and Hart had four shows on Broadway in 1926, two of them running simultaneously, and two of them with books by Herbert Fields. These last two were the successful ones. *The Girl Friend* was a somewhat stilted play about the ineffectual effort of corrupt gamblers to bribe the hero into throwing a 6-day bike race. Were it not for the popularity of the title song and "The Blue Room"—each on the top of the list of hit songs in 1926—it might not have done well at all. But the second of the Rodgers-Hart-Fields musicals in 1926 was a venture many years ahead of its time, completely unconventional in theme and treatment, *Peggy-Ann*. Years before Broadway or Hollywood became interested in psychiatry and dream psychology—14 years before Moss Hart wrote a famous musical comedy built around this material in *Lady in the Dark—Peggy-Ann* was a production that reached into and was stimulated by the writings of Sigmund Freud and his disciples. It required no little bravado to write a musical comedy on the subject of dream psychology in 1926. But it was almost reckless to develop the idea with a complete disregard of the *status quo* in the theater. The authors refused to use a chorus girl routine with which to open their show since this did not fit into the pattern of their play. As a matter of fact, *Peggy-Ann* had no singing or dancing at all for the first 15 minutes. And *Peggy-Ann* ended on an equally original and daring note: the concluding sequence was a slow comedy dance performed on a darkened stage.

Peggy-Ann was a fantasy in which reality became enmeshed with the dream world, the obvious intertwined with the outlandish. The story concerned the dream life of the heroine. Weary of her prosaic existence in Glens Falls, New York—and a humdrum future with Guy, the colorless boy friend to whom she is engaged—Peggy-Ann finds release in the wildest of dreams and fancies. Her imagination carries her off in a love escapade aboard a yacht, and brings her to New York where she marries a wealthy suitor. But during such proceedings things get confused. Absurdity piles upon absurdity, as so often happens in dreams. Modernistic dances (never before did musical comedy have dance routines edging so closely to the world of ballet!) assumed a kind of nightmarish quality. The stage lighting, which frequently was allowed to go awry, added to the over-all confusion. When Peggy-Ann makes her first flight to New York, the chorus (which follows in her footsteps) changes its dress from country to city attire in full view of the audience. In later episodes fish are made to speak (and in a pronounced London accent and inflection); Cuban race horses are interviewed; medicine pills appear as large as golf balls; policemen sport pink mustaches. At her wedding, Peggy-Ann is dressed merely in her step-ins, and a telephone book is used instead of a Bible during the ceremony. Peggy-Ann finally awakens to be made crushingly aware that she must accept the realities of Glens Falls and a future with Guy, and she faces that future stoically.

Though the critics described *Peggy-Ann* as "unique," "bright and fantastic" and "festive, funny, and fascinating," it did not at first attract many customers. The word

130

had spread that this show was arty, highbrow, and consequently a bore. But some of New York's arch-sophisticates—Dorothy Parker, Robert Benchley, Alexander Woollcott, among others—kept singing its praises both in the newspapers and magazines and by word of mouth. Before long, *Peggy-Ann* became the show in town that *had* to be seen, discussed, praised, or condemned. It had almost a year's run in New York before being successfully produced in London.

If *Peggy-Ann* antedated Moss Hart's *Lady in the Dark* by some 14 years, *A Connecticut Yankee*—the big Rodgers-Hart-Fields musical of 1927—preceded the Lerner and Loewe musical hit *Camelot* by more than 33 years. Both *A Connecticut Yankee* and *Camelot* were based on King Arthur and the Knights of the Round Table in legendary Camelot. But where Lerner and Loewe pointed up splendor and pageantry, Rodgers-Hart-Fields (basing their musical on Mark Twain's farce, *A Connecticut Yankee in King Arthur's Court*) sought out the comedy implicit in anachronisms and satire.

William Gaxton played the part of the Yankee who, in his dreams, steps from our own day into the 6th century. As "Sir Boss" in Camelot he creates a one-man revolution by introducing such unheard-of marvels as the telephone, the radio, and efficiency experts. In short order, the Camelot of King Arthur and his knights assumes the image of a 20th-century American city. King Arthur begins to resemble President Calvin Coolidge, while Merlin has fallen into the habit of speaking in American slang. The highways of Camelot are dotted with advertising slogans like "I would fain walk a furlong for a Camel."

"Set to as fresh and lilting songs as we may hope to find with well-turned lyrics," said Brooks Atkinson, "it makes for novel amusement in the best taste." *A Connecticut Yankee* stayed on Broadway for over 400 performances, toured the road for 16 months, was seen in Daly's Theater in London in 1929, and was revived in St. Louis and New York in 1936 and 1943 respectively.

The songwriting of Rodgers and Hart achieved a new level of excellence in *A Connecticut Yankee*. Never before had Lorenz Hart revealed such a virtuoso technique in his versification, such aptitude in sophisticated allusions, such a happy touch in the use of fresh images and figures of speech. "Our minds are featherweight, their togetherweight, can't amount to much" is the way Sir Galahad serenades Evelyn La Belle-Ans. In that number ("I Feel at Home with You") as in "On the Desert Island with Thee" and "Thou Swell" Hart's writing is so consistently brilliant that, at long last, the lyric is fully emancipated to become music's equal partner. Before Hart, a lyricist was rarely credited as co-author when an important song was referred to either in print or in conversation. In other words, when anybody referred to a show tune by Jerome Kern they identified it as a "Kern song" and never as a "Kern and Wodehouse song." The same held true with Victor Herbert, or Sigmund Romberg, and Rudolf Friml. But when Hart had finally succeeded in making the lyric an inextricable partner to Rodgers' melody, the creations of Rodgers and Hart were always identified as "Rodgers and Hart songs" and never merely as "Richard Rodgers' songs."

Rodgers kept pace with his partner, matching effervescent melodies to the light fantastic of Hart's verses. And they were as gifted in sentiment as in wit. One of the best numbers in *A Connecticut Yankee* was the ballad "My Heart Stood Still." Actually, this number had not been written for *A Connecticut Yankee*. Rodgers and Hart were cruising in a taxi in Paris when a near accident made Hart exclaim, "My heart stood still." Back at their hotel, Rodgers wrote a melody above which he penned the title "My Heart Stood Still" and turned it over to Hart to create an appropriate set of lyrics to melody and title. They first used this song in a revue produced in London by Charles Cochran. So well did the Prince of Wales like this number that whenever he visited a night club he asked the orchestra to play it for him. Through his influence the song became the rage of London. When, some months later, Rodgers and Hart began planning *A Connecticut Yankee* with Fields, they decided to find a place for this ballad in that show, achieving with it in America a success no less formidable than it had been in England.

Before the 1920's ended, Rodgers-Hart-Fields added two more major Broadway successes to their impressive skein. *Present Arms* (1928) was about Marines stationed in Honolulu in which "You Took Advantage of Me" was introduced. *Spring Is Here* (1929) was a gentle little comedy about two young people in love for which Rodgers and Hart wrote one of their greatest ballads, "With a Song in My Heart."

The last of the musical comedies by Rodgers-Hart-Fields was *America's Sweetheart* (1931), a satire on Hollywood and the movie business. Two youngsters— Geraldine and Michael—come to the motion-picture capital from St. Paul. Geraldine becomes a star of the silent films, a has-been when the talkies take over; then it is Michael's turn to achieve stardom. Geraldine was played by an arresting young lady named Harriet Lake. Like the character she portrayed, Harriet Lake was destined to go to Hollywood and reach the top of her profession, but under the assumed name of Ann Sothern. (A second young lady, playing a minor part, also made good in Hollywood later on—Virginia Bruce.)

It is, perhaps, poetic justice to find *America's Sweetheart* as the musical comedy bringing to a close one period in the Broadway career of Rodgers and Hart. In 1931 they went to Hollywood to work for 4 years for the medium and in the setting they mocked so gaily in that last musical comedy. It was in Hollywood that the triumvirate of Rodgers-Hart-Fields worked together for the last time. When Rodgers and Hart came back to Broadway in 1935—without Herbert Fields—a new era unfolded both for them and for the American musical theater.

The Great Sophisticate / 9

While the 1920's ended on December 30, 1929—and a far different political, social, and sociological climate prevailed during the ensuing decade—a number of highly gifted writers managed to keep alive in the musical theater of the 1930's some of the feverish spirit and the unconventional attitudes of the "roaring Twenties." The most significant of these was Cole Porter. In his lyrics and melodies—for like Irving Berlin he wrote both—he fixed the smartness and cynicism, the freedom in sex attitudes, the lack of inhibitions in speech and behavior, and the outright iconoclasm that had characterized the 1920's. He is the arch cynic to whom a crushing love affair was "just one of those things" and who could be true to his girl "only in my fashion." He is the dilettante who sprinkles throughout his lyrics cultural, literary, and geographical allusions of a well-read, well-educated, and well-traveled person. He is the nonconformist unafraid of the erotic, the exotic, or the esoteric. He is the sensualist who brings to his melodies throbbing excitement, purple moods, irresistible climaxes.

Most of all he himself is like a character from a novel of F. Scott Fitzgerald. All his life Cole Porter was the avid hunter of excitement, adventure, and gaiety; all his life he traveled under the banner of "anything goes." He was the sybarite to whom the good things of life was almost a religion. Provocative in his attitudes, unpredictable in mood and action, irresponsible in behavior, he was truly a living symbol of the decade in which he first achieved maturity as a song writer.

His background was unique among American popular composers in that he was born to wealth, and that his apprenticeship took place not in Tin Pan Alley but in the playgrounds of Europe. He was born in Peru, Indiana, on June 9, 1893 to a family that had accumulated vast wealth through speculations in coal and timber. A comprehensive academic education carried him through Yale, from which he was graduated in 1913. His musical training had also been all-inclusive, beginning with the violin and piano in boyhood, continuing at the Harvard School of Music after he left Yale, and ending some years after that at the Schola Cantorum in Paris with Vincent d'Indy. He had written a complete operetta (words as well as music) when he was only ten; a year later he had a piano piece published; at seventeen he had his first popular song issued in Tin Pan Alley, "Bridget"; by nineteen he had written two famous college songs, "Bingo Eli Yale" and "Yale Bulldog Song"; and in 1916 he completed his first score for a full-length Broadway musical comedy, *America First,* described in the program as "a patriotic comic opera," in which Clifton Webb was starred as a titled Englishman. *America First* was produced by Elizabeth Marbury, the same person who had just then scored such a decisive success as a co-producer of the first Princess Theater Show. She could hardly have realized then that in young Cole Porter she had another gilt-edge investment, since *America First* lasted only 2 weeks.

Possibly because of his disappointment in *America First*—more probably because the spirit of adventure and restlessness was already stirring within him—Cole Porter now enlisted in the French Foreign Legion, with whom he served in North Africa. Some say he carried a portable piano on his back with which he used to entertain his friends with improvised songs. In any event, it is a fact that he received the *Croix de guerre* decoration from the French Government for keeping high the morale of his regiment. When America entered World War I, he was transferred to a French officer's training school in Fontainbleau, after which he was assigned to teach French gunnery to American troops. He now rented a luxurious apartment in Paris, there to become the gracious host to the élite of the social, political, and artistic worlds. All the while he kept on writing smart, and often risqué, songs that delighted his guests no end. Immediately after the war, a few of these numbers appeared in the Broadway revue, *Hitchy-Koo of 1919*, without attracting notice; one of these, "When I Had a Uniform On" helped to launch the New York stage career of an outstanding Broadway comic, Joe Cook.

After the war, Porter married Linda Lee Thomas of the Social Register, and they set up a palatial home on Rue Monsieur in Paris. The garish furnishings (wallpaper platinum in color, mirrors extending from floor to ceiling, upholstery made from zebra skins, and so forth) were matched only by the splendor of the festivities taking place there. On one occasion, the Porters hired the entire Monte Carlo Ballet to entertain their guests; another time, on a moment's whim they transferred their guests by motor cavalcade from Paris to the Riviera for a gay week end. In 1923, the Porters rented the palace in Venice where the great English poet, Robert Browning, had died. Fifty gondoliers served as footmen, and a special night club was built outside the palace to accommodate 100 guests, whose various needs were attended to by a French chef, a Negro jazz band, and Elsa Maxwell devising for them all kinds of stunts and games. The 1920's were at hand, and the Porters were doing their best to set the tone for this high-living era.

It took Porter 6 years after *Hitchy-Koo* to get more of his songs performed on Broadway, and this happened in the *Greenwich Village Follies of 1924*. It took him all that time to develop that suave, provocative manner that would henceforth identify his best songs. But once that manner was established, he stood so sharply apart from

136

most of his colleagues on Broadway and Tin Pan Alley that he could not fail any longer to arouse enthusiasm. His identity first became crystallized in the sparkling musical comedy *Paris* (1928) which starred Irene Bordoni; and that identity revealed itself in such a slick, smart, and slightly suggestive song as "Let's Do It" which gained a new lease on life in 1960 as a beer commercial over radio and television. The Parisian setting of this musical suited Porter's temperament and background neatly. So did that of *Fifty Million Frenchmen* (1929) for which he wrote "You Do Something to Me," "You've Got That Thing," and "Find Me a Primitive Man," all three of which bear the Porter hallmark of culture and sophistication. (*Fifty Million Frenchmen* was the first of seven Cole Porter musicals for which Herbert Fields was either the sole librettist or a collaborator.) Porter's first unqualified song masterpieces came soon after that in two lesser Broadway productions: "What Is This Thing Called Love?" in *Wake Up and Dream* (1929) and "Love for Sale" in *The New Yorkers* (1930).

In the 1930's there were seven Cole Porter musicals on Broadway. Four were among the best of the period, and all four carried the mood and temper of the 1920's into the new decade. *The Gay Divorce* (1932) starred Fred Astaire as a hired co-respondent in a divorce action, a job he assumes most willingly since it means he can thereby woo and win the divorcee, the girl he loves. In this role, Astaire introduced one of Porter's greatest ballads, "Night and Day," a title later expropriated for the Cole Porter screen biography released in 1946. Porter's stimulus in writing this classic was said to have come from a hearing of rhythms of distant tom-toms while he was cruising down the Nile in Egypt.

Anything Goes (1934) teamed up Ethel Merman and Victor Moore aboard a transatlantic liner. Ethel appeared as a one-time evangelist become night-club singer, and in this capacity she introduced such Cole Porter delights as "Blow, Gabriel, Blow," "You're the Top," and "I Get a Kick Out of You." Victor Moore was cast as Public Enemy No. 13 who, in flight from the police, is disguised as a Reverend. When he learns to his horror that the police are not really after him because he is as harmless as a cream puff, he whines in a broken voice: "I can't understand this Administration!"

Victor Moore was also one of several stars in *Leave It to Me* (1938), a satire on the Soviet Union which Bella and Sam Spewack adapted from their own stage comedy, *Clear All Wires*. Here Victor Moore appeared as an American ambassador to the Soviet Union continually homesick for Topeka, Kansas, and continually longing for such American delights as a double banana split. In his efforts to get recalled he becomes embroiled in all kinds of serious international episodes of his own contrivance—only to discover that from each incident he emerges a hero. When he finally decides to take his job seriously and try to promote peace and better relations between the United States and the Soviet Union, he only manages to antagonize both countries and to bring his hapless diplomatic career to an end.

There were other stars besides Victor Moore in *Leave It to Me*. William Gaxton played an aggressive newspaperman. Tamara was the French girl who attracts him, and Sophie Tucker was the Ambassador's conniving, overambitious and overbearing wife. But the performer who stole the limelight was a little girl from Texas who—before *Leave It to Me* opened—had been none too impressive as a night-club entertainer or radio singer. Not much, then, had been expected from her Broadway debut. In one of the scenes she appeared at a wayside Siberian railway station, performing a mock strip tease while removing her ermine wraps, and all the while chanting in a baby voice, "My Heart Belongs to Daddy." The house went into an uproar, thereby proclaiming a new queen of musical comedy, whose reign would continue with ever increasing luster for many a year. She was Mary Martin. (Five young men, in fur jackets, were grouped around her in that scene. One of them was also making his New York stage debut here, but went unnoticed. But he, too, would soon see his name in lights: Gene Kelly.)

In *Du Barry Was a Lady* (1939) Bert Lahr was a washroom attendant in a night club, whose star entertainer was portrayed by Ethel Merman. In his dreams, Lahr becomes the lecherous monarch of France, Louis XIV; and Merman—a girl whom he had always doted upon secretly —becomes a lusty Madame Du Barry. The rowdy humor resulting from the king's indefatigable efforts to get Madame Du Barry into a rendezvous were made to order for Bert Lahr's rambunctious comic gifts. He played his part, as Richard Watts, Jr., said, "with the sort of spluttering indignant violence and leering impudence that makes him one of the best comedians in the world."

The Sober Thirties / 10

When the 1920's came to an end the economic bubble burst. The stock market collapsed, and a major depression was on. If the 1920's was a period of inebriation then the Thirties was the resultant hang-over. Unemployment was rampant: people sold apples on street corners, queued up before soup kitchens, inhabited shanties in improvised Hoovervilles. Labor was restive. Strikes erupted as labor unions sought to assert their power over management and to spread their influence among the working people. The government—conscious as never before of its obligations to provide work, food, and even culture to its citizens—embarked on a "new deal" under the dynamic leadership of a new President, Franklin D. Roosevelt. Government agencies sprouted into alphabet letters: the NRA, the WPA, the CCC, and so forth.

The era of the petting collegiate and the flapper, of the speakeasy and gangster rule, of the sophisticate and the cynic, of the lawbreaker and free spender was followed by that of more sober men and women with a healthier and more balanced set of values. The Thirties was an age interested in social and political problems, in crusades, in the common man. It preferred moderation to excess, became interested in mental stimulation, searched for economic and social panaceas.

The musical theater often became a sensitive sounding board, vibrating with the overtones of such points of view and aspirations and everyday problems. Two of the songs most often recalled as the theme music for these years of depression came out of the theater: "Brother, Can You Spare a Dime?" by Jay Gorney with lyrics by E. Y. Harburg, from *Americana* (1932) and the Rodgers and Hart song, "I've Got Five Dollars" from *America's Sweetheart*. Similarly, social themes, political problems, labor conflicts, the question of war and peace, the menace of Fascism often invaded the musical stage; and the humor and satire of the times often cut deeply into the overriding issues and personalities of this era.

The 1930's were hardly upon us when there came to Broadway a brilliant, scalpel-edged musical satire on (of all things!) war, a subject obviously remote from the often frivolous themes of the 1920 musical comedies. It was *Strike Up the Band!*, book by George S. Kaufman and Morrie Ryskind, lyrics by Ira Gershwin, and music by George Gershwin. It opened on Broadway on January 14, 1930. Here the book would have no traffic with the kind of contrived and artificial material to which musical comedies had so often been partial. Not for this production are the usual boy-meets-girl, boy-loses-girl, boy-gets-girl complications—dressed up in the fineries of pretty melodies, dances, costumes, and sets. Instead, the direction of text, lyric, and music was toward a profoundly serious subject, that of war, but reduced to the ridiculous by the kind of paradoxes and absurdities we associate with a Gilbert and Sullivan comic opera. An American manufacturer of chocolates is upset because Congress refuses to raise the tariff on Swiss confections. After taking a sleeping pill to calm his nerves, he dreams that he is the general of an American army invading Switzerland over the issue of chocolates. By stealing the enemy's secret signal (what else but a yodel?), the general can make an effective onslaught on the Swiss army and defeat it decisively. The American general becomes a hero, but only for a day. The newspapers back home disclose the appalling secret that all the while our pious-

141

minded American manufacturer has been using Grade B milk to make his sweets.

But more issues than one are annihilated in the brilliant text of George S. Kaufman and Morrie Ryskind. The musical laughed at American big business and the business tycoon, international diplomacy and treaties. This no longer was stock musical comedy, but one with a sharp and incisive political viewpoint. And the satire was found not only in the characters, the dialogue, and the situations, but also in Ira Gershwin's scintillating lyrics and in George Gershwin's remarkable music.

Given a more ambitious canvas than the routined emotions and developments for formal musical comedy had thus far provided him, George Gershwin revealed an enriched palette. His music often had the spice and sting of satire, as in the justly famous title song, a march reducing to mockery all the pomp and circumstance of military life; as in the less familiar march, "Entrance of the Swiss Army," which describes within musical terms the synthetic, hothouse variety of military force the enemy possesses; as in the patter song, in the vein of Gilbert and Sullivan, "If I Become the President." Gershwin also showed a new spaciousness in the finale in which he reviewed through a skillful interweaving of various thematic material all that had previously transpired in the musical comedy. Instead of the traditional thirty-two bar chorus, preceded by an equally formal verse, Gershwin produced in this finale an extended section in which songs, choruses, recitatives, and instrumental interludes were woven together into a single fabric. This was a new Gershwin—as far as musical comedy was concerned. But the old Gershwin—he of the incomparable ballads—was not absent, represented by songs like "Soon" and "I've Got a Crush on You."

None of their previous Broadway musicals had given the Gershwins the satisfaction, the sense of achievement that *Strike Up the Band!* did—even though it did not do well at the box office. They were here permitted to sidestep convention and formula; and the experience exhilarated them no end.

They were even more delighted with the musical comedy that came almost 2 years after *Strike Up the Band!*, a satire in a similar vein called *Of Thee I Sing* (1931). From the beginning of its conception with its authors—again George S. Kaufman and Morrie Ryskind—*Of Thee I Sing* was planned to be a new kind of musical theater in which all the parts—music, humor, routines, production numbers—were basic to the plot.

Where *Strike Up the Band!* concentrated on war and the international scene, *Of Thee I Sing* was concerned with the political and domestic problems in Washington, D.C. The point of departure here was a Presidential campaign. Candidates for top office are selected by the political bosses of one of the major parties in a smoke-filled hotel room: Wintergreen for President, portrayed brashly and robustly by William Gaxton, Throttlebottom for Vice President, with Victor Moore in perhaps the greatest role of his long career. The principal campaign issue decided on is "love." A beauty contest is held in Atlantic City to decide on "Miss White House," who will marry the President and become the First Lady. But after Diana Devereaux emerges the winner, and Wintergreen is swept into office, the latter falls in love and marries simple Mary Turner, to whom he first became attracted when he discovered she had a gift for making corn muffins. Since Diana is of French extraction, the fact that she is being jilted by the President results in international complications. President Wintergreen is about to be impeached when the electrifying news is announced that Mary is about to become a mother. No "expectant President" has ever been impeached. To save the office for Wintergreen, his Vice President poses a satisfactory solution to the problem by offering to marry Diana himself.

It is in the details, rather than the plot itself, that provide most of the acid commentary on American politics in the depression year of 1931. In those days the office of

Vice President was pretty much of a hollow shell. The Vice President was rarely seen or heard and his influence was nil. In *Of Thee I Sing* the pathetic little Vice President, in Victor Moore's incomparable portrait, cannot get to see the White House after his election save by joining a conducted tour; the public library in Washington will not give him a card unless he can come up with two references; in fact, he himself had been reluctant to run for that office because he had been afraid his mother would find out about it.

Political campaigns, the harangues in Senate, the hagglings of the Supreme Court are also victims of satirical attack. In the picturesque torchlight parade during the Presidential campaign, signs inform voters that "A Vote for Wintergreen is a Vote for Wintergreen," "Vote for Prosperity, and See What You Get," and "Even Your Dog Loves Wintergreen." The Senate becomes involved in a complicated debate whether Jenny, Paul Revere's horse, should get a long overdue pension; when informed that Jenny is dead, all members rise in silent tribute. Mary, the President's wife, cannot have her baby (or, rather, babies, since she has twins) unless the Supreme Court decides on the sex.

This was the most ambitious score Gershwin wrote for the popular theater. Numerous orchestral incidents commented, with telling strokes, on what was occurring on the stage. Choral numbers and extended vocal sequences and recitatives carried the plot along. The style of some of the melodies and recitatives went far from Washington in order to poke fun at grand opera, on the one hand, and the Viennese waltz, on the other; yet their relevancy is never lost. Grand opera is used to mock the stuffy proceedings in the Senate; the Viennese waltz to tell, with tongue-in-cheek sentimentality, about Mary's imminent motherhood. In the torchlight parade, "Wintergreen for President," Gershwin quoted snatches of Irish and Jewish tunes to emphasize that the candidate loved both these people with equal tolerance; to contribute a pronounced national or local flavor, Gershwin also interpolated tid-bits from "Hail, Hail, the Gang's All Here," "A Hot Time in Old Town Tonight," "The Stars and Stripes Forever," and "Tammany."

In the title number, the hit song, the word "baby" is used right after "of thee I sing" to transform a solemn patriotic hymn into a maudlin Tin Pan Alley tune. Thus with one stroke patriotic balladry and Tin Pan Alley songs are caricatured. "Vamp till ready" chords—long popular in vaudeville to introduce a song or a dance—set the stage, with wonderful incongruity, for a meeting of the Senate. There is a reminder of a Salvation Army hymn in the song "Posterity is Right Around the Corner." The flavor of the French music hall is found in the ditty in gibberish French, "Garçon, s'il vous plait"; Southland sentimentality is poured richly through the texture of "I Was the Most Beautiful Blossom." Gershwin never faltered in trying to find the exact musical equivalent for every shade and nuance of wit, humor, and malice of his text and lyrics.

This, then, was a far different musical comedy from the kind to which Broadway was accustomed in 1931. The critics went wild. George Jean Nathan (not usually free with his praises of musical comedy) said it was "a land-mark in American satirical musical comedy." *Of Thee I Sing* had the longest Broadway run of any Gershwin musical, and a second company took it on tour. It broke tradition on two counts. It became the first musical comedy to win the Pulitzer Prize for drama, and it was the first musical-comedy libretto to be published in book form.

Two more musicals of the 1930's had Washington, D.C. —specifically the White House and the Capitol—for their setting, and political and domestic issues as material for comedy and satire. *Let 'Em Eat Cake* (1933) was a none too satisfactory attempt by George S. Kaufman, Morrie Ryskind, and George and Ira Gershwin to produce an-other *Of Thee I Sing*. Here Wintergreen and Throttle-bottom run for re-election and are defeated. Wintergreen then becomes the leader of a successful revolution to overthrow the government and set up a dictatorship of the proletariat. When a tense international dispute arises, the issue is settled by a baseball game—America's team made up of the nine members of the Supreme Court. As umpire, Throttlebottom makes a poor decision, for which he must suffer death at the guillotine (imported for this purpose from France). But Mary Wintergreen manages to save his life. The republic is restored, and Throttlebottom is elected the new President.

There was occasional mirth and sparkle within the framework of these grim happenings, in numbers like "Comes the Revolution" and "Union Square"; and the score included a fine Gershwin song in "Mine." But *Let 'Em Eat Cake*—like most sequels—was only a faint carbon copy of the original. As Brooks Atkinson remarked sadly: "Their [the writers'] hatred had triumphed over their sense of humor."

In the Rodgers and Hart musical, *I'd Rather Be Right* (1937)—text by George S. Kaufman and Moss Hart—it is not a fictitious character who occupies the White House, but Franklin D. Roosevelt, America's President in 1937. This is the musical for which George M. Cohan was brought out of retirement. He enacted the role of the President, come to the hero, Phil Barker, in his dreams. Phil complains he cannot get married unless he gets a raise; and his employer will not give him that raise unless the national budget is balanced. The President promises him he will do all he can, but every effort to bring about a balanced budget is frustrated by selfish interests. The budget never does get balanced. The President convinces Phil to get married anyway and trust in both his own future, and in that of his country.

A racy exchange of dialogue satirized many of the agencies and activities in busy Washington in 1937: the "brain trust," the New Deal, Federal-subsidized theater, mounting taxes, politics and politicians, and so forth. When the Secretary of the Treasury complains to the

President he has no money left, the latter asks with the sharp edge of a complaining husband: "What did you do with all the money I gave you? Three hundred millions ought to last a week!" When the Postmaster General, James A. Farley, wants a man appointed Collector of the Port of New York, and when the President informs him one has already been appointed, Farley answers: "But not in *Seattle!*" Vivacious melodies and lyrics contribute further condiments to this satirical stew with "We're Going to Balance the Budget," "Labor Is the Thing," "A Little Bit of Constitutional Fun," and President Roosevelt's bits of confidential revelations in "Off the Record."

The depression and current events were also tapped for the material for musical productions in the 1930's.

The main action of Irving Berlin's musical comedy *Face the Music* (1932) to a text by Moss Hart, is an attempt by a New York police sergeant to lose a large amount of cash he had accumulated illicitly. And the quickest and most efficient way for him to lose that money is by financing a musical comedy. As it happens, the musical comedy becomes a success. All this was a convenient hook on which to hang the effects of the depression on the American way of life in 1932. Wall Street tycoons are made to take their meals in the Automat; Albert Einstein, the great scientist, is compelled to earn his living by appearing in vaudeville; the Roxy Theater, New York's then fabulous movie house, has to offer four feature films to attract customers; the Palace Theater, America's foremost vaudeville house, must provide free lunches with its shows. "Let's Have Another Cup o'Coffee," heard in the Automat scene, is one of the songs inspired by the depression; a second fine Irving Berlin number in this musical, however, was neither political nor social-minded, but a beautiful ballad, "Soft Lights and Sweet Music."

Graft and political corruption were treated in a later Irving Berlin musical comedy, *Louisiana Purchase* (1940), in which Morrie Ryskind's book was based on a story by Buddy De Sylva. Victor Moore appears as a U.S. Senator, sent down to New Orleans to investigate the shenanigans of its political bosses, one of whom is a Huey Long type of character enacted by William Gaxton. In an effort to silence the Senator from making an exposure, the big boss of New Orleans contrives to impugn the Senator's unimpeachable moral character by trying to get him involved with three fetching ladies. At first things look bad for the Senator, especially after he is photographed with a glamour girl on his lap. But he does manage to prove his innocence and to triumph over the slick crooks.

A third important Irving Berlin musical of this period concerned with political and social issues of the day was a revue, *As Thousands Cheer* (1933), in which Berlin helped Moss Hart with the book, besides contributing lyrics and music. *As Thousands Cheer* was as topical as the daily newspaper. Indeed, its format copied the various sections of a great daily by presenting songs, scenes, dances, episodes, and skits in sequences resembling the features of a newspaper—the news-column, the funnies, the society page, the lonely-hearts column, and so on. Characters in the revue were based on people in the news in 1933. Clifton Webb impersonated Mahatma Gandhi, John D. Rockefeller, Sr., and Prince Mdivani; Helen Broderick was seen as Aimee Semple MacPherson, the evangelist, and Mrs. Herbert Hoover; Marilyn Miller mimicked Barbara Hutton, the Woolworth heiress then being wooed by Prince Mdivani; Ethel Waters imitated the Negro chanteuse, Josephine Baker. The revue included a skit about the White House into which a new administration had set foot in 1933, and another about the Metropolitan Opera as it would be affected by radio sponsorship. Ethel Waters raised the temperature in the theater with a torrid rendition of "Heat Wave." But Berlin's most memorable song in *As Thousands Cheer* was "Easter Parade," introduced by Marilyn Miller and Clifton Webb in the first-act finale. The melody for "Easter

Parade" had not been written for this revue but was done in 1917 to a lyric entitled "Smile and Show Your Dimple." Since it had been a failure at the time, Berlin forgot about it until 16 years later when he used his lovely tune for a new lyric about Easter.

Another topical revue tapping the veins of current social, economic, and political problems—but this time a revue of the more intimate and informal kind—became one of the most successful productions ever seen on Broadway. *Pins and Needles* (1937) was originally planned as a highly modest undertaking. The International Ladies Garment Workers Union in New York wanted to stage an amateur show with Union members as its performers. It recruited several more or less nonprofessional writers to contribute sketches, lyrics, and the music. As a stage frolic for Union people, the revue aspired to speak of those topics closest to the hearts of its audience; and so the accentuation was on subjects both at home and abroad of most concern to an American worker. *Pins and Needles* was tried out in a vacation resort in Pennsylvania owned and operated by the Union. After that the revue was brought for several week-end performances into a small New York theater—the Princess, the very house in which and for which the Princess Theater Shows had been created in the 1910's. "Sing me a song of social significance" ran one of the numbers in the new revue. Songs of social significance predominated—songs like "One Big Union for Two," "It's Better with a Union Man," and "Doing the Reactionary." There were also sketches about politics in Washington, the tense situation in Europe, together with sentimental pieces about the simple pleasures of the working man and woman.

The points of view and commentaries, as well as many of the approaches and procedures, of *Pins and Needles* were so fresh and new and vigorous and timely that the revue caught fire with audiences and exploded into conflagration. It stayed on at the Princess Theater (soon renamed the Labor Stage) for several years, its run of more

149

than 1100 performances being the longest of any revue produced in New York. During this run new material was continually interpolated to keep step with changing headlines. To ridicule the Soviet-Nazi pact of 1939 a hilarious travesty on both Stalin and *The Mikado* of Gilbert and Sullivan was interpolated, "The Red Mikado." After Prime Minister Chamberlain returned from Munich with "peace in our time," a skit was introduced called "Britannia Waives the Rules."

The author of most of the lyrics and music to *Pins and Needles* was a newcomer to show business. He was Harold Rome, born in Hartford, Connecticut, on May 27, 1908. Rome was educated at Trinity College in that city, and later at Yale. In 1934 he was graduated from the Yale School of Architecture and came to New York to find a job. The depression, now at its peak, made jobs for apprentice architects virtually nonexistent. The one Rome managed to find paid so little that he had to find ways of supplementing his income. He did so by doing the only thing he knew outside of architecture: writing lyrics and melodies. Gypsy Rose Lee helped him get one of his lyrics published, and the Ritz Brothers used one of his songs in a movie. Since Rome was soon earning more from songwriting than from architecture, he decided at last to try to make his living exclusively from popular music. For three summers, between 1935 and 1938, he worked in an adult camp in the Adirondack Mountains, where he helped write material for and assisted in directing the weekly shows put on by a resident company. Meanwhile, in 1937, the International Ladies Garment Workers came to him with a proposition that he write musical numbers for their projected revue for Union members. He could hardly have foreseen that this seemingly humble assignment was his bridge to fame and wealth.

Identified by *Pins and Needles* as a writer of left-wing songs and materials, Rome was signed by the producer, Max Gordon, to create songs for another political-and social-minded revue, *Sing Out the News* (1938). For this production Rome created one of his best political songs in "Franklin D. Roosevelt Jones." (Here, as in all his other songs, Rome always wrote his own lyrics.)

During World War II, Rome served in the Army where he put on army shows and wrote orientation songs. After the war, Rome returned to the Broadway scene with the kind of political-social revue which had made him famous. *Call Me Mister* was also a box-office triumph. Though produced in 1946, it belongs within the ranks of the topical revues that had flourished so richly in the 1930's. Its main concern was the problem of readjustment facing millions of young Americans in 1946 on being mustered out of the Army. Army life was recalled sometimes wistfully, sometimes sardonically. But the revue also directed many a sidelong glance at the political and social scene. "The Senator's Song" was a caricature of the reactionary Southern Senator; "The Face on the Dime" was a Negro's poignant tribute to President Roosevelt. But the number that stopped the show nightly had little relation to either the military or the political life. It was a rollicking satire on the then prevalent craze for South American rhythms and dances, "South America, Take It Away," presented infectiously by Betty Garrett.

Call Me Mister was Harold Rome's last important association with intimate revues and political viewpoints. After 1946 he distinguished himself primarily as composer-lyricist for a number of nonpolitical, nonsocial musical comedies including *Wish You Were Here* (1952), *Fanny* (1954), and the first Western-type musical comedy, *Destry Rides Again* (1959).

Social significance which had penetrated the revue with *Pins and Needles* entered into the book musical with the provocative and exciting *The Cradle Will Rock* (1937), text, lyrics, and music by Marc Blitzstein. Described by Virgil Thomson as "the most appealing operatic socialism since *Louise*," and by Brooks Atkinson as "the most versatile triumph of the political insurgent theater," *The Cradle Will Rock* became one of the most dramatic events in the theater of the 1930's. Marc Blitzstein had formerly been a modernist composer of avant-garde concert music. But the depression had transformed him into a musician with a strong social consciousness and a politically left-wing viewpoint.

The entire action takes place in a night court of a community identified as Steeltown. The town's powerful citizens—headed by Mr. Mister, the symbol of capitalism —have joined forces in a "Liberty Committee" to frustrate the efforts of steelworkers to form a union. But despite the wealth and influence of the employers, and their often devious methods and maneuvers, the workers prove successful. Popular songs with catchy lyrics, ditties, parodies, the blues, ballads, torch, and patter songs—all within formats and structures familiar to musical comedy—were liberally scattered throughout the production to lighten the atmosphere.

The Cradle Will Rock was a production of the WPA Federal Theater—a government subsidized agency formed to bring economic relief to workers within the theater during the depression. The producer was John Houseman, and the director Orson Welles—both neophytes at the time. Soon after the dress rehearsal, in June of 1937, such pressure was brought to bear on the Federal Theater by powerful government officials and agencies against a play with a pronounced left-wing slant, that the decision was finally arrived at to cancel the production. But the cast did not receive notification of this cancellation until a few hours before curtain time on opening night. A feverish search ensued to find a nearby empty theater in which the play could be given without government auspices. Luckily that theater was found, and the cast and audience were transferred there. Since the scenery belonged to the Federal Theater, and no funds were available to pay the men in the orchestra, both had to be dispensed with. The performers appeared on a bare stage dressed in their regular street clothes. Marc Blitzstein, who played his score on the piano, made brief between-the-scenes comments to clarify some of the stage action. Strange to say, the play gained in dramatic force and emotional impact through this untraditional presentation, and *The Cradle Will Rock* became a box-office attraction. A producer was now found ready to finance a regular run on Broadway, which began on January 3, 1938. Still presented without scenery, costumes or orchestra—but this time through choice rather than necessity—*The Cradle Will Rock* stayed on Broadway for about 4 months. It was also performed in other parts of the country, and during the next decade was several times revived in New York.

Blitzstein's second left-wing musical comedy, *No for an Answer* (1941) was also closed down by the authorities, this time soon after its première. Since the end of World War II, Blitzstein has distinguished himself for musical dramas with operatic dimensions.

Fascism, the threat of war, and then the war itself cast their shadows over the Broadway musical stage, even as they did over the entire country during the closing years of the Thirties.

One of the most bitter diatribes against war was found in the musical comedy *Johnny Johnson* (1936), with which Kurt Weill made his bow as a composer for the American popular theater. Paul Green, author of book and lyrics, described this play as a "fable," and it is indeed a kind of a parable filled with social criticism. The hero is an American soldier during World War I who is convinced that this is a crusade to end all wars, and one in which he must play a role. He is simple, naive, human, honest—qualities that bring him all kinds of difficulties with his officers during the war and with his own integrity and ideals when the war ends. Because of his pacifist ideas he loses the girl he loves and is even confined to an asylum as insane. His bitterness deepens as he watches the world around him beginning to flex its muscles for a new global conflict. "The world," Brooks Atkinson explained, "has slapped him with its ultimate indignity. It can no longer find room for a completely honest man, for it has surrendered to the charlatans, opportunists, and rogues who are the captains and kings of destruction."

Though essentially a musical comedy whose main purpose was propaganda, *Johnny Johnson* had many a delightful comic interlude. One involved our hero in a military psychological test and another with a psychiatrist. Weill's music also passed from the realistic and the dramatic to the sentimental and the comic: sentimental in "To Love You and to Leave You" and "O Heart of Love"; the comic in "They All Take Up Psychiatry."

With *Johnny Johnson,* a Broadway musical-comedy composer of first importance made his debut. Kurt Weill was one of the many Germans seeking sanctuary in this country from the ruthless Nazi persecution of Jews. Before Hitler had come to power, Weill had started out his career in Germany as a composer of modern concert music for selective tastes. But he soon became a household name with operas in a popular, and at times a jazz, style. Born in Dessau, Germany, on March 2, 1900—and a child prodigy in music—Weill received his main music instruction at the Berlin High School of Music and privately with Ferruccio Busoni. At first a composer with extreme modern tendencies, Weill soon found himself being drawn more and more to the popular idioms, perhaps the result of having worked as a pianist in German beer halls when he was a music student. In any event, Weill came to the conclusion that the ivory tower was no place for him, that he was happier moving with everyday people and speaking to them through his music in an idiom they could best respond to. "I don't care about writing for posterity," is the way he put it. And so, Weill wrote operas like *The Protagonist, The Royal Palace, The Czar*

Has Himself Photographed, The Rise and Fall of Ma-hagonny, and a work that made him a world figure, *The Three-Penny Opera* adapted from John Gay's historic *The Beggar's Opera* that had been produced in 1728.

In his operas Weill did not hesitate to replace formal arias and ensemble numbers with popular ballads, music-hall tunes, popular dances like the tango and the shimmy, and American popular idioms like the blues and jazz. One of his numbers from *The Rise and Fall of Mahagonny* became a major song hit in Germany in the early 1930's, a piece not only with the English title of "Alabamy Song," but also with an English lyric, though sometimes only gibberish English.

The Three-Penny Opera, text by Bertolt Brecht, was his triumph. In the first year of its production it was given over 4000 performances in more than 120 German theaters. It soon reached an even wider audience through a motion-picture adaptation directed by G. W. Pabst. In the United States, in 1933, it was a failure. But two decades later it returned to conquer. An off-Broadway production—libretto revised and modernized by Marc Blitz-stein, but the Weill music retained intact—opened in 1954 and stayed on for more than half a dozen years and for over 2250 performances. During this period one of its tunes, "Mack the Knife" (or as it is sometimes also known, "Moritat") achieved a formidable phonograph-record sale on two different occasions. In 1955 it received over twenty different recordings; and in 1959 it helped to make the reputation of the young popular singer, Bobby Darin.

Weill fled from Germany the morning after the Nazis set the Reichstag in Berlin aflame. He visited Paris and London, finally coming to the United States in 1935. He immediately took out his first citizen papers, began to study English, and haunted the Broadway theater to get a first-hand education in the musical stage in this country. Then in 1936 he received his first Broadway assignment with *Johnny Johnson.* One year after that came

The Eternal Road, a pageant of Jewish history by Franz Werfel, directed by the renowned German master, Max Reinhardt.

Then in 1938 came *Knickerbocker Holiday.* There no longer could be much question but that Weill—who had made his first attempt to speak in his music with an American accent in *Johnny Johnson*—had now an unmistakable American identity in his songwriting.

The evils of Fascism, the regulated State, and dictatorial rule are accented in *Knickerbocker Holiday,* though its setting is New Amsterdam in 1647, and its main character is the peglegged Peter Stuyvesant, portrayed by Walter Huston. Stuyvesant, Governor General of New Amsterdam, is a dictator who sets up a semi-Fascist State. His councilors are all ruthless men ready to exploit the people for their own end, but they in turn are but the tools in the hands of Stuyvesant himself. Brom Broeck— in love with Stuyvesant's young wife, Tina—represents the Dutch people who espouse liberty passionately and are violently resentful of dictatorial authority.

As the middle-aged husband of attractive Tina, who has married him against her will, Stuyvesant remarks on this January-May marriage in "September Song," probably the one number with which Weill's name will most often be associated. Huston, of course, was no singer. He had a rough, nasal, rasping voice. Weill kept that nonsinging voice in mind when he wrote his melody with its unusual progressions.

The author of book and lyrics was one of America's leading playwrights, here writing for the musical-comedy stage for the first time. He was Maxwell Anderson, recipient of the Pulitzer Prize for *Both Your Houses* in 1933, and of the Drama Critics Award for *Winterset* in 1936 and *High Tor* in 1937.

Europe exploded into war in the fall of 1939, and America was drawn into the conflict after Pearl Harbor in the winter of 1941. The American uniform now became a more or less familiar sight on the American musical stage. Two of Cole Porter's musical comedies in the early 1940's had such military trimmings. *Let's Face It* (1941) was an updated version by Herbert and Dorothy Fields of an old Broadway stage comedy, *Cradle Snatchers*. Three inductees at Camp Roosevelt, in Long Island, become involved with three ladies from nearby Southampton—those women trying thereby to punish their respective husbands for their wandering eyes and ways. One of these soldiers is played by Danny Kaye (now a full-fledged stage star by virtue of his success in *Lady in the Dark* earlier the same year). Here he delivers one of his best double-talk, tongue-twisting routines, "Melody in Four F" about the trials and tribulations of army conscription. *Something for the Boys* (1943) also touched on military life in the United States. Ethel Merman appeared as Blossom Hart, one-time chorus girl turned defense worker in Texas, in a plant a stone's throw from Keeley Field. When Sergeant Rocky Fulton falls in love with her, his girl friend relays to the Commanding Officer of Keeley Field some unfounded gossip that leads him to declare Blossom and the boardinghouse where she lives off limits. But Blossom proves herself a heroine when she discovers she is a human radio—through carborundum fillings in her dental bridgework. Thus she is able to save one of the army planes, and its flyers, from destruction.

The most triumphant of all the war-outfitted musicals was Irving Berlin's revue, *This Is the Army*. In 1942—as earlier in 1918 with *Yip, Yip, Yaphank*—Berlin was fired with the ambition to create an all-soldiers' show. He lived for a while in a barracks at Camp Upton (the same camp where he had been stationed during World War I), to get material for songs, sketches, dances, comedy, and production numbers. Once again—as in 1918—he created a vast, varied picture of army life as seen from the eyes of an inductee. *This Is the Army* also carried a reminder of 1918 in one of its most poignant scenes. Dressed up in his old World War I uniform, Berlin revived the hit song of *Yip, Yip, Yaphank,* "Oh, How I Hate to Get Up in the Morning," supported by a chorus that included six men who had also appeared with him in the earlier show.

After opening on Broadway on July 4, 1942, *This Is the Army* was made into a movie, toured the United States, and then visited all the combat areas of Europe, the Near East, and the Pacific. It was seen by more than 2½ million American soldiers. It earned over $10,000,000 for the Army Emergency Relief and another $350,000 for British Relief agencies. For this monumental achievement, Irving Berlin received from General George C. Marshall the Medal of Merit.

In musical comedy the means was more important than the end, the parts more significant than the whole. The story, the characters, the situation were generally just the excuse for offering songs, dances, routines, and stars. Putting together a musical comedy was a kind of jigsaw puzzle in which the producer started out with many different pieces which he had to fit together into a picture.

Beginning with the 1920's a new concept of musical theater was arrived at in which the procedures of musical comedy were reversed. In this new approach, the producer started out with a good play in which the main interest lay in story, background, characters, and situations. Everything else had to be an inextricable part of the dramatic exposition. The new genre aspired to be an art form through the projection of dramatic truth, insight into and depth of characterization, while borrowing the resources of music and dance to project and intensify mood and feeling.

This new kind of production was the musical play.

The musical play can be said to emerge with *Show Boat* in 1927, book and lyrics by Oscar Hammerstein II, music by Jerome Kern. When Kern first read the Edna Ferber novel of the same name, and wanted to make it into a musical production, everybody thought he had gone berserk (including Miss Ferber herself). *Show Boat* was an atmospheric novel whose strength lay in its colorful background and strong characterizations. How could you possibly use material like this for a musical comedy?

How could you introduce coy chorus girls, agile tap dances, scene-stopping star routines, and the other paraphernalia of musical comedy in a story rich with authentic American atmosphere?

These were some of the questions Kern's friends asked him when he confided his intention to make *Show Boat* into a musical. His answer was simple and to the point. He had no intention of writing a formula-ridden musical comedy with all the familiar trappings. He wanted something else: a musical with a logical story and arresting people in it, a musical in which all the elements served the play. The humor, he felt, had to spring naturally from a character or a situation; the songs had to be basic to the story; the production numbers were to be used only when the plot demanded them. After he had elaborated some of these ideas to Edna Ferber she agreed to permit him to go ahead with an adaptation, for which Kern recruited Oscar Hammerstein II.

Both Kern and Hammerstein were fully aware that they were forging new trails. They went toward their goal unflinchingly, uncompromisingly. Florenz Ziegfeld, who had agreed to be the producer, soon became convinced he had a white elephant on his hands: a show much too highbrow for popular consumption. He continually procrastinated about getting the play on the boards. The delays were exasperating, but they allowed the authors more time in which to work out their materials to their full satisfaction.

Finally, *Show Boat* opened at the Ziegfeld Theater in New York on December 27, 1927, in the kind of spaciously designed and handsomely mounted structure for which Ziegfeld had become so famous. To the surprise of all, *Show Boat* proved a sensation. Robert Garland called it an "American masterpiece," and Richard Watts, Jr., referred to it as a "triumph." Audiences were just as enthusiastic. Far from being an artistic adventure for the discriminating few, *Show Boat* turned out to be a delight for the masses. Its Broadway run of almost 2 years averaged a weekly gross of $50,000. A national tour between June 1929 and March 1930 played to sold-out houses throughout the country. *Show Boat* returned to Broadway for a second run in 1932, besides playing in London and Paris. In 1929 it was made into a silent motion picture with synchronized sound.

The triumph did not end there. It would be impossible to compute the many millions of dollars *Show Boat* has earned since its birth. It is continually revived—in theaters, outdoor auditoriums, marine shells, even opera houses. A New York revival in 1946 enjoyed a run of over 400 performances, with half a million people passing more than $2,000,000 through the box office. *Show Boat* has been heard in special concert versions, and was twice more adapted for motion pictures after the 1929 silent version. Numerous recordings of the complete score sold millions of discs. Kern himself adapted the musical material into a symphonic work entitled *Scenario,* which has been performed by some of America's foremost symphony orchestras. In short, *Show Boat* has become both a gilt-edge investment and an inextricable part of our cultural life. It is a stage classic, whose grandeur and eloquence seem to increase with the passing of time.

It is a nostalgic chapter from America's past. Its period is the closing decades of the 19th century, its main setting *Cotton Blossom,* a showboat plying up and down the Mississippi River, stopping at little towns to give performances. Cap'n Andy is the owner of the boat. His daughter, Magnolia, falls in love with a gambler, Gaylord Ravenal, and she elopes with him to Chicago. But Gaylord cannot adjust himself to married life just as he cannot give up his gambling ways. Though they are still in love with each other, and though Magnolia is about to have a child, they separate. After the birth of a daughter, Kim, Magnolia earns her living singing the songs she had learned on her father's showboat. In time she becomes a stage star and Cap'n Andy hears her perform at the Chicago Fair Midway. After the passage of many years, Magnolia and Kim return to the *Cotton Blossom,* where they find a contrite and repentant Gaylord awaiting them, now willing and happy to assume the responsibilities of a husband and a father. And it is Kim who now becomes the star of the *Cotton Blossom,* singing her mother's songs.

It took courage to set a story like this for our popular musical stage in the 1920's, since some of the subsidiary material invaded dangerous territory. The story went to great lengths to describe not one but two unhappy marriages, while the second of these touched on the sensitive subject of interracial relationship. The Negro, and his difficult life in the South, was treated not with the customary humor and sentimentality of the American musical theater but with realism and compassion. The play opened with the scene showing Negroes lamenting their hard lot as they lift huge bales of cotton, and a climactic point in the story comes with the song "Ol' Man River" which speaks of the tragedy of an oppressed race.

But beyond the willingness of Hammerstein and Kern to face squarely every issue posed by their play—however provocative or unusual that issue might be—they also had the creative gifts with which to flood their writing with warmth, tenderness, romance, and beauty. In *Show Boat,* Oscar Hammerstein II—ever a skillful workman, and in 1927 one of the theater's most successful librettists and lyricists—became more than just an adroit craftsman. Here he transcends the techniques and skills of his trade to arrive at the higher purposes and the deeper insights of a true poet and a fine dramatist. And Kern tapped creative veins new even for him. His lyricism was touched with a new glow; his sentiment acquired a new kind of humanity; and his writing was filled with a fresh dramatic impact. His songs were lifted to the elevation of genuine folk music. This happened most of all in "Ol' Man River," in which many of the qualities that characterize the Negro spiritual were caught and fixed—and so successfully that many today think it is an American

162

folk song. Edna Ferber can never forget when Kern first sang and played this song for her. "I give you my word my hair stood on end, the tears came to my eyes, and I breathed like a heroine in a melodrama."

But the score overflowed with other riches. There were three unforgettable love songs, "You Are Love," "Make Believe," and "Why Do I Love You?" And there were two other numbers, both which helped make a star of Helen Morgan, appearing as the half-caste, Julie. Sitting atop a piano—her identification as a torch singer—she shot a quiver through the audience with her throbbing rendition of "Can't Help Lovin' Dat Man" and "Bill."

"Bill" was the only song not written directly for *Show Boat,* the only song for which Oscar Hammerstein did not provide the lyrics. It was written by Kern and P. G. Wodehouse for *Oh, Lady! Lady!* one of the Princess Theater Shows, but it was dropped from that play since it seemed too subtle in mood and too original in melodic structure to enjoy popular appeal. An attempt was later made to place "Bill" in *Sally,* and again it was discarded. But when Helen Morgan was chosen to play Julie in *Show Boat,* Kern realized that his song had finally found its singer; and it was for Helen Morgan that Kern decided to interpolate "Bill" into the *Show Boat* score.

The wide gulf separating *Show Boat* from most of the other musical comedies of the 1920's could have been spanned only by a man like Jerome Kern. From the beginning of his career he had been more concerned with a score as a whole than with any individual song, something which most certainly was not the case with other Broadway composers of the same period. Kern's sound instincts for good theater led him to seek out a way to make each of his numbers relevant to the play; to find the "gimmick" (as Otto Harbach once said about him) "to make a song logical within a play." Oscar Hammerstein has also written that "he didn't think a score important unless it is linked to a good libretto. . . . He was always more intense about story and characteriza-

163

tion than about music." Such an attitude was virtually unknown in the 1910's and 1920's when composers were not too particular about the texts given them for musical settings, nor even the lyrics for their melodies.

Such a serious approach to the musical theater and to his craft made it possible for Kern to consider Edna Ferber's *Show Boat* as a musical, when practically everybody else thought the project quixotic. The same qualities also led him, in the years following *Show Boat,* to seek out unusual subjects for other musicals, and to treat them in unusual ways.

In *The Cat and the Fiddle* (1931) Kern once again worked with an unusual story, text, and lyrics, this time by Otto Harbach. The main love plot, set in Brussels, involves an American girl crazy about jazz and a serious European composer working on an opera. Before they can fall in love they must first resolve their differences in musical tastes, which they do. *The Cat and the Fiddle* pursued a strange course by dispensing with chorus girls, production numbers, and comedy; all its resources were directed toward plot and characters. And in his score, Kern digressed from the familiar and the expected by—at one point in his music—introducing a fugal passage, and at others by using a charming canzonetta, "The Night Was Made for Love" as an integrating motive. The latter was a warm, glowing melody that proved Kern did not lose the popular touch, increasingly ambitious though his musical approaches were becoming; further proof came with songs like "She Didn't Say Yes" and a number that is too little appreciated, "Poor Pierrot."

In his attempt to emphasize that he was departing sharply from musical comedy, Kern had designated *The Cat and the Fiddle* as "a musical love story." *Music in the Air* (1932)—book and lyrics by Oscar Hammerstein II—was characterized as "a musical adventure." This production was also unusual for its time, even though setting and characters remind us of the kind of stuff we used to see in operettas. The setting is the picturesque little Bavarian town of Edendorff. The characters include a village schoolmaster and the girl he loves; a big-town theater producer; a glamorous prima donna. But the treatment of this material was highly individual—at least in 1932. In his music Kern created several numbers with an authentic German folk-song personality; others resembled beer-hall tunes. But some, while unmistakably American, were inextricably intertwined with the situations from which they sprang or the characters who sang them: "I've Told Ev'ry Little Star" and "The Song Is You." Hammerstein, for his own part, contributed a feeling of naturalness to his lyrics and dialogue, and a warmth to his character portrayals, which injected into his play the vitality of a living organism. "Mr. Kern and Mr. Hammerstein," said Brooks Atkinson about *Music in the Air,* "have discovered how musical plays, which used to be assembled, can now be written as organic works of art. . . . At last musical drama has been emancipated."

Kern's last successful Broadway musical, *Roberta* (1933) was, on the other hand, a musical following accepted patterns and glorifying, of all things, a fashion show. Its main appeal rested in three wonderful Kern songs, lyrics by Harbach: "Smoke Gets in Your Eyes," "Yesterdays," and "The Touch of Your Hand." Kern's last appearance on Broadway with a new production took place in 1939 with a failure, *Very Warm for May*—a show that would have been permanently forgotten if still another of Kern's song masterpieces had not been born there, "All the Things You Are."

After 1939, Kern's music was written exclusively for the screen where, on two occasions, he received Academy Awards (for "The Last Time I Saw Paris" and "The Way You Look Tonight"). Kern died in New York City of a heart attack on November 11, 1945.

Encouraged and stimulated by *Show Boat,* others besides Kern made a conscious effort to change musical comedy into musical play. Some of these productions were favored by audiences and proved successful. Others —either because they were ahead of their times, or because their aspirations were higher than their achievements—fell by the wayside. Nevertheless all of them were in one way or another milestones along a road stretching toward a new and vibrant stage art—an art that finally achieved fulfillment in 1943 with *Oklahoma!* of Rodgers and Hammerstein.

As early as 1928, Rodgers and Hart tried to do something completely new in the musical theater—and failed. With Fields as librettist, they wrote *Chee-Chee,* which they described as "a new form of musical show, in which all the songs were a definite part of the progress of the piece, not extraneous interludes without rhyme or reason." They refused to list the names of the separate musical numbers in the program as was then—and still is —general practice. As the program went on to explain: "The musical numbers, some of them very short, are so interwoven with the story that it would be confusion for the audience to peruse a complete list." These musical episodes included, with the basic songs, numerous motives and transitional passages to identify characters and situations, intensify an emotion, or underline a piece of stage business in the manner of a Richard Wagner leitmotiv. "The music," said Gilbert Gabriel, "is truly ingratiating, often lovely." But *Chee-Chee* was a failure because, first of all, the Oriental text was about a highly disagreeable subject that has no place for discussion on the musical stage, and, second of all, because it was a bore. "It was a brave thing to do," is the way Richard Rodgers now speaks of it, "but so is a swim across the Atlantic Ocean, and it was just as foolish." But *Chee-Chee,* nevertheless, did suggest some new musical approaches which Rodgers and Hart themselves would apply to their musicals a decade later.

In 1928, another musical (and another box-office disaster) was a portent of things to come within the musical theater. *Rainbow*—book and lyrics by Laurence Stallings and Oscar Hammerstein II, and music by Vincent Youmans—was years in advance of its own day in trying to carry to musical comedy some of the values of good drama. A "romantic play," as the program called it, *Rainbow* was a poignant and at times exciting folk drama with music. The setting of California during the gold-rush days of 1849 was the impulse to set into motion some unusual American dance sequences of ballet dimension, some penetrating American characterizations, and some fine Youmans music in which several choral incidents had the throbbing vitality of genuine folk music.

Arthur Schwartz and Howard Dietz made an interesting experiment in musical playwriting in 1934 with *Revenge with Music*. This was an attempt to make a musical comedy out of the same famous Spanish novel of Pedro de Alarcón, *The Three-Cornered Hat,* which had previously been made into an opera by Hugo Wolf and a ballet by Manuel de Falla. It was a saucy tale about the attempts of the governor of a Spanish province to make love to the wife of a humble miller; and, by reciprocity, of the efforts of the humble miller to make love to the governor's wife. But as a musical comedy for Broadway *Revenge with Music* did not quite come off and lacked conviction (it failed once again to make much of an impression when revived over television almost a quarter of a century later). But it did have a highly unusual text, and it did boast two wonderful Arthur Schwartz songs in "You and the Night and the Music" (introduced by Libby Holman playing the role of the miller's wife) and "If There Is Someone Lovelier than You" (sung by Georges Metaxa in the part of the miller). In subsequent musical productions, however, Arthur Schwartz made no further effort to digress from musical-comedy formulas—the best being two that starred Shirley Booth, *A Tree Grows in Brooklyn* (1951) and *By the Beautiful Sea* (1954).

Strike Up the Band! and *Of Thee I Sing*—the two satires with Gershwin's music already discussed in the preceding chapter—also pointed to new horizons with the kind of subjects they chose as text and in the fresh new manner of treating this material as play and music. Gershwin's most successful union of music and drama, however, came with his epical Negro folk opera, *Porgy and Bess* (1935). Since this is an opera and not a musical comedy or a musical play—in that it is set *throughout* to music, even though some revivals have preferred to abandon operatic recitatives for spoken dialogue—it does not come in for treatment in a book like this concerned with the popular stage. But it is important to notice how this eloquent musical drama is deeply rooted in Tin Pan Alley—as well as in Negro folk art—with numbers like "It Ain't Necessarily So," "There's a Boat that's Leavin' Soon for New York," and the blues, "A Red-Headed Woman Makes a Choochoo Jump Its Track," as well as in the jazz background to some of the choruses and the jazz colorations to some of the orchestration.

Porgy and Bess represented Gershwin's farewell to the Broadway stage. (While an opera, it was produced by Broadway's Theater Guild, in a Broadway theater.) Gershwin's last years, like those of Kern, were spent in Hollywood working for the movies. He died in the motion-picture capital on July 11, 1937, following an unsuccessful brain operation.

Cabin in the Sky (1940) was still another musical which, in the years immediately preceding *Oklahoma!*, left the well-beaten track. Like *Porgy and Bess* it derived its strength and originality from the Negro. Its excellent music was the work of Vernon Duke who, under the name with which he was born (Vladimir Dukelsky) had written outstanding concertos, symphonies, and tone poems. He first became attracted to American popular music just after World War I, in Constantinople, where he had come from his native Russia en route to the United States; and what had aroused this interest was a copy of the sheet music of Gershwin's "Swanee." After coming to the United States he was encouraged by Gershwin to try writing in a popular style; and it was Gershwin who had coined for him the name of "Vernon Duke" for these popular efforts. In the early 1930's some of Vernon Duke's songs were heard in such intimate revues as *Three's a Crowd, Shoot the Works* (1931), and *Americana* (1932). In 1932 he had his first hit song, "April in Paris," introduced in the revue *Walk a Little Faster* (1932), still the number by which Duke is most often remembered. *Walk a Little Faster* was the first Broadway show for which Duke wrote the entire score. *Cabin in the Sky*, 8 years later, was his first book musical.

The text by Lynn Root, lyrics by John Latouche (his first for the Broadway theater), the choreography by George Balanchine, the performance of an all-Negro cast that included Ethel Waters, Todd Duncan, and Katherine Dunham, together with Vernon Duke's music, were all of one piece. *Cabin in the Sky* was a poignant Negro legend set in musical terms. Lucifer, Jr., and the Lawd's General are competing for the soul of Little Joe, a humble Negro always getting into all kinds of trouble. Through Petunia's efforts—and despite the allure and temptations offered by Georgia Brown—the forces of good triumph over evil in gaining for Joe admission to heaven. "The folk characters of the play," this writer has said elsewhere, "were rarely permitted to degenerate into vaudeville humor, gawdy spectacle, or outright caricature. Every element in the production maintained dignity." As for Vernon Duke, he achieved new heights as a popular composer with songs like the title number, "Honey in the Honeycomb" and "Takin' a Chance on Love," the last of which, as sung by Ethel Waters, proved a showstopper night after night.

But it was Rodgers and Hart, in the period between 1936 and 1942, who were probably most significant in bringing to our popular musical theater a new artistic stature and maturity. With their restless imagination and their daring they continually sought out new areas for stage cultivation. As Richard Rodgers said soon after his

169

return from Hollywood: "I should like to free myself for broader motifs, more extended designs—but within the framework of the theater." And *Time* Magazine commented in 1938: "As Rodgers and Hart see it, what was killing musical comedy was its sameness, its tameness. . . . They decided it was not enough to be just good at the job; they had to be constantly different, too. The one possible formula was, Don't have a formula; the one rule for success, Don't follow it up."

The *new* Rodgers and Hart appeared for the first time in *On Your Toes* (1936), on whose text they themselves collaborated with George Abbott. For plot, characters, situations, the writers went to the then esoteric world of serious ballet. Their hero, Phil Dolan III (portrayed by Ray Bolger in his first Broadway starring role) is the son of a vaudeville hoofer who wants to become a ballet dancer. At first he makes a ludicrous spectacle of himself by appearing in a hilarious travesty on the classic ballet, a variation of the Scheherazade theme. But when, Frankie—one of his pupils and a girl with whom he is in love—creates a ballet in modern style and tempo (and in which he stars with the ballerina, Vera) he finds the proper medium for his terpsichorean gifts.

This ballet sequence, in a modern idiom and tempo, brings *On Your Toes* to its climax; it was the first important and successful effort by a Broadway musical to introduce serious dance. This was done so well that henceforth ballet and musical comedy would join hands in a happy partnership. The modernistic ballet in *On Your Toes,* called "Slaughter on Tenth Avenue," was choreographed by George Balanchine, here stepping into musical comedy for the first time after a distinguished career as ballet master of the Diaghilev Ballet and the Ballet Russe de Monte Carlo. This was a jazz ballet satirizing gangster stories. Its protagonists are a hoofer and his girl, both in flight from gangsters. They find a temporary refuge in a Tenth Avenue café where the girl is killed, but the hoofer rescued by the police. For this extended

170

dance sequence, Rodgers wrote one of his most ambitious orchestral scores, one that has since retained its popularity in the symphonic-jazz repertory. When *On Your Toes* was revived in 1954, it was "Slaughter on Tenth Avenue," more than any single element, that had retained its one-time appeal. As Richard Watts, Jr., said: "A sizable number of jazz ballets have passed this way since it first appeared, but it still is something of a classic in its field, and the music Mr. Rodgers wrote for it continues to seem one of the major achievements of his career." Besides this extraordinary ballet music, Rodgers also contributed two significant songs, one a perennial favorite, "There's a Small Hotel," and the other in a blues style, "Quiet Night."

For *Babes in Arms*, one year later, Rodgers and Hart wrote their own book without collaborative assistance. Here they planned to emphasize youth—since the main story concerned the efforts of some children to put on a show. Their reason is that since their parents are vaudevillians always on tour, and since they must shift for themselves most of the time, the local sheriff has threatened them with work camp. They hoped that their show would bring in enough money to make them self-sufficient until their parents get back. That show did not relieve their financial plight, though it did prove artistically rewarding. When their personal situation becomes most critical, the fortuitous circumstance of a transatlantic flyer making a forced landing on their farm becomes the instrument by which the children manage to solve their problem.

Youth had a holiday. Most of the performers were youngsters, the two stars—Mitzi Green and Wynn Murray—being only sixteen. The show-within-the-show, put on by the kids, was a youthful escapade in which ingenuity and talent overcame the handicap of limited costumes and stage facilities; for example, in a Turkish scene all the costumes needed for Turkish garb were provided by a few towels. One of the ballets "Peter's Journey"—

again choreographed by Balanchine—amusingly depicted such Hollywood stars as Clark Gable and Greta Garbo. The whole production thrust aside many musical-comedy fads and tricks, "in favor," as Robert Coleman said, "of novelty and freshness." *Babes in Arms,* in the opinion of John Mason Brown, was "a zestful, tuneful, and brilliantly danced affair," bubbling over "with the freshness and energy of youth." And then there was Rodgers' music in which his invention was rarely richer or his lyricism fresher, with songs like "Where or When," "My Funny Valentine," "The Lady Is a Tramp," "Johnny One Note," and "I Wish I Were in Love Again."

After *Babes in Arms* came the political satire *I'd Rather Be Right* (1937). This, in turn, was followed in 1938 by *I Married an Angel,* adapted by Rodgers and Hart from a Hungarian play. Its hero marries an actual angel (Vera Zorina was this angel in her first Broadway starring part) only to discover to his horror that being married to someone who is the embodiment of truth, goodness, and virtue is by no means the happy arrangement he originally thought. *The Boys from Syracuse,* also in 1938, was the first time that Shakespeare had been tapped for musical-comedy treatment, the Shakespearean play here being *The Comedy of Errors.*

The most exciting, the boldest, and in many ways the greatest of all the Rodgers and Hart musicals of this period was *Pal Joey* (1940), book by John O'Hara, adapted from his own stories originally published in *The New Yorker.* The setting is Chicago's unsavory South Side, and the disreputable characters get enmeshed in all kinds of skullduggery, opportunism, blackmail, and other sordid dealings and adventures. The musical theater, so long sanctified for escapism, is here subjected to a vigorous treatment of realism. When first produced, *Pal Joey* proved too strong a dose for a public so long fed on innocuous sweets, and it rejected it. But when *Pal Joey* was revived in 1952 it not only enjoyed the most extended run of any revival in the history of the Broadway theater

172

but was also the recipient of numerous awards, including that of the Drama Critics Circle as the best musical of the year, and eleven of the sixteen Donaldson Awards, the first time that one play gathered so many Donaldson honors. To critics, many of whom had previously regarded the musical somewhat highhandedly, *Pal Joey* now loomed as a genuine work of art, "a masterpiece in the musical theater." And Rodgers' best songs gained prominence on the Hit Parade, notably "Bewitched, Bothered, and Bewildered" and "I Could Write a Book." Of by no means incidental importance is the fact that it was in the title role of *Pal Joey* that Gene Kelly first became a star.

The last Rodgers and Hart musical was *By Jupiter* (1942), a frothy and irreverent treatment of a mythological subject: the invasion by the Greeks of Pontus, where women are the warriors and the men stay home to cook and clean. With *By Jupiter* the collaboration of Rodgers and Hart ended on a note of triumph after a quarter of a century. The show ran for more than a year, and it could have stayed on Broadway much longer than that if Ray Bolger, its star, had not left the show to entertain American troops in the South Seas.

For some time before 1942, it had become apparent to Rodgers that his partnership with Hart was doomed. Larry Hart may have been a genius whose intellectual brilliance, foresight, knowledge of the stage, and sound creative instincts helped usher in a new epoch of the American musical theater; whose lyrics were incomparable in their day for poetic grace and technical skill, incisive wit, and sophisticated attitudes. But he was also an irresponsible, erratic, ungovernable and completely unreliable little man. He was the kind who liked to do tomorrow what should be done today, who made a fine art of procrastination, who continually had to be badgered to get down to work, who rarely kept appointments and never came on time. Rodgers, on the other hand, was precise, methodical, and systematic, most punctilious about meeting deadlines. To a workman with such a temperament, a collaborator like Hart could prove to be a continual source of irritation. Nevertheless, because of Rodgers' drive and perseverance, Hart kept his nose to the grindstone, and though he hated working with a lusty passion he managed to complete his assignments.

Then came the day when it became all too apparent that Hart was through. Self-conscious about his pygmy size (he was only 5 feet tall) and frustrated by several broken love affairs, Hart succumbed to depressions from which he tried to escape through drink. There were times when Hart had to be hospitalized for alcoholism. He now became more erratic in his behavior than before, more unpredictable in his moods, more unreliable in meeting commitments. Part of *By Jupiter* had to be written in the hospital. When that show opened in Boston, Hart disappeared for several days on one of his binges.

In an effort to revive Hart's will to work, Rodgers decided to revive for Broadway one of their supreme achievements of the 1920's—*A Connecticut Yankee*. It reopened on November 17, 1943, almost a year and a half after *By Jupiter*. Somehow Hart managed to get hold of himself long enough to write a few new lyrics (including "To Keep My Love Alive") and help make some timely changes in the text. Then he fell apart completely. On opening night he walked up and down the back of the theater muttering to himself. Then he disappeared for a few days. He was finally found in his bed—unconscious. He never recovered. Five days after the New York reopening of *A Connecticut Yankee*, Larry Hart was dead.

The era of Rodgers and Hart was over. Together they had written music for 27 stage productions (and 8 movies). With their never-ceasing search for new plots and formats they carried into the theater a fresh, invigorating breeze that cleared away some of the cobwebs and layers of dust collecting on musical comedy for so many years. For their musicals, they wrote about a thousand songs, more than a dozen of which are classics.

But where Rodgers was concerned, if one glorious epoch had ended with Larry Hart, a still more glorious one was about to unfold with a new collaborator. For 25 years Rodgers and Hart had dominated the Broadway stage. For the next 17 years theater history would be shaped by Rodgers and Hammerstein.

Oh, What a Beautiful / 12
Mornin'

In 1942, the Theater Guild approached Rodgers about making a musical out of one of their productions—Lynn Riggs' *Green Grow the Lilacs*. When Rodgers, in turn, consulted Lorenz Hart, the latter was not in the least bit interested. He was weary physically and spiritually; he was depressed; he felt he needed a prolonged holiday in Mexico. Besides, he was not sure *Green Grow the Lilacs* had the makings of a good musical. That was the moment Rodgers knew that "a long and wonderful partnership" was over and that he had to seek a new collaborator.

It was then that Rodgers asked Hammerstein to work with him. They were, of course, no strangers to each other in 1942. They had been friends for years, had moved in the same social spheres; in fact, many years earlier they had even been collaborators. When they met for the first time Rodgers was thirteen, Hammerstein twenty. The boy Rodgers had come in 1915 to attend a Columbia Varsity Show in which Hammerstein, then a student at Columbia, was singing several songs and appearing in a few sketches. After the show, the two were introduced to each other. Rodgers was in awe of Hammerstein because the latter was older, an upper classman, a performer in the Varsity Show, and most of all a member of a distinguished theatrical family. Oscar Hammerstein's grandfather, also bearing the same name, was a famous

176

opera impresario; his father, William, was manager of one of New York's leading vaudeville houses, the Victoria on 42nd Street; his uncle, Arthur, was a noted Broadway producer.

Four years after their first meeting, Rodgers set two of Hammerstein's lyrics to music for an amateur show. In 1920, Hammerstein was a member of the Columbia University committee that had chosen the script and music of Rodgers and Hart for the annual Varsity Show.

They did not work together after 1919, but they did meet frequently on and off Broadway. Rodgers followed Hammerstein's rapidly mounting success with no little admiration, and perhaps a suggestion of envy, while he himself was struggling ignominiously with failure. After graduating from Columbia law school, and working for a while as a law clerk, Hammerstein received his first job in the theater from his uncle Arthur, to serve as assistant stage manager for the Broadway show, *You're in Love*, at a salary of $20 a week. This was in 1917. In 1920, Oscar Hammerstein II made his debut as a writer of musical-comedy books and lyrics with *Always You*, which was badly received by the critics and lasted only 67 performances. *Tickle Me*, also in 1920, did somewhat better; and the Vincent Youmans–Herbert Stothart operetta, *Wildflower*, became in 1923 Hammerstein's first major success.

By 1942—when, after almost a quarter of a century, Rodgers and Hammerstein revived their writing partnership—Hammerstein was, to be sure, a giant on Broadway. He had worked with some of Broadway's most distinguished composers, including Friml, Youmans, Kern, Gershwin, and Romberg. He had helped create such stage classics as the operetta *Rose-Marie* and the musical play *Show Boat*. His lyrics had adorned some of the most successful songs of the 1920's and the 1930's.

But by 1942 Hammerstein had also suffered a number of disasters both on Broadway and in Hollywood which had encouraged even his best friends to think he was

177

through. In Hollywood, in the middle 1930's, four of Hammerstein's pictures had been scrapped before release, two others were box-office disasters, and two more just broke out even. Producers were saying that Hammerstein could not "write his hat." On Broadway he suffered three successive flops, and to add bitters to an already galling potion, he had several more appalling failures in London. By 1942 Hammerstein had become pretty much convinced that his successes were now a thing of the past, that he had lost his touch. "I kept going through inner conceit," he said. And it was only that "inner conceit" that made him listen sympathetically to Rodgers' suggestion that they team up for the Theater Guild production.

It was after this first Rodgers collaboration had restored Hammerstein to his winning stride—had even started him off on a new career in the theater that would dwarf most of his previous efforts—that he inserted the now-famous advertisement in *Variety,* whose blazing headline read: "I've Done It Before and I Can Do It Again." Under this caption Hammerstein enumerated, not his earlier successes, but his subsequent failures: *Very Warm for May* (7 weeks); *Ball at Savoy* (5 weeks); *Sunny River* (6 weeks); *Free for All* (3 weeks); *The Gang's All Here* (3 weeks); *East Wind* (3 weeks); and *Gentleman Unafraid* (1 week).

One of the reasons why Hammerstein was so eager to work with Rodgers on the new Theater Guild project was that, by a curious coincidence, he himself had long been wanting to make a musical out of *Green Grow the Lilacs.* In fact, he had once tried to get Jerome Kern interested in doing the music. After Kern turned him down, Hammerstein—still convinced that the play could be made into a fine musical—attempted to buy the necessary rights from the Theater Guild. On that occasion, Hammerstein was informed that the Guild was already negotiating with Rodgers and Hart on such an adaptation.

Thus Hammerstein was able to bring to his new assignment with Rodgers the same kind of excitement and exhilaration he had once carried to *Show Boat*. "What happened between Oscar and me," Rodgers has said, "was almost chemical. Put the right components together and an explosion takes place. Oscar and I hit it off from the day we began discussing the show." It was a marriage of words and music, heaven-made. They were both of the same temperament—hard-working, idealistic, sober, calculating, methodical, and humanitarian. Hammerstein, like Rodgers, was compulsive about meeting schedules and keeping appointments. Like Rodgers, Hammerstein was a man bored by café society and night life, preferring a retiring existence in which happiness was derived from a good job well done. After half a lifetime with the careless, happy-go-lucky and completely undependable Larry Hart, Hammerstein represented to Rodgers tranquillity, emotional stability, and a security he had thus far not known in working for the theater.

And so Rodgers and Hammerstein went to work on the musical play that finally arrived on Broadway as *Oklahoma!*, to become one of the theater's monumental achievements.

Long before they wrote their first lyric and melody—"Oh, What a Beautiful Mornin'"—Rodgers and Hammerstein had arrived at an all-important decision—the kind Hammerstein and Kern had to reach with *Show Boat*. The flotsam and jetsam of musical comedy would have to be abandoned in translating a sensitive, poetic folk play for the musical theater. Musical comedies traditionally opened with a big, resplendent, stage-crowded scene. Their new musical would have to begin simply and unpretentiously: a single character would be seen on the stage (a woman churning butter), and from off-stage would come the strains of "Oh, What a Beautiful Mornin'." Musical comedies traditionally thrust a dazzling line of chorus girls from the stage aprons early in the production, most usually with the rise of the curtain. Since the Riggs play did not call for the presence of such a chorus until halfway through the act, Rodgers and Hammerstein decided to delay its appearance that long. Most musical comedies expected the music be written before the lyric—that's the way it had been with Rodgers and Hart—since the lyric was something functional tacked on to the melody. But so determined were Rodgers and Hammerstein to make each lyric an essential part of the text that they concurred at once for Hammerstein to write the lyrics first. Musical comedies avoided villains and murder, considering them completely antipathetical to escapist theater. But the Riggs play had villains *and* a murder, and Rodgers and Hammerstein had no intention of deleting them. Finally musical comedy considered ballets poison at the box office. But American folk ballets, Rodgers and Hammerstein were convinced, were an inextricable part of their show.

"We realized," as Hammerstein said, "that such a course was experimental, amounting almost to the breach of an implied contract with a musical-comedy audience. I cannot say truthfully that we were worried by the risk. Once we had made the decision everything seemed to work right and we had the inner confidence people feel when they have adopted the right and honest approach to a problem."

If Rodgers and Hammerstein were not worried by their unusual course of action, others connected with the production were. It is now one of the legends of the theater how everybody associated with *Oklahoma!*—except Rodgers and Hammerstein, and Theresa Helburn, the Theater Guild executive who had conceived the project in the first place—was convinced that though it might become excellent art it would also be a financial calamity. All around Broadway, the new Theater Guild production was being described as "Helburn's Folly." It is also a theater legend now how the process of gathering the needed capital of $83,000 was long and laborious. Most of those who did make a financial investment did so out of friendship for Miss Helburn or indebtedness to the Theater Guild; but always with the sinking feeling they were throwing sound currency down a sewer. Even when the play tried out in New Haven, the rumor was circulated that this was a lemon. The production was too long and too static, it had no comedy, no stars, no sex appeal. "No Girls, No Gags, No Chance" was the way one Broadwayite put it.

As soon as *Oklahoma!* opened on the historic evening of March 31, 1943, the gagster who had coined the above phrase could have added two additional words to his succinct evaluation: "No Tickets." *Oklahoma!* had proved, on opening night, a stunning stage experience such as one does not often encounter in a lifetime of playgoing. From the moment the curtain rose and the first strains of "Oh, What a Beautiful Mornin'" were heard—down through the final rousing scene with the presentation of the title number—the audience sat spellbound as a new kind of stage art unfolded with incomparable beauty and majesty. Here, as Lewis Nichols said, was a "folk opera"; here, as Burton Rascoe wrote, was a musical "fresh, lovely, colorful, one of the finest musical scores any musical play ever had"; here, in John Anderson's opinion, was a production "beautiful and delightful . . . fresh and imaginative, as enchanting to the eye as Richard Rodgers' music is to the ear." The next morning the queues started forming outside the St. James' Theater box office—and they kept on forming for the next 5 years!

The Lynn Riggs play, faithfully adapted by Hammerstein, was set in the Midwestern Indian country at the turn of the present century. Laurey is in love with Curly, and though he reciprocates her affection he is too shy and retiring to make his true feelings known; in her presence he assumes a hostile attitude. To anger Curly, Laurey accepts an invitation to attend a picnic with Jud Fry, a disreputable creature. One of the attractions of the picnic is for a man to bid for a girl's lunch box in an open auc-

tion and thus share the repast with her. When Curly out-
bids Jud, Laurey knows how he really feels about her.
From then on their romance flourishes. Curly proposes
and is accepted. At their wedding, Jud—all the worse for
drink—attacks Curly with a knife. In the ensuing brawl
Jud is killed as he falls on his own open blade. A trial is
hastily improvised by the local judge. Curly is found
innocent and permitted to go off with his bride on their
honeymoon to a land soon to become known as Oklahoma.

The romance, the tensions, and the drama from the
play arise from the love affair of Curly and Laurey. Most
of the humor arises from still another love triangle, this
time engaging Ado Annie, a young man named Will, and
an Oriental peddler. Ado Annie is a girl who just "cain't
say no," and who believes that in love its "all 'er nothin'."
The Oriental peddler takes his love where he finds it;
finding it with Ado Annie he is none too serious about
his intentions. Will, however, loves Ado Annie and wants
to marry her. But he faces a seemingly insurmountable
obstacle when Ado Annie's father insists he raise the
sum of 50 dollars cash so he can marry her. When the
peddler finds the hot breath of an impending marriage
on his neck, he sees to it that Will gets the 50 dollars,
and Ado Annie.

Hammerstein managed to find humor even in the des-
picable character of Jud, thus carrying bright soft, light
hues to an otherwise black portrait. The humor is found
in an extended song episode, "Pore Jud."

If the humor came only from characters and situations,
so did the dances and the songs. The dances, with choreography by Agnes De Mille, were imaginative American folk ballets germane to the story. And the songs were
similarly often in the style of folk art, with lyrics by Hammerstein that were direct, simple, at times colloquial, and
frequently poetically eloquent. In "Oh, What a Beautiful
Mornin'," lyricist and composer brought a new song dimension to the musical theater. The expression and the
technical means of both melody and lyric were of the

simplest and the most elementary, yet touched with such beauty and poetic grace that it rises to the elevation of genuine folk music. Other songs also had the same simple appeal and approach, also assumed the identity of Western folk songs and dances: the title song, "The Surrey with the Fringe on Top," "The Farmer and the Cowman," and "Kansas City." Only the main love song, "People Will Say We're in Love," was in the style and structure long favored by musical comedy; and it is perhaps no coincidence that this is the only musical number in the production in which the old method of writing melody before lyric prevailed. For all the other songs, Rodgers fashioned his melody to the demands of Hammerstein's lyrics.

But the score of *Oklahoma!* consisted of more than songs. Through the play, musical fragments were interspersed—sometimes as a background to the dialogue; sometimes to heighten an emotion; sometimes to accentuate a mood; sometimes to serve as a transition from one episode in the play to the next. Thus music was called on to perform a far more important function in telling the story and delineating character than our musical theater had thus far known. Using musical episodes in this fashion would henceforth be a basic method for Rodgers and Hammerstein.

Oklahoma!, then, was in every way a revolutionary event in the musical theater. The musical play, first found with *Show Boat*, was here finally realized—a vital, vibrant American art form. *Oklahoma!* made stage history on several other counts as well. Its Broadway run of 5 years and 9 weeks (2,248 performances) and its New York box-office grossage of $7,000,000 broke all existing records. A national company toured for 10 years, performing in about 250 cities, before an audience exceeding 10 million, and grossing another $20,000,000. In addition, the New York company, after closing shop on Broadway, toured 71 cities. Companies were formed to present this musical play in Europe, South Africa, Scandinavia, Australia, and for the Armed Forces. In London its run was

183

the longest in the 300-year history of the Drury Lane Theater.

Oklahoma! introduced to the recording industry the now standard practice of issuing an entire score of a Broadway musical success on phonograph records; over a million such albums were marketed, a phenomenon in this era before the long-playing disc. In 1955, a magnificent Todd-AO screen production of *Oklahoma!* (the first time that process was used) was released, and in time grossed about $8,000,000 domestically. In all, *Oklahoma!* yielded a profit of over 5 million dollars on its original investment of $83,000. Each reluctant investor of $1,500 was compensated with a return of more than $50,000.

After the curtain had fallen on the opening-night performance, Rodgers, Hammerstein, and their many friends celebrated at Sardi's Restaurant on 44th Street, where Broadwayites traditionally congregate. There Rodgers met Lorenz Hart. Hart congratulated Rodgers and added: "You have at least another *Blossom Time*, Dick. This thing of yours will run forever." Then he disappeared in the crowd. In my biography of Richard Rodgers I remarked that it could well be said that the first day Rodgers started to work with Hammerstein was also the day Hart's life really ended; after that he just went through the motions of living. Less than 8 months after *Oklahoma!* opened, Hart was dead. In all probability, the knowledge that *Oklahoma!* had finally accomplished—and *without* him—what he had been reaching for all his life with Rodgers, may have proved more deadly to Hart than his fatal pneumonia.

In view of the magnitude of their artistic and financial achievement, it is easy to understand why Rodgers and Hammerstein should have become the foremost spokesmen for and exponents of the musical play. Their confidence and their courage bolstered by the fantastic victory of *Oklahoma!*, they could proceed to bring to reality their vision of what a musical play should be.

But before Rodgers and Hammerstein wrote their second musical play, Hammerstein had a pet stage project of his own realized. It was an all-Negro musical play, *Carmen Jones*, an updated, Americanized adaptation of Bizet's opera *Carmen*. Bizet's music was used with no alterations and additions, and with only minor deletions, decked out with new contemporary lyrics. The setting of 19th-century Seville of the Bizet opera became an American Southern town during World War II. Seductive Carmen Jones falls in love with Joe, a corporal, and steals him from Cindy Lou. Joe goes AWOL from his army camp, and the lovers flee to Chicago, where Carmen Jones falls in love with Husky Miller, a pugilist. When Joe realizes that he has lost Carmen Jones, he murders her outside a sports arena, on the night of Husky's championship bout.

The same kind of tenuous, but nonetheless recognizable, relationship that exists between the story in Bizet's opera and that devised by Hammerstein can also be found between the main arias of the opera and the songs of *Carmen Jones.* The famous "Habanera" became "Dat's Love," and the no less popular "Toreador Song," "Stan' Up and Fight"; the Seguidille was made into "Dere's a Café on de Corner," the "Flower Song" into "Dis Flower," and Micaëla's Air into "My Joe."

Carmen Jones opened on December 2, 1943 and remained for almost 2 years. Coming as it did on the heels of *Oklahoma!*, it proved another "memorable milestone," as Robert Garland said, "in the upward and onward course of the great American showshop."

The successor to *Oklahoma!* was *Carousel*, produced on April 19, 1945. To this day it is one of the most poignantly beautiful and most radiant of all the Rodgers and Hammerstein musical plays; and by the same token it is one of the imperishable masterworks of the American theater. "When the highest judge of all hands down the ultimate verdict," said Brooks Atkinson in 1954 after

185

witnessing a revival of *Carousel,* "it is this column's opinion that *Carousel* will turn out to be the finest of their creations. . . . *Carousel* is a masterpiece that grows in stature through the years."

Carousel was adapted from *Liliom,* a play by Ferenc Molnar about a barker in a Hungarian amusement park. But the time and place—as well as the names of the characters—were changed; and so was a good deal of the basic story. Reset in the United States in the year 1873, *Carousel* became an American play, most of whose characters were New England fishermen and mill girls. Billy Bigelow, an irresponsible barker in an amusement park, falls in love and marries sensitive Julie Jordon. In marriage, as out of it, he is a happy-go-lucky and shiftless bully. But when he discovers his wife is about to have a baby, he is filled with pride and a sense of responsibility. The necessity to get money to secure his child's future leads him to attempt a holdup; and when he is caught he commits suicide. In heaven, Billy is told that only through his soul's redemption can he gain admission, and he is given one day back on earth to achieve that redemption. He returns to find his daughter grown up, about to be graduated from school. The sympathy, understanding, and tenderness he brings her—she can now go ahead and face life with head held high!—is the means by which Billy's soul is redeemed.

It is not hard to see why this musical play is such a favorite with so many, why each new revival seems to uncover in it new beauties. Nowhere else did Rodgers and Hammerstein bring such humanity and compassion, such penetration into the motivations of characters, such a glow of warm feeling as here. Hammerstein's verses and dialogue achieved an even higher level of poetic beauty and mellow wisdom than in *Oklahoma!.* And for Rodgers, *Carousel* represented a leap forward in his musico-dramatic concept. The famous opening waltz for orchestra, played under the opening scene, is a symphonic prelude of concert caliber. Some of the songs—

like "Soliloquy," Billy's famous narrative when he learns he is about to become a father—have the dramatic impulse and the structural expanse of an opera aria. A new expressiveness enters Rodgers' lyricism in songs like "If I Loved You" and "June Is Bustin' Out All Over," while in "You'll Never Walk Alone" he created one of his most effective inspirational numbers. As if this were not enough achievement for a stage composer, he found a new creative range and scope in extended musical passages combining song, recitative, and dialogue set against music; and in brief instrumental interludes that stray in and out of the play like welcome visitors to remind us of past happenings.

After *Carousel* came one of the most unique experiments in the history of our musical theater, *Allegro* (1947). It sought to explore new areas for musicals in the same way that some of the avant-garde playwrights were doing for the spoken drama. *Allegro* was not always successful in what it tried to do, but there was about it a breathless kind of excitement that comes from exploring a brave, new world. Oscar Hammerstein wrote his own text as well as the lyrics, one of the few instances in which he was not adapting somebody else's play. The hero is Dr. Joseph Taylor, the son of a small-town physician who is spurred on by an overambitious wife to discard the high ideals of the medical profession for wealth and social position. But in the big city he finds only disillusionment, and he returns to his town to assume the humble practice of medicine among his own kind of people.

One of the many innovations in *Allegro* was to use a kind of "Greek chorus" to comment on what is happening, or to point out some moral; sometimes speech was used for this purpose, and sometimes a song. Another innovation was to dispense with most of the sets, properties, and costuming to permit the action to take place mainly on a bare, or semi-bare stage. A third radical departure was to use colors, thrown on a large screen backstage, and with it lighting, to set moods and heighten emotions. A fourth novelty was to tell Joe's story often through dances (including an unusual "psychiatric ballet") and music; and the latter consisted not merely of formal musical-comedy songs (such as "The Gentleman Is a Dope" and "A Fellow Needs a Girl") but also large choral episodes, and extended cantatas for solo voices, chorus, and orchestra.

Allegro did not sit well with the audiences, and it had a comparatively short life. But the critics loved it, describing its "lyrical rapture" and "stunning blend of beauty, integrity, imagination, taste, and skill." But, in reality, *Allegro* was not a well-integrated or completely convincing work of art, and some of the innovations had the appearance of stunts rather than basic artistic procedures. All the same, rarely before or since has the musical theater provided such a provocative and stimulating evening.

Then, having had a brief rendezvous with failure, Rodgers and Hammerstein once again took Broadway by storm—with *South Pacific* (1949). It was anticipated on Broadway with a fanfare of publicity bugles proclaiming that here was something very special, even from the authors of *Oklahoma!* and *Carousel.* Word from out-of-town tryouts kept spreading the news that all the elements of musical theater had been jelled by stage director, Joshua Logan, into a production of incomparable enchantment, starring the inimitable Mary Martin with Ezio Pinza, the latter in his first appearance in the Broadway theater after triumphs in opera. Consequently, by the time *South Pacific* opened at the Majestic Theater, on April 7, 1949, it had amassed the largest advance sale recorded up to then, about a million dollars.

Anything less than a masterpiece would have been a letdown. Fortunately, *South Pacific was* a masterpiece that stunned the first-night audience—and uncountable audiences after that. Some diehards of the entertainment world—veterans like Arthur Hammerstein and Michael

Todd—went all out and called it the greatest show ever seen on Broadway, perfect in every respect. The critics were one in singing its praises. "An utterly captivating work of theatrical art," was the way Richard Watts, Jr., described it; "a thrilling and exultant musical play," said William Hawkins.

South Pacific was an adaptation by Hammerstein and Joshua Logan of James A. Michener's book of stories in the Pacific during World War II—*Tales of the South Pacific,* winner of the Pulitzer Prize for fiction. Ensign Nellie Forbush, portrayed by Mary Martin, is an American nurse stationed in a small Pacific island with members of American Naval and Marine units. She falls in love with Emile de Becque, a middle-aged French planter who had settled on the island long before war had broken out (De Becque being the role filled by Pinza). But when Nellie discovers that De Becque had once been married to a Polynesian and is the father of two Eurasian children, she refuses to have anything more to do with him. Heartbroken at this rejection, De Becque joins Lieutenant Joseph Cable on a dangerous war mission to penetrate a nearby island still held by the Japanese. Cable is killed, but De Becque returns safely after relaying back information enabling an American task force to make a successful invasion of several Japanese-held islands. On his return, De Becque finds Nellie waiting for him. She is feeding and playing with his children, ready to let bygones be bygones. A secondary love interest in the play concerns Cable and a Tonkinese girl, Liat, whom he meets on the off-limits island of Bali Ha'i.

More than one danger signal flashed for the authors in making their adaptation. But with their now customary recklessness in doing the unexpected, they dashed past the red lights toward the destinations demanded by their story and characters. Their hero was a middle-aged, slightly gray man, defying a time-honored precept of the musical theater that romance belonged exclusively to the young. The love affair of Cable and Liat raised a racial problem the musical theater preferred to avoid. Such issues were met squarely; in the song "Carefully Taught," Rodgers and Hammerstein made an eloquent sermon for racial tolerance.

For Rodgers, *South Pacific* was still one more step forward in making music reflect the personal traits of the characters. "Bali Ha'i" and "Happy Talk" caught some of the mysterious, exotic personality of Bloody Mary, the Tonkinese mother of Liat; "A Cockeyed Optimist," "I'm Gonna Wash that Man Right Outa My Hair," and "I'm in Love with a Wonderful Guy" were the kind of songs a girl like Nellie, from America's Midwest, would naturally and instinctively enlist to echo her inmost feelings. The sophistication and romantic character of De Becque could be discovered in his two love songs, "This Nearly Was Mine" and "Some Enchanted Evening," while the simplicity and sincerity of Cable echo in "Younger than Springtime."

Once again—as in *Oklahoma!* and *Carousel*—Rodgers and Hammerstein had brought a new aesthetic experience to theatergoers. And the response of audiences was little short of cyclonic. For most of the 5 years it stayed on Broadway (specifically 1925 performances, only 323 less than the record previously compiled by *Oklahoma!*) tickets were so hard to come by that anecdotes and jests sprouted like wild mushrooms about the ways and means people employed to get a pair. The story went that for a fee as a public speaker Justice Hugo Black, of the U.S. Supreme Court, simply wanted two seats for *South Pacific;* that, at a luncheon honoring Rodgers and Hammerstein, Carlos P. Romulo said, "Let's hope the Lord will make it easier for these two gifted men to get into heaven than it is for us to get into *South Pacific";* that when the concert singer Igor Gorin was asked to substitute for the ailing Lawrence Tibbett at Carnegie Hall he declined because he had tickets for *South Pacific* for the same evening.

In many ways, *South Pacific* amassed formidable records of its own. In New York, 3½ million people paid over $9,000,000 at the box office. The several year tour of a national company brought in many more millions of dollars. The Todd-AO screen production proved the greatest financial success of any screen adaptation of a Rodgers and Hammerstein musical, its domestic gross of more than 16 million dollars being the sixth highest in the history of talking pictures. In its stage version, *South Pacific* played 2½ years in London, after which the company went on tour for another year and a half. Australian and Danish companies opened on the same evening, and stayed for several years. In 1955, *South Pacific* was singled out in Madrid as the greatest box-office success the Spanish theater had known. Sheet music sold over 2,000,000 copies, the long-playing disc of the original-cast performance of the score almost 2,000,000 records. The name "South Pacific" received royalties from cosmetics, dresses, lingerie. *South Pacific* grabbed every theatrical prize in sight, including the Pulitzer Prize for drama, the New York Drama Critics Award as the best musical, seven Antoinette Perry, and nine Donaldson Awards.

The King and I (1951) was as far removed from *South Pacific* geographically as a South Pacific island can be from Siam. The habit of Rodgers and Hammerstein always to try something new, something radically different from a preceding success, still held true. It required a hardy and adventurous spirit to embark on a project like *The King and I*. Here was a musical completely foreign to American backgrounds, experiences, and characters; all the people in that play were Orientals except for four Anglo-Saxons, who were English. Here was a musical with no visible love interest engaging the two principal characters; they do not even kiss once. Here was a musical ending with the death of one of them.

Even its point of departure had defied tradition. *The King and I* was one of the first important musicals adapted from a motion picture, reversing a procedure so long in practice of transforming Broadway musicals into movies. The picture was *Anna and the King of Siam,* starring Rex Harrison and Irene Dunne, released in 1946, a non-musical film in turn derived from a novel by Margaret Landon. It was the brilliant English stage star, Gertrude Lawrence, who was the first to come up with the idea of changing the movie into a musical play; and she, in turn, convinced Rodgers and Hammerstein to make the change. Naturally, Gertrude Lawrence saw herself as Anna. Casting the part of the hero, the swaggering king of Siam, presented, however, a problem, since nobody along Broadway seemed to fill the specifications. But one day, at auditions, a huge man with an Oriental head and regal bearing tried out for the part. He sat on the floor and sang gypsy songs to his own accompaniment. The moment they heard him, Rodgers and Hammerstein knew they had found their king. The candidate was Yul Brynner, up to now a bit player on Broadway and a television director. He was so much the Siamese king to the manner born that, even though he was playing opposite Gertrude Lawrence in what was possibly the most sensational performance of her life, he was never obscured by her brilliance.

Anna is a prim, dignified, appealing little English schoolteacher brought to Siam in the early 1860's to teach Western culture to the king's princes and princesses. Her first reaction to the king is that he is a despot, a dictator who brooked no contradiction, and who was a child in his moods and whims. For his part, the king found Anna disconcertingly stubborn and dogmatic about her Western ideas. In time, however, each found in the other much to admire. Though attracted to each other, their attachment could remain only of the mind and not of the heart since a gulf separated their cultures and social positions. Meanwhile, as a teacher, Anna came to love deeply the king's many children. When her anger against the king's broken promise makes her want to leave Siam for good and return to England, she finds it hard to part from her brood. The king is reluctant to see her go, especially since it was through her common sense and ingenuity that a sensitive diplomatic dilemma in Siam was resolved. She does stay on, because the sudden death of the king had made her indispensable to the children.

Six carloads of the most sumptuous Oriental sets, and resplendent costumes made from silks imported from Thailand, helped make *The King and I* a spectacular visual experience. The eye was further delighted by a stunning ballet sequence conceived by Jerome Robbins in which the American story of Harriet Beecher Stowe's *Uncle Tom's Cabin* was recreated in the simple, literal, ingenuous terms of the Siamese dance. But *The King and I* was also a feast for the ear, with a score arresting in its melodic, harmonic, and instrumental invention; in its projection of the most subtle moods and most delicate nuances of feeling; in its varied imagination. Sometimes the music was delicately touched with Oriental spices which gave it a most welcome tang, as in the ever-delightful little march for the royal princes and princesses; in the haunting ballad, "We Kiss in a Shadow"; in the background music for the ballet in which only percussive instruments (including Oriental woodblocks and ancient cymbals) were used. At times the musical imagination had a dramatic sweep, as in the king's extended narrative, "A Puzzlement"; sometimes it had the aesthetic impact of a German art-song, as in the sensitive beauty of "Hello, Young Lovers"; and sometimes it had the recognizable Richard Rodgers charm, as in "Shall We Dance?" and "I Whistle a Happy Tune."

Rarely before had our musical stage discussed an Oriental setting and people with such good taste and maturity, with such respect for exotic customs and dress, such tolerance for exotic behavior. As Hammerstein had said when first he began writing the text, "What was required was an Eastern sense of dignity and pageantry— and none of this business of girls dressed in Oriental costumes and dancing out onto the stage and singing 'chingaling-aling' with their fingers in the air." What Rodgers and Hammerstein put on their stage was not a travesty or an empty spectacle feasting on Oriental splendor, but, as Richard Watts, Jr., said, "an East of frank and unashamed romance, seen through the eyes . . . of theatrical artists of rare taste and creative power, and it [was] made something far more than a lovely exotic panorama by the ability of the authors to create characters possessing human dignity."

The King and I was the third Rodgers and Hammerstein musical to exceed a run of a thousand performances (*Carousel* almost hit that mark with 890 performances). A half year before that engagement was over, its star, Gertrude Lawrence, died of cancer, bringing to conclusion one of the most lustrous careers in the theater of our times—and with one of her most poignant, most unforgettable characterizations.

After *The King and I*, Rodgers and Hammerstein attempted—at times consciously, at other times subconsciously—to return to musical comedy on three successive occasions. The first was with *Me and Juliet* (1953), a backstage story of life in the Broadway theater during the run of a successful musical comedy. The authors tried to carry over into their story of the complicated love life of two sets of characters their own excitement over and enthusiasm for the stage. Familiar to time-honored practices in musical comedy were the happy resolution of the plot; the Broadway type dance numbers realized by Robert Alton (a man long skilled in the more formal kind of musical-comedy routines); and slick and sleek songs like the hit number "No Other Love," a tango which the composer had derived from the background music he had previously written for the television documentary, *Victory at Sea*. Rodgers and Hammerstein had taught their public to demand something more significant, something more permanent than such entertainment—and they became victims of their own good teaching. *Me and Juliet* lasted less than 400 performances, earned only a modest profit, and has been forgotten.

There was also a good deal of musical comedy in *Pipe Dream* (1955) and *Flower Drum Song* (1958), and by the same token both were "minor key" Rodgers and Hammerstein creations. The former was an adaptation of a novel of John Steinbeck presenting an odd assortment of screwball characters in Cannery Row, an offbeat section of San Francisco. Rodgers' score included a fine inspirational number in "Everybody's Got a Home but Me," an above average ballad in "All at Once You Love Her"; Hammerstein's text boasted one or two hilarious scenes set in a flophouse, including a farcical episode entitled "The Bum's Opera." But *Pipe Dream* had little else. It was so vigorously rejected by the critics and audiences that it suffered the shortest run of any Rodgers and Hammerstein production (246 performances).

While *Flower Drum Song* was not much better as stage art than *Pipe Dream*, it had far more substantial values as entertainment. It told the story of the rivalry in San Francisco's Chinatown between the old and the new generations of Chinese, and between Eastern and Western culture. A song like "I Enjoy Being a Girl" (presented excitingly by a new star, Pat Suzuki); a buck and wing dance that followed the number, "Don't Marry Me"; a strip tease in a night club—all this is musical-comedy trappings which masters like Rodgers and Hammerstein knew how to make dramatically effective. As a moneymaker *Flower Drum Song* carried Rodgers and Hammerstein back to the top of their profession; it was their first musical since *The King and I* to be made into a movie. But for those whose memories glowed with the wonder and radiance of *Oklahoma!*, *Carousel*, *South Pacific* and *The King and I*, the *Flower Drum Song* still proved to be a letdown.

But in *The Sound of Music* (1959)—whose advance sale of over $3,000,000 broke all precedent—Rodgers and

Hammerstein once again set out to do a musical play with characters, situations, and conflicts unusual for the popular stage. The characters were the members of the Trapp Family—a group of choral singers headed by Baron George von Trapp and his wife, Maria, who actually had lived in Austria in the era before World War II and had toured the world of music in choral concerts. The unusual incidents in *The Sound of Music* emerged from the fact that the play was set in Austria just before and during the Nazi occupation (or *Anschluss*) in 1938, its story centering around the courageous efforts of the anti-Fascist Baron to elude the menace of storm troopers and finally to flee with his family to freedom. This is heavy, even somber, stuff for musical-stage treatment, demanding on the part of Rodgers new musical approaches. He met this challenge with an unaccompanied choral *Praeludium* instead of an overture for orchestra, and with the injection into an otherwise popular score of several chants simulating church music. But the dark and menacing shadows hovering over the play were continually lightened with charm, grace, and a happy glow. The core of the story was the love affair between Maria Rainer, a postulant in an abbey (enchantingly played by Mary Martin) and the widower, Baron George von Trapp, father of seven bright-faced children. She comes to the household to teach them music and in that capacity, and with the aid of the children, she offers a disarming little number called "Do, Re, Mi" which regularly met an ovation from the audience. She wins the heart of the children, and after that she wins the Baron as well. Thus *The Sound of Music* was at times grim with foreboding and touched with drama and tragedy; but at other times it was radiantly romantic, winningly sentimental, sweet and caressing. Some of its songs were the best Rodgers and Hammerstein had written since *The King and I;* besides "Do, Re, Mi" the score included the title number, an outstanding inspirational number in "Climb Ev'ry Mountain" and "My Favorite Things."

196

The Sound of Music was the greatest artistic and box-office triumph enjoyed by Rodgers and Hammerstein since *The King and I*—testimony (if such be needed) that the masters had not lost their golden touch. It ran on Broadway for more than three years. Then in a remarkable screen adaptation starring Julie Andrews it went on to become the biggest moneymaker in the history of motion pictures besides capturing the Academy Award as the best film of the year, and selling 8 million disks of the sound track recording, an all-time high.

Tragic to say, *The Sound of Music* proved the last triumphant chord to a majestic collaboration. On August 23, 1960, Oscar Hammerstein II died of cancer. The Rodgers and Hammerstein partnership was over—and so was an epoch in the American musical theater the like of which we are not liable to witness for many years to come.

Musical Comedy in Excelsis / 13

The musical play, then, came fully into its own in the 1940's. But this did not mean that musical comedy was displaced. On the contrary—the 1940's made Broadway exciting and alive with some extraordinary musical comedies. Good entertainment still had a strong pull at the box office, just as long as that entertainment was smart, adult, and fresh. The best of the 1940 musical comedies were that. In a Sunday article in the *New York Times,* Howard Taubman mentioned some of the ingredients that go into the making of outstanding musical comedy: "A fresh idea, a consistent point of view, an unhackneyed sense of fun, a showcase for personality, a feeling for individuality of style in music, dancing and staging." The musical comedy was able to survive the competition of the musical play—even thrive in spite of that competition —because it was capable of meeting these specifications.

Lady in the Dark (1941) was a musical comedy about psychoanalysis 15 years after *Peggy-Ann* of Rodgers-Hart-Fields. Moss Hart's play had as its heroine a woman editor of a fashion magazine who undergoes psychoanalytic treatment. Much of the production was devoted to her dream sequences. The play moved continually from the realistic world of the heroine's business and love life to the unreal world of her feverish, fretful dreams and dream recollections of her childhood and youth. As that editor, Gertrude Lawrence gave a stunning virtuoso performance; and in a minor role, Danny Kaye demonstrated for the first time in the Broadway theater his immense potential as a comic, particularly when his glib, athletic tongue gave a breathless delivery of a song, "Tchaikovsky," made up almost entirely of complicated names of Russian composers. The music for *Lady in the Dark* was by Kurt Weill, while Ira Gershwin was the lyricist. For the dream sequences, Weill wrote a sensitive number, "My Ship," used as a kind of link among various episodes; in another, in which the heroine dreams about a preposterous circus, she sings the haunting "The Saga of Jenny," the lament of a lady who could not make up her mind.

Kurt Weill's *One Touch of Venus* (1943)—this time, book and lyrics by S. J. Perelman and Ogden Nash—was, perhaps, not quite the excitingly different musical comedy that *Lady in the Dark* had been, but it proved an even greater box-office attraction. Mary Martin appeared as a statue of Venus come to life, with resultant complications to poor Rodney who falls in love with her and deserts his own girl friend, Gloria. As Venus, Mary Martin popularized two distinguished Weill tunes, "Speak Low" and "How Much Do I Love You?" The musical comedy ends happily for all the principals as Venus reverts to her former status as an inanimate statue, and Rodney and Gloria become reconciled.

One of the most sensational musical comedies of the 1940's was Irving Berlin's *Annie Get Your Gun* (1946). Though by 1946 Berlin had already become the top man of his trade—it is doubtful if anyone, anywhere, could match his achievements in Tin Pan Alley, on Broadway, and as the unofficial musical laureate of World War II —*Annie Get Your Gun* posed a challenge for him. This was a production by a new firm then recently founded by Rodgers and Hammerstein to put on their own musical plays and sometimes the works of other writers. This meant that composer-lyricist Irving Berlin was working under and for one of America's leading song composers and the dean of American lyricists. Besides, Jerome Kern had originally been selected to write the music, a project that did not materialize, due to Kern's sudden death. Thus composer Berlin was stepping into the shoes left vacant by America's aristocrat of song.

Irving Berlin met this double challenge not only by writing his best and most versatile score but also by achieving the greatest box-office triumph of his career. The run of 1147 performances achieved by *Annie Get Your Gun* was one of the longest in Broadway history.

Annie Get Your Gun starred Ethel Merman as the brash, swaggering backwoods girl, Annie Oakley, who was handier with a gun than with things like book learnin' or men. As the star of Buffalo Bill's Wild West Show she falls in love with Frank Butler, head of Pawnee Bill's show, a rival outfit. A merger between the two companies also helps bring about the satisfactory union of Annie and Frank.

It was a grand spectacle throughout, with Ethel Merman giving one of her most exciting performances. Such a combination could only spell out musical comedy *in excelsis*. And Irving Berlin was never better, his touch never surer, both in melody and lyrics. His songs were romantic ("They Say It's Wonderful"), sentimental ("The Girl that I Marry"), spicily good-humored ("You Can't Get a Man with a Gun"), discreetly pornographic ("Doin' What Comes Natur'lly"), animal-spirited ("I Got the Sun in the Morning" and "Anything You Can Do"), and even touched with a kind of exaltation ("Show Business"). Few musical comedies had such a profusion of song hits. But there was much more to make *Annie Get Your Gun* an irresistible package of the most wonderful entertainment. There was remarkable choreography by Helen Tamiris that included a colorful dance by Sioux Indians and the brilliant sets and costuming by Jo Mielziner. "Seldom is seen in the theater an offering in which everything is just as it should be," said Vernon Rice.

Annie Get Your Gun dwarfs the stature of Irving Berlin's next two musical comedies, though each had sound entertainment values. For *Miss Liberty* (1949), Robert Sherwood—the eminent American dramatist who was a three-times winner of the Pulitzer Prize—wrote his first musical-comedy libretto. Against the setting of New York and Paris in 1885, *Miss Liberty* described some of the attempts in New York to raise the money for a base to the Statue of Liberty which had been presented to the United States by France. Subsidiary plots touched upon the bitter rivalry between two powerful New York newspapers, the *Herald* and the *World;* also on the romance of a breezy young reporter and the French girl he brings back from Paris as the one who had been the model for the Statue, but who in reality was just a fraud. Berlin's score included such lilting tunes as "Let's Take an Old-Fashioned Walk," a bit of nostalgia for Paris in "Paris Wakes Up and Smiles," and an inspirational number based on words by Emma Lazarus inscribed on the base of the Statue of Liberty, "Give Me Your Tired, Your Poor."

Call Me Madam (1950) was all the richer for having Ethel Merman in the leading role. She is an American woman Ambassador sent to the mythical kingdom of Lichtenburg, a character modeled in part after the real-to-life American Ambassador and Washington party giver, Mrs. Perle Mesta. Washington politics, diplomatic red tape, international intrigue are all strands neatly woven into a fabric whose main design was the love interest between our woman Ambassador and the Lichtenburg Prime Minster, between her young assistant and a Lichtenburg princess. "She is one of the joys of the world," wrote Richard Watts, Jr., of Ethel Merman's robust, earthy, uninhibited portrait of a woman Ambassador. To her the principal Berlin songs were assigned: "You're Just in Love," "The Best Thing for You," and "The Hostess with the Mostes' on the Ball." A fourth song—chanted by three Congressmen—was a hymn to Dwight D. Eisenhower, "They Like Ike." When this song was first heard in *Call Me Madam,* Eisenhower was still 2 years away from the White House. It is not too much to say that his path to the Presidency was at least partially cleared by this exultant paean which was used so effectively during his Presidential campaign of 1952.

Fantasy was the keynote of two of 1940's best musical comedies, both of them produced in 1947. "I don't believe," once said E. Y. Harburg, the lyricist, "the theater is a place for photographic reproduction. That's why I'm attracted to fantasy, to things with a poetic quality. Through fantasy, I feel that a musical can say things with greater effectiveness about life. It's great for pricking balloons, for exploding shibboleths. Of course I want to send people out of the theater with the glow of having a good time, but I also think the purpose of a musical is to make people think."

In this spirit he wrote with Fred Saidy the book and lyrics of *Finian's Rainbow*, for which Burton Lane created the music. *Finian's Rainbow* was a marriage of fantasy and satire, of old Irish legends and modern American social and political problems. Finian and his daughter Sharon come from the mythical Irish town of Glocca Morra to Rainbow Valley, in Missitucky, in southern United States. They carry a crock of gold, stolen from Og, a leprechaun. With such a framework we get stinging side glances on racial prejudice in the South, left-wing Socialism, TVA, sharecropping, corrupt legislators, the idle rich, and a reactionary Negro-hating Southern Senator who turns black through the necromancy of the leprechaun. If social and political criticism and satire contribute bite and sting to the play, the love of the leprechaun and a beautiful deaf-mute who "speaks" by dancing, contributes a heart-warming infusion of tenderness. It is the glamour and the poetry of Irish lore, and the tenderness of romance, that are found in the two hit songs, "How Are Things in Glocca Morra?" and "Look to the Rainbow," just as it is the barbs and thrusts of social criticism that we hear in some of the other numbers, all of them particularly attractive because of Harburg's flashing lyrics, such as "The Begat" and "When the Idle Poor."

Fantasy devoid of any satirical overtones made *Brigadoon* also an unadulterated delight in 1947. Surely at least part of the historic significance of this musical comedy is the fact that it was the first stage success of Lerner and Loewe—Alan Jay Lerner, librettist and lyricist, and Frederick Loewe, composer. But even if Lerner and Loewe had not, a decade later, stunned show business with *My Fair Lady*, their *Brigadoon* would still have earned them a place of honor in the theater.

Frederick Loewe, born in Vienna on June 10, 1904, was raised to be a concert artist. He was taught the piano by some of Europe's foremost teachers, including Ferruccio Busoni and Eugen d'Albert, and in 1923 he received the important Hollander Medal for piano playing. One year later he came to the United States to pursue a career in music. He made such little headway that, in outright disgust, he decided to give up serious music for good. For about a decade he knocked around the country earning his living as best he could in a great variety of occupations. He played the piano in a Greenwich Village night spot, was a riding instructor in a New Hampshire summer resort, worked as a prize fighter in a Brooklyn athletic club. In the West he was a gold prospector, cowpuncher, and delivered mail on horseback. In the early 1930's he was again occupied as a popular pianist, at times in a German beer hall in the Yorkville section of New York, at other times on cruise ships. But by the early 1930's he was also beginning to write popular songs. One of these was "Love Tiptoed Through My Heart," heard in a Broadway play, *Petticoat Fever*, in 1934; another, "A Waltz Was Born in Vienna" was used as a dance number by Gomez and Winona in the *Illustrators Show* in 1934. In 1937 Loewe wrote a complete stage score for the first time, for *Salute to Spring* produced in St. Louis. One year after that he wrote the songs for his first Broadway musical, *Great Lady,* which struggled through 20 performances before closing down.

Then, one day in 1942, Loewe was introduced to young Alan Jay Lerner at the Lambs Club in New York. Lerner was 24 years old at the time. Born to wealth, he received a comprehensive academic education in New York, England, and at Cambridge, Massachusetts. At Harvard, from which he was graduated, he had demonstrated a ready gift for writing humorous sketches and verses by contributing to two Hasty Pudding Shows. After his graduation from Harvard he worked for radio where over a 2-year period he completed about 500 scripts.

When their paths crossed at the Lambs Club, neither Loewe nor Lerner had sound reason for optimism about their respective talent or their future in the theater. Their decision to work together changed all that.

Their first effort was a musical comedy written for a Detroit stock company in which Dorothy Stone was starred. Their second, *What's Up,* was their Broadway debut (in 1943), a farce in which Jimmy Savo played an East-Indian potentate; its life span was 8 weeks. In 1945 they brought to Broadway a delightful fantasy, *The Day Before Spring,* which some critics liked for its bold attempt to invade the female psyche and the fresh way in which the ballet sequences exploited dream psychology. Financially, this production also proved a deficit—and thus gave little warning that with their very next musical comedy the team of Lerner and Loewe would hit a jackpot.

That musical comedy was *Brigadoon.* Brigadoon is a magic Scottish village which one day every hundred years comes out of the Highland mists to resume life the way it had been lived there in 1747 when it had suddenly disappeared off the face of the earth. Legend dictates that whoever stumbles upon Brigadoon during its one-day existence each century must become a part of its activity. This happens to two present-day Americans. They become so infected with the spirit of the romantic past that, in short order, they become authentic Briga-doonites. One of these two Americans even falls in love with a Scottish lass. "The plot works beautifully," wrote Brooks Atkinson. "Mr. Lerner organized the story. He does not get down to the details of the fairy story until the audience has already been won by the pleasant characters, the exuberant music, and the prim though fiery dances. After that the incantation is complete and easy." Loewe's melodies enhanced the sweetness of the setting and the charm and quaintness of the characters. Some of his tunes had a dash of Scottish sauce to provide a piquant flavor: "Come to Me, Bend to Me" and "The Heather on the Hill." Others—and these included a hit song of 1947, "Almost Like Being in Love"—might be of an American recipe, but they were blended beautifully into the Scottish dish.

Besides being the greatest box-office success of their career up to that time, *Brigadoon* earned for Lerner and Loewe laurels from the Drama Critics Circle, the first time a musical comedy received such an award as the best play of the season.

Like Irving Berlin, Cole Porter realized the greatest triumph of his fabulous Broadway career in the 1940's, and it came with *Kiss Me Kate* (1948).

Kiss Me Kate was the second of two significant American musical comedies based on Shakespeare, the first having been *The Boys from Syracuse* by Rodgers and Hart. But in using *The Taming of the Shrew*, Bella and Sam Spewack, the librettists, adroitly used a Shakespeare comedy within the context of a contemporary American story with contemporary American characters. A 20th-century troupe of actors is presenting the Shakespeare comedy in Baltimore. Its two principals, Fred and Lilli, had once been man and wife. But now they are divorced and though each has his or her own new amatory interest, they are still sentimental about each other. The play then shifts nimbly from the Baltimore of today—and the love problems harassing the hero and heroine—to old-time Padua and the troubles of Petruchio and his shrew of a wife, Kate. Since Fred is playing Petruchio, and Lilli, Kate, they sometimes forget they are playing Shakespearean roles. Within their actual performance they give vent to their pent-up anger at or romantic ardor toward each other, just as within an actual performance of the Shakespeare play they finally realize they cannot live without each other.

Cole Porter's lyrics and melodies are of the palpitant present, just as Shakespeare's humor and poetry belong to the past. But there is never a feeling of incongruity. The score—the best of Porter's Broadway career, one of the best, indeed, in all Broadway history—was in the composer's best sophisticated, satirical, or sensual styles, ranging from such languorous numbers as "So in Love" and "Were Thine that Special Face" to such more flippant and at times risqué attitudes as "I Hate Men," "Too Darn Hot," "Always True to You," "Brush Up Your Shakespeare," and a delightful parody of Viennese operetta waltzes, "Wunderbar."

Kiss Me Kate has been acclaimed globally. Its Broadway engagement of over 1000 performances was followed by a comprehensive coast-to-coast tour, a brilliant motion picture, and performances halfway around the world in over a dozen foreign translations. It was the first American musical comedy given in Poland, its more than 200 performances always playing to capacity houses. It was the most successful American musical comedy ever produced in Germany and Austria up to that time; at the Volksoper, in Vienna, it proved the foremost box-office success in the more than 60-year history of that theater.

The two musical comedies by Cole Porter that followed *Kiss Me Kate* returned to the Parisian setting he knew so well, to which he was so sympathetic, and with which he had made his first bid for success on Broadway. *Can-Can* (1953) was a nostalgic backward glance at Bohemian Paris of 1893 and the efforts of the French police to close down a Montmartre café because it featured the "shocking" can-can dance. Cole Porter's sentimental tribute to the city of love, light, and the good life, "I Love Paris," and several other songs in a French vein such as "C'est magnifique" and "Allez-vous en" enhanced a delightful production that included a hilarious take-off on an Apache dance, a sensational can-can dance, a burlesque duel on a Parisian rooftop, a comic ballet in the Garden of Eden, and some particularly arresting sets and costumes by Jo Mielziner. *Can-Can* was later made into a color-splashed, eye-filling movie starring Frank Sinatra, Shirley MacLaine, and Maurice Chevalier. It was a rehearsal in Hollywood of the can-can dance from this screen production that inspired a violent denunciation from the Soviet Prime Minister, Nikita Khrushchev, during his first visit to the United States in 1959.

While *Silk Stockings* (1955) was essentially a mirthful commentary on Soviet red tape, bureaucracy, and political way of life, it also boasted a Parisian background. *Silk Stockings* was the musical-comedy adaptation of the motion-picture comedy, *Ninotchka,* that had starred Greta Garbo—the adaptation made by George S. Kaufman, Leueen McGrath, and Abe Burrows. The heroine, Ninotchka, is a female Soviet agent sent to Paris to bring home a wayward Soviet: a composer writing a score for a French picture who is overstaying his leave in the delightful French capital. Her first contacts with the joys of Paris—and touched for the first time by romance in her associations with a dashing American theater agent played by Don Ameche—Ninotchka soon also tends to prolong her Parisian visit willy-nilly. Three Soviet agents are now dispatched to bring her back to Russia. But once she does return, her American boy friend helps her escape back to Paris, and freedom.

A nostalgic number like "Paris Loves Lovers" helped bring a French accent to this musical comedy, just as a ballad like "All of You" underlined its romantic element. But the cream of the production was found in the jests about things Soviet. The three Soviet agents—Ivanov, Brankov, and Bibinski—provide a devasting caricature of Soviet citizens which runs the gamut from subtle satire to broad burlesque. In asking for a copy of "Who's Who in the Soviet Union," one of the commissars gives it the title of "Who's Still Who." When an American is informed that the world-famous Soviet composer, Prokofiev, is dead, he remarks innocently, "I didn't even know he had been arrested." In such a spirit of undisguised malice are some of Cole Porter's amusing parodies of Russian folk music and two sprightly numbers, "Too Bad" and "Siberia."

Young Lochinvars ⁄ **14**
from the West

A new breed of composer appeared on the Broadway scene in the 1940's. From their fertile pens came some other of the remarkable musical comedies produced during that decade, and in the ensuing two decades. These composers differed from earlier colleagues in that they received their basic professional training, and realized their first major victories as songwriters, not in Tin Pan Alley or on the Broadway stage, but within the motion-picture studios of Hollywood. Among these young musical Lochinvars come out of the West to invade Broadway were Harold Arlen, Frank Loesser, Jule Styne, and Meredith Willson.

While it is quite true that Harold Arlen had had some Broadway stage experience before going to Hollywood, it was only after he had made his mark writing songs for the screen that he was able to score just as decisively in the theater. Born in Buffalo, New York, on February 15, 1905, young Arlen spent much of his boyhood playing the piano in night clubs and on lake steamers. He then formed a jazz combination of his own for which he did all the arrangements. With this group he went to New York City in 1927 to appear in a night spot. After that, in 1930, Arlen timidly put a toe into Broadway waters when his song "Get Happy" appeared in the *9:15 Revue,* sung by Ruth Etting in the first-act finale. The show was a failure, but the song was a hit and helped land for Arlen a job writing songs for revues put on by The Cotton Club, a Harlem night spot where Duke Ellington and his orchestra appeared. Arlen's first important songs were here introduced, including the deservedly famous "Stormy Weather," which Ethel Waters introduced and helped make famous. Between 1930 and 1932 Arlen's songs cropped up in two editions of the *Earl Carroll Vanities* and in several other revues and musical comedies. In 1937, *Hooray for What!*, starring Ed Wynn, became the first book musical for which Arlen wrote a complete score.

But thus far there was nothing particularly impressive about his achievements in the Broadway theater, nor was his career there a success story. But his work in Hollywood during the next half dozen years helped make Arlen one of the most significant and original new song composers to appear in American popular music in some years. Usually with E. Y. Harburg as his lyricist, Arlen wrote for the screen a number of truly remarkable songs which are still as popular today as they were when first heard: "It's Only a Paper Moon," "Happiness Is a Thing Called Joe," "Let's Fall in Love," "Blues in the Night," "That Old Black Magic," and "Over the Rainbow." The last won the Academy Award in 1939 after Judy Garland had introduced it in *The Wizard of Oz*.

Then in 1944, Arlen, with Harburg as his lyricist, returned to Broadway after an absence of seven and a half years. Since this return was made with *Bloomer Girl*, he came with flying banners: *Bloomer Girl* ran for more than 650 performances. This was a period piece set in the little town of Cicero, New York, in 1861. The "bloomer girl" was an actual historical character: Amelia Bloomer (in the play she is called Dolly), a feminist who led a spirited fight for Women's Rights, Temperance, and the practicability of having women wear bloomers in place of hoop skirts. She and her sister Evelina get involved in the Abolitionist movement. Though Evelina is in love with a Southern gentleman, Jeff Calhoun, she does not hesitate to help one of Jeff's slaves escape in the Underground. The play ends as the Secessionists fire on Fort Sumter. By that time Jeff has come around to Evelina's way of thinking and has freed his slave. With a wonderful Civil War ballet created by Agnes De Mille; a spectacular production number built around the song "Sunday in Cicero Falls"; a compelling scene developed from episodes from *Uncle Tom's Cabin;* and musical numbers like "I Got a Song" and "T'morra, t'morra," *Bloomer Girl* belonged at the top of the best musicals of the 1940's.

After *Bloomer Girl,* Arlen divided his activity between Broadway and Hollywood. His Broadway successes included two musical comedies with Caribbean settings. *House of Flowers* (1954)—book and lyrics by Truman Capote in his first assignment for the musical theater—took place in the West Indies during a Mardi Gras festival. It took full advantage of that locale to feature exciting native dances and a frenetic voodoo rite. Arlen's music, similarly, had pronounced West Indian flavors, numbers like "Two Ladies in de Shade of de Banana Tree." *Jamaica* (1957) was the musical comedy in which Lena Horne made her first Broadway appearance in a starring role. The show became a frame for her remarkable performing gifts and her irresistible personality. She was heard in eight musical numbers, and she had the audience well in the palm of her hand in the plangent blues, "Take It Slow, Joe," the ballad, "Cocoanut Sweet," and the calypso-like ditties "Ain't It the Truth?" and "Push the Button."

Whereas Arlen had completed some writing for Broadway before his chores for and successes in Hollywood, both Frank Loesser and Jule Styne did not make their Broadway debuts until their reputations as composers had been solidly fixed in the motion-picture capital. And when, at long last, they did make that stage debut, it proved a resounding success.

That of Frank Loesser came with *Where's Charley?*

(1948). An old chestnut of the professional and amateur stage—Brandon Thomas' farce, *Charley's Aunt*—was here freshened and refurbished as a musical comedy by George Abbott. This business of having a man masquerade as a woman, wearing female garb and assuming feminine attitudes and mannerisms, is something which long before 1948 had been worn to shreds. But as Charley, Ray Bolger managed to make this routine consistently funny. And his suave way in delivering a song like "Once in Love with Amy" (in which he had the audience participate), and his charming and slick performance with a tap-dance routine, brought dimension to what might otherwise have been a perfunctory musical comedy; transformed it into a stunning production that played to capacity audiences for almost 800 performances.

Frank Loesser was a New York boy, born on June 29, 1910. Though his family was musical (his brother, Arthur, became successful as a concert pianist and teacher) Frank did not receive any formal music instruction. Nevertheless he was a musical child, and sought to express that musical nature by playing the piano by ear, becoming a virtuoso on the harmonica, and by singing. His academic education ended abruptly after a single year at the College of the City of New York. For several years after that he held various poorly paying jobs, all of them distasteful. He was a process server for a law firm; he played the piano in a mountain resort; he did reporting for a small-town newspaper; he was the knit-goods editor of a journal; he performed press-agent chores; he even tasted foods in restaurants. But if his heart belonged anywhere it was in writing verses, and lyrics for songs. Finally he did manage to land a job as lyricist in Tin Pan Alley where his first song was published in 1931. It was "In Love with the Memory of You," the melody by another youngster, William Schuman, now one of America's foremost serious composers and President of the Juilliard School of Music. Loesser's
212

first hit followed in 1934 with "I Wish I Were Twins," music by Joseph Meyer.

The song brought him a Hollywood contract where, for the next few years he wrote a number of lyrics to songs by some of the screen's most productive and eminent songsmiths: "Says My Heart" with Burton Lane; "Small Fry" with Hoagy Carmichael; "Jingle, Jangle, Jingle" with Joseph J. Lilley.

Thus far Loesser had confined himself exclusively to writing lyrics. World War II made him a composer as well. Soon after Pearl Harbor he wrote music and lyrics of "Praise the Lord and Pass the Ammunition," which sold over 2,000,000 records and 1,000,000 copies of sheet music. Shortly after that, on the request of the Infantry, he produced one of the war's most poignant ballads in "The Ballad of Rodger Young." Then as Private First Class in Special Service he created songs for the WAC, Bombardiers, Service Forces, and one which became an official anthem of the Infantry, "What Do You Do in the Infantry?"

After the war, Loesser kept on writing both music and lyrics in his assignments for the screen. He had become one of Hollywood's ace composer-lyricists when *Where's Charley?* introduced him to New York theater audiences.

Having made his Broadway bow with a box-office smash, Loesser followed it up with one of the triumphs of our musical theater: *Guys and Dolls* (1950). The authors described this musical comedy as "a fable of Broadway." Stories and characters by Damon Runyon were here translated into musical-comedy idiom by Jo Swerling and Abe Burrows. The jerks, screwballs, and nonconformists who populated Damon Runyon's Broadway—tinhorn gamblers, small-time night-club entertainers, Salvation Army do-gooders, and their ilk—were given the breath of life. The brisk and exciting pace of George S. Kaufman's direction, particularly in the opening scene, a pantomime of Broadway life and movement; Michael

Kidd's remarkable ballets, the best inspired by a crap game in a sewer; Jo Mielziner's sensational sets; and most of all Loesser's versatility as composer and lyricist—all this combined to make *Guys and Dolls* a very model of what the ideal musical comedy should be.

Nathan Detroit is a tinhorn gambler who, for 14 years, has been engaged to Adelaide, a night-club entertainer. Each time they are about to get married, a crap game frustrates their plans. Consequently, poor Adelaide is suffering from a psychosomatic cold and chronic sneezes, as she poignantly explains in one of the wittiest songs found in musical comedy, "Adelaide's Lament." But theirs is not the play's main love story. That entangles Sky Masterson, a gay blade and high liver, with—of all people!—Sarah Brown, a Salvation Army lass. Their romance has dramatic ups and downs: "up" when Sarah discovers to her amazement that she has fallen in love with a character like Sky; "down" when she learns that the only reason he has taken her to Havana was to win a bet. Both love affairs reach a happy resolution by the time the final curtain descends. But romance is only incidental to the racy picture provided of New York life, to the insight into the strange impulses and unique motivations governing the lives of some of the city's more picturesque citizens.

Loesser's talent with flashy, witty, or functional lyrics —and his consummate skill and seemingly inexhaustible inventiveness with melodies of many moods—was never richer. In a romantic vein we get ballads like "I've Never Been in Love Before" and "I'll Know"; for satire we have the extraordinary three-voice canon, "Fugue for Tinhorns," in which three gamblers pick their winners from a racing form sheet, and Adelaide's psychosomatic lament; wit and levity effervesce like bubbles in champagne in the title number, and in two night-club routines by Adelaide and her girls, "Take Back Your Mink" and "A Bushel and a Peck."

Guys and Dolls is one of Broadway's big success stories. Its run of over 1000 performances netted more than $12,000,000 dollars. Another million dollars came in an advance from Samuel Goldwyn for a stunning motion-picture adaptation starring Marlon Brando, Frank Sinatra, Jean Simmons, and Vivian Blaine, the last re-creating for the screen the role of Adelaide she had helped make famous on the stage.

Jule Styne's Broadway debut took place with *High Button Shoes* in 1947. Born in London, England, on December 31, 1905, Styne had come to Chicago as a boy to make there some concert appearances as a piano prodigy. A scholarship enabled him to get a thorough musical schooling at the Chicago Musical College, after which he made a living playing the piano in various Chicago dance bands, including one which he himself had organized and for which he wrote all the arrangements. Late in the 1930's he went to Hollywood to work as an arranger, serve as vocal coach for stars like Shirley Temple and Alice Faye, and write background music for the films. Before long he was writing popular songs to Sammy Cahn's lyrics, beginning with "I've Heard that Song Before" which Frank Sinatra introduced in a movie short. The first song hit by Styne and Cahn was "I Don't Want to Walk Without You" in 1941. After that came a string of impressive song successes, among which were "It's Been a Long, Long Time," "Let It Snow," "There Goes That Song Again," "Give Me Five Minutes More," and "I'll Walk Alone."

In 1944, Styne and Cahn were contracted to write songs for a musical comedy, *Glad to See You*, which was Broadway bound but never reached there. *High Button Shoes*, however, did go to Broadway and stayed there for over 2 years. Phil Silvers (long before he became television's favorite conniver as Sergeant Bilko) was the star. As Harrison Floy, a swindler, he comes to New Brunswick, New Jersey, home of Rutgers University, in 1913. With a partner-in-crime he defrauds the innocents of that community with whatever shady deal two scheming minds can contrive. In the process he is called on to deliver a lecture to the local bird-watcher society; to engage in a burlesque fight with a football star; to do a series of impersonations; and to fix the big college football game of the year. To all this Phil Silvers brought the bounce and verve and gusto he had stored up after a lifetime playing in burlesque theaters. But nostalgia, as well as Phil Silvers, was an attraction in this musical comedy. Amusing recollections were provided of female fashions in 1913, the perversity of a model-T Ford, and best of all of Mack Sennett's Keystone Kops in a brilliant farcical ballet conceived by Jerome Robbins. Two good songs by Styne and Cahn were also strong assets, "Papa Won't You Dance With Me?" and "I Still Get Jealous."

Jule Styne became a kingpin among Broadway musical-comedy composers with four smash successes after *High Button Shoes: Gentlemen Prefer Blondes* (1949), *Bells Are Ringing* (1956), *Gypsy* (1959), and *Do, Re, Mi* (1960). In the first of these, Anita Loos' vivacious novel of the same name was made into a musical production re-creating the frenetic 1920's through its two principal female characters, two gold-digging flappers en route to Paris. The personal philosophy of one of them, Lorelei Lee, is neatly summed up in two of the show's best musical numbers, "Diamonds Are a Girl's Best Friend" and "A Little Girl from Little Rock," the means by which Carol Channing became a star.

Bells Are Ringing, text and lyrics by Betty Comden and Adolph Green, proved a field day for its star, Judy Holliday, in her first appearance in musical comedy. As a matter of fact, this production was a kind of old-home week for Comden, Green, and Judy Holliday. Many years earlier they had been members of The Revuers, a night-club act for which Comden and Green wrote the material. *Bells Are Ringing* was the first time that the three of them worked together since those days.

216

As an operator in a telephone-answering service in Manhattan, Judy Holliday, as Ella Peterson, manages to overhear the problems besetting the lives of her clients. She is driven helplessly by a compulsion to set things right for them, with resultant confusion for all concerned. One of her clients is a playwright, Jeff, with whom she falls in love—and ultimately wins; another is a dentist eager to write popular songs; a third, a "method" actor who aspires to be another Marlon Brando. The efforts of a bookie, taking bets on the horses, to use the office of the answering service as his base of operations contributes further hilarity. Styne's graceful tunes were still another significant element in a satisfying whole—as in the three hit numbers, "Just in Time," "The Party's Over," and "Long Before I Knew You"—though he was equally successful in a lighter style. "Drop that Name" was a vivacious commentary on people who come to swank parties and casually let it be known what famous people they rub elbows with; and "I'm Going Back" is a song calculated to end all similar sentimental numbers of returning home.

Gypsy was based on the autobiography of Gypsy Rose Lee, the famous burlesque strip-tease artist; the adaptation was made by Arthur Laurents. Ethel Merman assumes the part of a ruthless, overambitious mother of two promising young actresses. One of them is Gypsy Rose Lee, and the other June Havoc (named in the musical Louise and Claire, respectively). Gypsy becomes a burlesque queen while her sister sacrifices a stage career for a successful marriage, The opportunities afforded by this story to provide a glimpse at backstage life in burlesque and other facets of show business are vividly provided, and reach a climactic point of interest in the number "You Gotta Have a Gimmick" in which three strip-tease performers explain the art of their noble profession. Another song, "Let Me Entertain You," is a recurrent tune used for each reappearance of Gypsy Rose Lee and June Havoc, first when they audition for vaudeville, then when they are established performers, and finally as the sexy musical background for one of Gypsy's strip performances. "Everything's Coming Up Roses" and "Together, Wherever We Go" are songs in the hit class, whose never failing impact is due as much to Ethel Merman's delivery as to Styne's skill in composition.

In *Do, Re, Mi*—book by Garson Kanin and lyrics by Betty Comden and Adolph Green—Phil Silvers made a welcome return to musical comedy after an absence of almost a decade. As Hubie Cram—an irresponsible con artist who tries to become a big shot in the jukebox industry only to end up as ignominiously as he had started out—Silvers is in his element. As Henry Hewes wrote: "He mimics the variety of dated performances you might find on the Late Late Show. His delivery is at one minute neo-Cohan, at another Jolsonesque, and at yet another Duranteistic. And his antics as he supervises a recording session, getting the singer to relax, and demonstrating to each musician how to play the songs, are hilarious." Other characters besides Hubie seem to have stepped right out of the zany, offbeat Broadway world of *Guys and Dolls*. These include three ex-hoodlums who are encouraged by Hubie to leave retirement and get rich in the jukebox business. They end up making the business a racket and discovering a new singing star. The comedy tunes, "It's Legitimate" and "Adventure," and the ballads "Cry Like the Wind" and "Make Someone Happy" represent the best of Styne.

The personal history of Meredith Willson differs sharply from that of Arlen, Loesser, and Styne. Willson went to Hollywood and Broadway by route of serious music. First he was for many years the flutist of the New York Philharmonic Orchestra; after that he became a composer of symphonic music introduced by some of our leading orchestras. Only then, in 1940, did he begin working for motion pictures by writing a score first for Charles Chaplin's *The Great Dictator* and after that the background music for *The Little Foxes*. He also achieved note over radio with many leading network programs originating in California—as conductor, genial and often amusing commentator, and creator of novel and unusual musical features; as a composer of hit songs, the best being "You and I" and "May the Good Lord Bless and Keep You"; and as the author of such humorous books as *And There I Stood with My Piccolo*.

A native of Mason City, Iowa—born on May 18, 1902— Willson often enjoyed telling his friends anecdotes about his Midwestern boyhood. One of those delighted with these tales was Frank Loesser who suggested that Willson use this material for a musical comedy. Willson did just that—writing the text and lyrics as well as the music —and he called it *The Music Man* (1957).

The Music Man did not give much promise of being anything exceptional when it opened on Broadway. It was well-known that other producers had turned it down; that the out-of-town tryouts had not been spectacular. But on opening night *The Music Man* lifted its audience out of its seat with its very opening scene—a brilliant bit of stage business on a moving train in which lyric and melody were beautifully synchronized with the rhythm of the train. From that point on, the audience readily succumbed to the inescapable charms of this show that was so unashamedly sentimental, homey, small-town and old-fashioned. A rousing finale inspired an unprecedented demonstration. As *Variety* reported it: "The audience broke out spontaneously into applause to the even rhythm of the music. Nothing like it has ever been seen on Broadway." River City, Iowa, in 1912, is its setting. And the hero is a mountebank, Harold Hill (magnificently played by Robert Preston) who travels from town to town encouraging its inhabitants to form and finance boys' bands. He then absconds with the money entrusted to him for the purchase of musical instruments and uniforms. But in River City he meets a lovely librarian and piano teacher, Marian, to whom he loses his heart; and his enthusiasm is also captured by a group of music-loving kids. He now goes about seriously the business of creating a boys' band. Much of what happens then may be pure corn, much of it may be razzle-dazzle, especially the closing scene where the boys' band appears in full regalia to make raucous but enthusiastic music. But the whole thing has an infectious spirit about it that proved irresistible, a spirit nicely caught in the show's main song, "Seventy-Six Trombones," a melody that Willson uses again but more wistfully and tenderly in Marian's number "Goodnight, My Someone."

Having found in Americana a bountiful source of musical-comedy material, Meredith Willson went on to write another outstanding show with early American characters and settings: *The Unsinkable Molly Brown* (1960). Molly Brown—given a cyclonic performance by Tammy Grimes—is a character out of America's past. She is a wild, uninhibited, backwoods girl from Missouri who can neither read nor write. But she went on to make her fortune in the mines of Colorado; to become a pillar of society in Europe where she even turns down an offer of marriage from a prince; and to come home after being one of the few survivors of the ill-fated *Titanic* that collided with an iceberg in the Atlantic in 1912. Richard Morris' book had a noisy, rowdy air to it that helped to accentuate Molly's earthy, boisterous individuality. And Willson's spirited and tuneful score boasted a melody with the catchy and irresistible impact of "Seventy-Six Trombones"—Molly Browns' root-toot-tooting chant, "I Ain't Down Yet."

The George Abbott Touch / 15

Some of the newer composers of musical comedies during the 1940's and 1950's came out of the West. Still others—also newcomers, and representatives of the younger generation—were from the East and became prominent in George Abbott productions. The quarter of a century that George Abbott worked with musical comedy—as stage director, as librettist, as a discoverer of creative talent—has been so fruitful that the "George Abbott touch" is now a recognized hallmark of success in musical comedy. He has introduced to musical comedy new techniques of production, new stylings, a new sense of pace and timing, a new feeling of excitement, a new burst of energy. Brooks Atkinson once described Abbott as "the recognized panjandrum of the Broadway musical carnival." Then he added: "Give him exuberant material in the vernacular and he can put together a rousing, professional entertainment. He can translate the exuberance into comedy, dancing, uproar, sentiment, and revelry, and exuberate the audience accordingly."

Abbott made his bow in the theater as an actor, and only then did he pass on to become the stage director of some of the sprightliest, liveliest, and brightest non-musical comedies seen on Broadway in the 1920's and 1930's. Occasionally he also wrote plays, at times in collaboration with others. But whether as stage director or author he brought to the footlights an irresistible exuberance and energy, a breathless motion; and with these came a concentration of style and an adroitness of stage technique no less powerful or dynamic. It is no coincidence that some of the best comedies of the 1920's and 1930's carry George Abbott's name either as stage director or author, or both: *Chicago* and *Broadway* in 1926; *Three Men on a Horse* and *Boy Meets Girl* in 1935; *Room Service* and *Brother Rat* in 1936.

After he had made his mark, and left a permanent impress on stage comedy, he turned his attention to the musical theater. It was Rodgers and Hart who were responsible for this transition. When they returned from Hollywood in 1935 and were asked to write the music for *Jumbo,* they invited George Abbott to help direct that production. A year later, while working on the text of *On Your Toes,* Rodgers and Hart felt their play needed tightening of structure and an acceleration of pace. They called on George Abbott as collaborator to make the necessary revisions. As Rodgers recalls: "George straightened out the story line and kept it straight through the turmoil and upheaval of rehearsals and out-of-town tryouts."

Abbott worked with Rodgers and Hart on several more musicals, including *The Boys from Syracuse,* and with Rodgers and Hammerstein on *Me and Juliet.* In the 1940's he staged Jule Styne's *High Button Shoes* and Frank Loesser's *Where's Charley?,* among several other musical-comedy hits.

One of those other "hits" introduced a new composer to Broadway. The hit was *On the Town,* the composer, Leonard Bernstein. Bernstein, born in Lawrence, Massachusetts, on August 25, 1918, was the *Wunderkind* of American music. Before his initiation into musical comedy he had achieved world-wide fame as a conductor of symphony orchestras, and as a composer of symphonic and ballet music. In whatever area he ventured he made a spectacular splash with his maiden effort. His debut as conductor—when, in 1943, he was a last-minute replacement for the scheduled conductor of the New York

Philharmonic for a Sunday afternoon concert—was an event to reach the front pages of the country's newspapers. His first symphonic work, the *Jeremiah Symphony*, selected by the N.Y. Music Critics Circle as the best new American composition of the year, was performed by the major American symphonic organizations, and was recorded by Victor. His first ballet, *Fancy Free*, instantly became a staple in the contemporary American dance repertory.

And so it was with his first musical comedy. *On the Town*, which opened on December 28, 1944, was a financial and theatrical triumph. It had the impressive New York run of 463 performances; it was sold to the movies even before it opened on Broadway (a highly attractive motion picture starring Gene Kelly and Frank Sinatra, released in 1949); it was revived simultaneously by two off-Broadway productions in 1959 when Walter Kerr said "it still stands as one of the most original, inventive, and irresistibly charming of all American musicals."

On the Town grew out of the ballet, *Fancy Free*. The ballet scenario—the work of the brilliant young choreographer, Jerome Robbins—described a brief shore leave in Manhattan of three sailors. Adolph Green and Betty Comden elaborated this slim idea into a musical-comedy text that was a veritable carnival of New York scenes and backgrounds. Jerome Robbins devised some ballets—the first time he worked in musical comedy. The extended stage version now followed three sailors on their 24-hour New York leave as they go gaily "on the town." One of them espies the picture of "Miss Turnstiles" in the subway and decides she is the girl he wants. With the help of his two buddies, he goes hunting for her. They scour the city—from one end to the other, from Times Square to Coney Island, from a Broadway night club to Central Park West. En route, one of the sailors finds his soul mate in a female taxi driver, and the other in a young anthropology student. "Miss Turnstiles" finally turns up in a studio in Carnegie Hall taking singing lessons.

223

George Abbott set the whole production spinning like a gaily colored top, from the rise of the first curtain. After that, street scenes, gags, dances, songs, followed one another with the speed of lightning. In an equally racy style, Bernstein's songs proved to be some of the best Broadway had heard in some time. They included poignant ballads ("Lucky to Be Me" and "Lonely Town") and facetious, witty items ("I Get Carried Away" and "I Can Cook, Too"). As a composer who had made the critics sit up and take notice with his *Jeremiah Symphony*, Bernstein was, of course, completely at home and at ease writing background music for ballets that was symphonic in style and treatment, impressive in musical values, yet never losing contact with theater audiences accustomed to lighter musical diversions than symphonies. Bernstein's music in *On the Town* sounded fresh and vital to the ears in 1944, and still stayed that way in 1959. "Mr. Bernstein's tunes are certainly better—much, much better—than any that have been produced for Broadway this season," said Brooks Atkinson in reviewing one of the 1959 revivals.

Bernstein's next musical comedy proved an even more stunning experience in its vitality and in its impact on audiences. This was also a play about New York, and like its predecessor it also profited no end from George Abbott's stage direction. *Wonderful Town* (1953) used material and characters long made familiar to magazine readers through Ruth McKenney's stories; also to theatergoers through the nonmusical stage adaptation formerly made by Joseph Fields and Jerome Chodorov and entitled *My Sister Eileen;* also to moviegoers through a boisterous nonsinging motion picture made out of that play, starring Rosalind Russell. Fields and Chodorov rewrote their eminently successful play as a musical comedy, and Betty Comden and Adolph Green prepared the lyrics to Leonard Bernstein's music.

In *On the Town*, New York had been invaded by three sailors. In *Wonderful Town* it is now two little girls

224

from Ohio come to the metropolis to seek out its opportunities for advancing their respective careers. Eileen wants to be an actress; her sister, Ruth, a writer. They find an apartment in a basement in New York's colorful Greenwich Village where they forthwith become members of a motley group of eccentrics that includes an ex-football star who always goes around in athletic shorts, a magazine editor, a newspaperman, a night-club owner, a landlord who is an abstractionist painter on the side, the manager of the 44th Street Walgreen Drug Store, and members of the Brazilian Navy. The girls encounter a far greater variety of adventures than they had bargained for, as well as countless mishaps and annoyances, not the least of which is the continual blasting for a subway underneath their apartment. But they survive to gain their ambitions.

Once again the George Abbot touch made a production explode into perpetual pyrotechnics like a Fourth-of-July fireworks display. *Wonderful Town* opens with a frenetic ragtag dance by Greenwich Village characters. The excitement thus engendered is not allowed to die down but, on the contrary, continues to mount toward pandemonium. The result is a musical comedy full of "organized bedlam and insanity" as Brooks Atkinson described it. The storm center is Rosalind Russell, whose performance as Ruth swept through the play with the irresistible force of a cyclone. And Bernstein's music was in harmony with the uproarious spirit of performance, staging, and text. He showed a fine hand for satire in numbers like the popular "Ohio" (a parody on sentimental songs about home) and "My Darlin' Eileen" (a take-off on sentimental Irish ballads); he demonstrated a keen sense of wit in "One Hundred Easy Ways" (Ruth's sure-fire formula for losing a man) and "Story Vignettes." And he betrayed a sensitive feeling for nostalgia and sentiment in "A Quiet Girl."

Bernstein's habit of starting at the top and then proceeding from that point to still greater heights held true

225

in musical comedy. In every way *Wonderful Town* out-stripped *On the Town*. It stayed on Broadway for about a hundred performances more than its predecessor. It was acclaimed by the Drama Critics Circle as the best musical comedy of the season, while Bernstein's score received special honors from the Antoinette Perry and Donaldson Awards. It was acclaimed in performances by a national company throughout the United States, and was produced successfully in several European capitals. In 1958 it received a robust television production over the CBS network.

In two other extraordinary musical comedies of the 1950's—*The Pajama Game* (1954) and *Damn Yankees* (1955)—George Abbott was not only the stage director, but also collaborator in the writing of the text. The score for both musicals was the work of a young, new team of songwriters—Richard Adler and Jerry Ross. Adler and Ross was a unique combination in that they collaborated on both the music and the lyrics. Neither one was a professional musician, though Dick Adler was the son of Clarence Adler, an eminent concert pianist and teacher. And neither had had much traffic with success until they joined forces to write such smash song hits as "Rags to Riches" (which climbed to the top rung of the "Hit Parade" in 1953 and sold over a million copies of sheet music and records), "Teasin'," "Now Hear This," and "The Newspaper Song." In 1953 they wrote a few songs for the *John Murray Anderson Almanac*, a Broadway revue, their first appearance in the theater before striking oil a half year later with *The Pajama Game*.

The Pajama Game violated sound musical-comedy practices on several counts. Most of its talent came from comparative unknowns: Griffith and Prince, the producers; Bob Fosse, the choreographer; Carol Haney, one of the stars; and Adler and Ross, creators of the score. It opened in May, a month avoided by musical comedies like the plague, since a show must weather the summer months before having had a chance to establish itself. Finally, its plot revolved around labor problems in a Midwestern manufacturing plant, a subject not usually rich in musical-comedy values.

Based on a delightful novel by Richard Bissell, *7½¢*, *The Pajama Game* was a realistic picture of life and complications (amatory as well as labor) at the Sleep-Tite Pajama Factory. The Union demands for its help a raise of 7½ cents an hour. Turned down by the management, the Union brings about a slowdown in production, and after that a strike. For Sid Sorokin, superintendent of the plant, this labor war is also a personal problem, since he is in love with Babe Williams, head of the Union Grievance Committee. But Sid manages to gain access to the private books of the firm by feigning interest in the bookkeeper. Thus he learns that the boss has for months been charging all his accounts an increased price covering the cost of the pay boost demanded by the Union. With this information at hand, he can bring about peace between labor and management, and in his own private life with Babe. With two show-stopping numbers, Carol Haney became a Broadway luminary. One was a strip tease performed during a Union picnic; the other an arresting routine in gam outfit, "Steam Heat." And two solid song hits placed Adler and Ross with Broadway's top tunesmiths: "Hey, There" and "Hernando's Hideaway." These and other elements in a brilliant production helped make *The Pajama Game* what one critic called "a royal flush and grand slam all rolled into one." The royal flush was a run of more than a thousand performances (the eighth musical in Broadway history to reach the magic circle). The grand slam came with a motion-picture adaptation in 1957 starring Doris Day, but otherwise utilizing most of the members of the original stage cast.

Damn Yankees became the ninth Broadway musical to roll up more than a thousand performances. Based on the best-selling novel of Douglass Wallop, *The Year the*

Yankees Lost the Pennant, Damn Yankees brought the age-old Faust legend into a modern yarn about baseball. Joe Boyd, a rabid rooter for the Washington Senators, is so weary of the poor showing made regularly by his favorite team that he is ready to trade his soul to the Devil for a pennant. The Devil transforms Joe into a star ballplayer on whose shoulders the Senators are carried to the pennant. But homesick for his wife (from whom he has necessarily been separated) and despite the physical enticements of a beautiful witch, Lola, he refuses to play in the World Series. Instead, he reverts to his former (and now completely welcome) status as a middle-aged married baseball fan.

In keeping this musical comedy moving with the speed of an uncontrolled locomotive, George Abbott created, as Maurice Zolotow said, "a feeling of perpetual motion" through the "adroit multiplication of hundreds of large and small movements." Gwen Verdon, as Lola, practically stole the show with her exciting dances and her languid, seductive rendition of "Whatever Lola Wants." The latter was one of the show's two top musical numbers. The other was "Heart," with which the hapless manager of the Senators tries to inspire his bedraggled team before Joe arrives to make it a winner.

The partnership of Adler and Ross came to a sudden, tragic end in 1955 when Jerry Ross, a lifelong victim of bronchiectasis, died at the age of twenty-nine.

George Abbott, who had helped bring Adler and Ross their first resounding Broadway successes, also helped uncover for Broadway a new major musical talent in Bob Merrill. Like Adler and Ross, Merrill had written several catchy songs before his Broadway debut. "If I Knew You Were Comin' I'd of Baked a Cake" sold over a million records in 1950 and was followed by "Truly, Truly Fair," "Doggie in the Window," and "Honeycomb," the last making a singing star out of Jimmie Rogers. For all these, and subsequent songs, Merrill was his own lyricist.

After that, Merrill worked in Hollywood on the first four-way contract ever given by MGM: as producer, composer, writer, and publisher.

His first Broadway show was *New Girl in Town* (1957), which George Abbott had adapted from Eugene O'Neill's Pulitzer Prize drama of 1922, *Anna Christie*. Gwen Verdon's performance as Anna and songs like "Sunshine Girl," "Look at 'Er," and "Did You Close Your Eyes?" made *New Girl in Town* a winner. Merrill's second Broadway musical comedy was also a Eugene O'Neill play bedecked with song and dance—this time, *Ah, Wilderness!* Renamed *Take Me Along* (1959), and starring Jackie Gleason, it had much of the heart-warming sentiment, touching emotion, and engaging humor of the popular O'Neill comedy. Jackie Gleason and Walter Pidgeon performed an infectious little soft-shoe dance to the title song; a macabre dream sequence was portrayed within ballet terms; puppy love found voice in the piquant duet, "I Would Die" and mature love more poignantly in "Promise Me a Rose."

(Bob Merrill's greatest Broadway success, however, came with a production directed not by George Abbott but by Gower Champion. It was *Carnival*, a musical-comedy based on the charming motion picture *Lili*, which opened on April 13, 1961. Anna Maria Alberghetti was here starred as the gamine Lili, involved in a poignant romance with a puppeteer, set against the background of a southern European countryside circus. A novel note is introduced in this production by dispensing with the drawn curtain before performance time. When the audience enters the theater it sees a set stage depicting a tent show, all lit up. Thus, as Howard Taubman reported, "the mood is set with a touch of quiet magic. . . . The lights go down, and there is no music from the pit. Pierre Olaf in careless carnival costume strolls out and sits under the proscenium wall, playing a wheezy phrase on a concertina." And the magic thus evoked persists throughout the performance. At times sentimental, at times humorous, at times dramatic, and at times filled with what Mr. Taubman described as "show business razzle-dazzle," *Carnival* proved a triumph, "rich in enchantment," as Richard Watts, Jr., said of it. Bob Merrill's score was one of the many strong suits of this spellbinding entertainment—with songs like "A Very Nice Man," "Always, Always You," and "Mira." Another valuable contributor were the dances choreographed by Mr. Champion, including a frenetic "Carnival Ballet.")

There was no mistaking the George Abbott touch in one of the greatest musical-comedy successes of the 1950's: *Fiorello!* (1959). "Fiorello" is Fiorello H. La Guardia, New York's Fusion Mayor, one of the city's most colorful, provocative, and rambunctious sons. The musical comedy (text by Jerome Weidman and George Abbott) is his biography. John Chapman regarded *Fiorello!* as one of the best musicals about New York since *Guys and Dolls.* It captured every desirable prize, including the Pulitzer Prize and the Drama Critics Award, together with numerous Antoinette Perry and Donaldson Awards.

In the prologue, Mayor La Guardia is seen reading the comics to kids over the radio during a newspaper strike. After that his career as a blustering little iconoclast is traced from his early days of law practice in Greenwich Village, in 1914, when he was a champion of the poor and the underprivileged; through his election to Congress, service in World War I, and two marriages; and up to the time he is elected New York's Mayor. One of the rewarding attractions of the musical comedy was the way it helped unfold a rich panorama of the political and social life of the city during those years; another was Tom Bosley's amazingly faithful re-creation of Mayor La Guardia both in appearance and in mannerisms.

Still another new pair of songwriters was brought to the fore by this George Abbott production: Jerry Bock, composer, and Sheldon Harnick, lyricist. Jerry Bock had previously worked with another lyricist, Larry Holof-

230

cener, with whom he wrote songs and special material for many important radio and television programs. They contributed three songs to an unsuccessful Broadway show, *Catch a Star*, before being called on to contribute a complete score. That was for *Mr. Wonderful* (1956), starring Sammy Davis, Jr., in his famous night-club routines, and it included two song hits, the title number and "Too Close for Comfort."

Jerry Bock teamed up with Sheldon Harnick for *The Body Beautiful* (1958), which lasted only 2 months on Broadway. But their work attracted the interest of the producers, Robert E. Griffith and Harold S. Prince, as well as that of George Abbott. And when the three men were planning *Fiorello!*, they decided to gamble on the yet unproved gifts of this young duo. The young pair of songwriters came through with flying colors, especially in two satirical numbers—unquestionably the high moments in the production—"Little Tin Box" and "Politics and Poker."

The writing combination of Jerome Weidman, George Abbott, Jerry Bock, and Sheldon Harnick joined forces again to bring still another facet of New York's past into musical comedy in *Tenderloin* (1960). Based on Samuel Hopkins Adams' novel of the same name, *Tenderloin* detailed the efforts of a Presbyterian minister (a role in which Maurice Evans turned for the first time from Shakespeare and other serious dramatic roles to musical comedy) to clean up a disreputable neighborhood in New York in the 1890's. As a period piece, *Tenderloin* carried a good deal of nostalgic interest, but it was also rich in satire, humor, and even broad burlesque.

Broad burlesque was the dominant keynote in still another George Abbott show to bring a new and young pair of songwriters to prominence. The show was *Once Upon a Mattress* (1959); the songwriters, Mary Rodgers, composer (daughter of Richard), and Marshall Barer, lyricist. *Once Upon a Mattress* was a farcical treatment of the old, familiar fairy tale, *The Princess and the Pea.*

As Princess Winifred, Carol Burnett (in her musical-comedy debut) revealed herself as a worthy member of that regal line of grand comediennes that included Fanny Brice and Beatrice Lillie. *Once Upon a Mattress* tried out at a summer adult camp in Pennsylvania before it profited from the magic directorial touch of George Abbott. Then it opened in an off-Broadway production in downtown New York where it proved so popular that it had to be moved uptown for a prosperous engagement on Broadway before going on an equally successful road tour.

A Vital, Vibrant / 16
American Art

The impact of Rodgers and Hammerstein on the musical theater was decisive. Cole Porter put it this way: "The most profound change in forty years of musical comedy has been—Rodgers and Hammerstein." The example they set in the kind of material they chose for their productions, in their consistently adventurous attitudes in developing this material, in their restless search for ever richer and deeper values in the musical theater —all this sparked other writers to similarly bold innovations. More and more librettists started to enlarge the scope of their activity in writing for the popular stage by seeking out plays with vital dramatic appeal, plays not afraid to invade the world of ideas, or even of vital social problems. More and more composers were encouraged to write for such plays music with an altogether new amplitude of style. In short, more and more of Broadway's musical-comedy writers were impelled by the success of Rodgers and Hammerstein to write musical plays.

For Kurt Weill, the demands of the musical play upon his creative gifts were easily met. He was a consummate musician with a comprehensive training behind him; in the past he had written ambitious operatic scores. The two compelling dramas for which he wrote music in the late 1940's taxed neither his technique nor his imagination. One was *Street Scene* (1947), a "folk play with music," as the program described it. It was based on

233

Elmer Rice's deeply moving Pulitzer Prize drama of 1929 of life in a New York City tenement among the poor and the depressed, among those tortured by frustrations, shattered hopes, elusive dreams. Murder is the climactic point of the drama, whose prevailing theme is disenchantment. Anna Maurant is accused by her husband, Frank, of carrying on an affair with a milkman. She is a middle-aged woman who has long suffered neglect and apathy at the hands of her husband; the flattering attentions given her by the milkman prove food and drink to a sadly deflated ego. One day, finding his wife in the milkman's company, Frank murders both. Meanwhile, their daughter, Rose, has fallen in love with an idealistic college student, Sam Kaplan. Sam is ready to give up his dreams and ambitions, to exchange school for a job so that they can get married. The tragedy within Rose's own household convinces her she can never ask Sam to make such a sacrifice. She flees from the neighborhood with her little brother, to seek a new life elsewhere.

The elemental passions surging through the Rice play are intensified by Weill's music. It is an integrated musical texture of haunting emotional impact; it is an inextricable part of the dramatic action. "Not until *Street Scene*," Weill once said, "did I achieve a real blending of drama and music in which the singing continues naturally where the speaking stops, and the spoken word as well as the dramatic action, is embedded in the over-all musical structure." While the score is studded with numbers to haunt the memory—songs like "Lonely House" and "Somehow I Never Could Believe," lyrics by Langston Hughes—no single number gives the play its over-all emotional impact. That comes from the integrated musical texture which courses through the play and catches all the nuances and overtones of the cataclysmic tragedy that destroys these little people. "Kurt Weill," said Rosamond Gilder in *Theatre Arts*, "turned *Street Scene* into a symphony of the city. . . . His music reflects the hot night, the chatter and gossiping housewives, the sound of children at play, the ebb and flow of anonymous existence."

In *Lost in the Stars* (1949), Weill found another stark and powerful play. The original source in this case was Alan Paton's novel of racial conflicts in South Africa, *Cry the Beloved Country*, adapted by Maxwell Anderson, who also provided the lyrics. The novel is filled not only with dramatic struggle and tragedy but also with warm compassion, human understanding, with hope and tolerance and faith in man and a better world. Weill's music illuminated these feelings, and also endowed them with deeper tones.

In South Africa, Absalom, the son of a humble Negro parson, leaves his hometown for Johannesburg. There he falls in love with Irina, gets involved in a robbery, and is apprehended by the police for the murder of a white man. Brought to trial, he is sentenced to be hanged. Just before the execution, the father of the white murdered man visits Absalom's father. Through their common grief a wonderful bond of understanding is forged.

Here, as in *Street Scene*, music is so germane to the action—and particularly in the choral writing does it acquire artistic significance—that some critics have called *Lost in the Stars* an "opera." (It has, as a matter of fact, been successfully introduced in the regular repertory of the New York City Opera Company.) Songs like "Oh Tixo, Tixo" and the title number catch the immeasurable sorrow of a pastor who learns that his son is a murderer. Lighter episodes like "Trouble Man" and "Who'll Buy?" also help to throw illumination on characters. But the most stirring music of all is that for the chorus—the chorus being used in the style of the Greek classic drama for the purpose of commentary. Perhaps nothing more stirring or eloquent has come out of the popular Broadway theater than pages like "Cry the Beloved Country" and "A Bird of Passage," the first a lament about Absalom's lost childhood, the other a religious pronouncement about the life of man.

235

Lost in the Stars was Weill's last Broadway musical play. He died in New York City on April 3, 1950. His career in the theater had come to a full circle. Just as in Germany his aim had been to make out of opera a popular form of entertainment, so on Broadway, in his last plays, he aspired to make popular-stage entertainment *into* opera.

The transition from musical comedy to musical play was made by Marc Blitzstein, Frank Loesser and Lerner and Loewe through the adaptations of highly successful stage plays. That of Blitzstein came with Lillian Hellman's bitter, vitriolic play about a decaying Southern family, *The Little Foxes*, which Blitzstein renamed *Regina* (1949), and for which he wrote book and lyrics as well as the music. In *Regina*, Blitzstein passes from the social and political protests of the 1930's to shattering musical drama. Where *The Cradle Will Rock* was an indictment of capitalist society thundered from a soapbox, *Regina* is an overwhelming tragedy about a deceitful, avaricious, hate-torn family destroyed by its own vices. The eclectic musical style that had characterized his score for *The Cradle Will Rock* is also evident here. When the text demands it, Blitzstein can write a spiritual, or ragtime, or a musical-comedy tune. But he can also progress to an expansive and compelling aria, to Handel-like recitatives, and even to modernistic "song speech." "With *Regina*," says Leonard Bernstein, "we have a kind of apex, a summation of what Blitzstein was trying to do. The words sing themselves, so to speak. The result is true song—a long, flexible, pragmatic, dramatic song."

Frank Loesser's graduation into the musical play came with *The Most Happy Fella* (1956), text by Loesser himself (who, of course, also contributed lyrics and music), derived from Sidney Howard's Pulitzer Prize play, *They Knew What They Wanted*. Though Loesser is reluctant to have this play called an "opera," his vast musical score is of operatic proportions since it embraces over thirty basic numbers besides numerous orchestral transitions, and episodes played under the dialogue. Almost three quarters of the play has music in one shape or form. Some of it consists of the hit-song variety of Tin Pan Alley and musical comedy, for which Loesser had long since proved his gift—"Standing on the Corner" being the most popular. Some of it consists of arias, duets, recitatives, canons, choral episodes, dances, parodies, folk hymns, and instrumental interludes. Loesser's attempt, explained Don Walker (who orchestrated the score), was "to create a form so you can say in music that which might be too emotional for dialogue. We pass into dialogue only for those developments that are not emotional in content, such as exposition."

Thus Loesser, through an amazingly wide gamut of musical style, was able to explore many shades of feeling: humor, tenderness, gentleness, sorrow, simple humanity. "He has taken an aging play," said Robert Coleman, "and turned it into a timeless musical." Or, to quote Brooks Atkinson: "He has told everything of vital importance in terms of dramatic music. . . . His music drama . . . goes so much deeper into the souls of its leading characters than most Broadway shows, and it has such an abundant and virtuoso score in it that it has to be taken on the level of theater."

In Howard's play, the emphasis was on Tony's growing maturity, when he is made to realize that he must compromise with ethics and ideals for the sake of the happiness of those around him. Loesser changed the stress, concentrating on the indefatigable hunt of lonely people everywhere for love and companionship.

The hero, Tony, is a middle-aged winegrower in Napa, California. While visiting San Francisco he meets Rosabella, a waitress, and falls in love with her on sight. Too shy to make his feelings known, he returns home and begins to correspond with her. When asked for his photograph, Tony, afraid of losing her, sends that of his handsome hired hand, Joe. Rosabella is now willing to come to Napa and marry Tony, to the latter's extreme delight. But on her arrival she is dismayed to discover Tony's deception. Nevertheless, they get married and Tony does everything he can to win Rosabella over to him with tenderness, consideration, and a heart overflowing with love. Rosabella submerges her disappointment by falling in love with Joe. Tony, however, is all-forgiving, and Rosabella learns to forget Joe and to love Tony for his sweetness and generosity.

The Lerner and Loewe musical play, *My Fair Lady* (1956)—one of the all-time artistic and commercial triumphs of the American stage—grew out of Bernard Shaw's brilliant comedy-satire, *Pygmalion*. With such a remarkable and witty text as the point of departure, *My Fair Lady* went on to be an ideal realization of what a musical play can become when each element of the stage serves the text with respect and humility. Alan Jay Lerner's adaptation and lyrics, and Frederick Loewe's music, were only two of many all-important elements in a remarkable whole. Added to these were Moss Hart's direction, Hanya Holm's choreography, Cecil Beaton's costuming, Oliver Smith's sets, and the engaging performances of Rex Harrison as Henry Higgins, Julie Andrews as Eliza, and Stanley Holloway as her Cockney father. Each supplemented the other into an artistic pattern so integrated that the elimination of any one would have broken the over-all design. And nowhere are these varied elements more exquisitely synchronized than in a scene like the "Rain in Spain"—a climax of the play—when song, acting, direction, dialogue, and pantomime all become one inextricable unity.

Shaw's plot was a modern adaptation of the Greek legend in which Pygmalion fashions a statue of Galatea, so beautiful that he falls in love with it as if it were a human being. Moved by Pygmalion's pleas, Aphrodite finally gives the statue life and, to Pygmalion's delight, Galatea becomes a flesh-and-blood woman.

In *Pygmalion* and in *My Fair Lady*, Pygmalion appears

in the person of Professor Henry Higgins, an eminent phonetician; Galatea, as Eliza Doolittle, an ignorant little Cockney flower girl. On a bet, the professor decides to transform Eliza into a lady of high social standing. He has her live in his house and undergo a most rigorous training in speech, dress, and manners. The experiment proves highly successful. At a gala social evening at the Embassy, Liza passes herself off as a duchess. The test over, Liza leaves the professor, intending to marry a rich man-about-town. Shaw never makes it clear within his play whether she actually marries him, though in a preface to a later edition of the play he insists she did, and became a proprietress of a successful flower shop. But in *My Fair Lady*, Professor Higgins cannot forget Liza, having become "accustomed to her face." In the closing scene she returns to him for what can now be assumed to be a permanent arrangement.

Shaw intended *Pygmalion* as a satire on class and social distinctions. In *My Fair Lady* the acid of such criticism is diluted by a welcome addition of glamour and tenderness. The setting of the play—London in 1912—is picturesquely evoked not only in the stunning sets and costumes but also in such evocative pieces of Continental music by Loewe as the "Ascot Gavotte" and the "Embassy Waltz," and in the Hanya Holm ballets for which each of these serves as the background. The higher strata of English life is vividly depicted in scenes such as these. But the lower strata is not neglected—represented by Eliza and her lovable but irresponsible Cockney father, and by such rollicking Cockney numbers as "Get Me to the Church on Time" and "With a Little Bit of Luck." And just as the opposite poles of English society provide contrast to characters and background, so do sentiment on the one hand and sophisticated satire on the other reflect opposing moods. We get sentiment in the hit songs "On the Street Where You Live," "I've Grown Accustomed to Her Face" and Liza's radiant "I Could Have Danced All Night." We get wit and satire in two of

Professor Higgins' best numbers, "A Hymn to Him" and "Why Can't the English?"

Few musicals before or since were hailed with such raptures as *My Fair Lady* was when it thundered into the Mark Hellinger Theater on March 15, 1956. Brooks Atkinson went all out by calling it "one of the best musicals of the century . . . close to the genius of creation." William Hawkins described the première as a "legendary evening." With this kind of send-off, *My Fair Lady* proceeded to smash record after record: in the length of its Broadway run, outdistancing *Oklahoma!*, the previous holder of this record, on the evening of June 13, 1961; in Broadway box-office receipts from 3,000,000 customers; in the financial returns from a formidably successful national tour begun on March 18, 1957 where box-office precedents were broken in city after city; in the number of companies presenting it in different parts of the civilized world, including the Soviet Union in 1960; in its over-all income of $33,000,000 in its first 4 years; in the 3,000,000 disc sale of the original-cast recording which, in itself, contributed about $15,000,000 to the till.

In a carefully planned attempt to bring to Broadway a second *My Fair Lady*—as if lightning can be made to strike twice in the same place!—most of its basic ingredients were combined into a new dish called *Camelot* (1960). Once again book and lyrics were by Lerner, and the music by Loewe; once again Moss Hart was the stage director, Hanya Holm the choreographer, and Oliver Smith, scenic designer; once again Julie Andrews played the heroine, with Robert Coote of the *My Fair Lady* cast playing a subsidiary role; once again, Robert Russell Bennett served as orchestrator, and Franz Allers as musical director. One thing alone was lacking—a Bernard Shaw play as the source of the text. And this, as Howard Taubman remarked shrewdly, spelled the difference between *My Fair Lady* and *Camelot*.

Camelot settled down to a long Broadway run guaranteed by its unprecedented advance sale of $3,500,000. In the harrowing task of shaping a second *My Fair Lady*, two of its collaborators were sent to the hospital in Toronto during the out-of-town tryouts—Moss Hart with a heart attack and Alan Jay Lerner with a severe case of bleeding ulcers. But the overstrained efforts of all concerned notwithstanding, in spite of the seemingly limitless funds expended on making the production the last word in visual beauty, in spite of the sometimes brilliant work of individuals and sometimes brilliant episodes, scenes, and songs, *Camelot* was no *My Fair Lady* because it lacked consistency of viewpoint, coherence of design, a oneness of conception.

A musical setting of T. H. White's novel, *The Once and Future King*, *Camelot* became confused in the way it should retell the Arthurian legend. It could not decide whether to be fantasy, glamorous romance in the manner of old-world operettas, or satire in the sophisticated attitudes of Shaw—and so it became a little of each. Yet if it was not the consistent masterwork that *My Fair Lady* had been, *Camelot* had a good deal to recommend it: fabulously mounted scenes; poignant performances by Richard Burton as King Arthur, Julie Andrews as Guinevere, and Robert Goulet as Sir Launcelot; several highly attractive dance sequences and some pleasing songs including the title number, "How to Handle a Woman," and "What Do Simple Folk Do?" *Camelot* may not have been a lady as fair as the one in whose footsteps she tried to follow, but nonetheless she was an attractive person whose presence on Broadway was a definite adornment.

An altogether new concept in musical-play writing came in 1957 with *West Side Story*—book by Arthur Laurents, music by Leonard Bernstein, lyrics by Stephen Sondheim, and choreography by Jerome Robbins. Rarely before has a grim social problem been treated in our popular musical theater with such compelling realism and force, with such uncompromising dramatic truth. Never before has the ballet been used so extensively and called on to perform such a vital role in telling the story. Never before has the music of a popular production caught the neuroticism, high tensions, and the bitterness of the play on the one hand, and its characters, on the other. "This musical show," said a London critic when *West Side Story* was produced in that city, "begins a new age in the theater."

West Side Story was Shakespeare's *Romeo and Juliet* in a present-day setting, with present-day characters and social issues. Instead of old Verona, Manhattan's West Side today is the setting. Instead of the rivalry between the Capulets and the Montagues, the conflict involves two teen-age gangs. Romeo becomes a New York youngster by the name of Tony; Juliet, a Puerto Rican girl, Maria. A variation of the famous balcony scene from *Romeo and Juliet* is found in an episode on a fire escape in a New York tenement.

Tony is a member of the Jets, a teen-age gang determined to keep Puerto Ricans out of their territory. The opposing gang, the Sharks, is Puerto Rican. As the curtain rises, two rival gangs are protagonists in a sinister dance set against the black background of an empty warehouse. The ominous mood previously established by a discordant, neurotic overture is here deepened. Both gangs decide to confer at a dance in a nearby gymnasium to decide on place, time, and weapons for a "rumble," or street battle. At the gymnasium, ballet once again becomes a part of the dramatic action: the imminent gang war is translated into dance terms, and a breathtaking mambo carries the scene on to an overwhelming climax. But a lighter note is sounded in these grim developments. Maria, sister of the leader of the Sharks, and Tony, one of the Jets, meet at the dance and fall in love. Since each is a representative from the enemy camp, their love affair must henceforth be conducted in secrecy. Something of the forlorn hopes and tattered dreams of these two helpless lovers is captured in an exquisite dance episode, "Somewhere." When they finally agree to get married,

242

they do so by improvising a mock marriage which they themselves take most seriously. This takes place inside the bridal shop where Maria is employed, and the dummies serve as witnesses. But their romance and happiness are doomed, as even they themselves had suspected from the beginning. In the gang war that finally explodes, Tony kills Maria's brother, and after that Tony himself becomes the victim of an avenging Shark.

"The subject is not beautiful," said Brooks Atkinson. But then he emphasized the fact that in spite of this, "what *West Side Story* draws out of it is beautiful. For it has a searching point of view. . . . Everything . . . is of a piece. Everything contributes to the total impression of wildness, ecstasy, and anguish."

West Side Story was a tremendous box-office success on Broadway in two separate engagements; went on a highly profitable national tour; embarked on a tour of Israel, Africa, and the Near East early in 1961; and was made into a motion picture. That such immense financial rewards could come to a musical like this one—in which the musical theater abandons the traditional ivory tower to grapple with problems and ideas germane to present-day living—is an eloquent testimony that the musical play has come of age; that its place in the American theater is now indestructible; that it has truly become a vital, vibrant American art.

Musical Play vs. / 17
Musical Comedy

With the operetta dead and the revue dying, the musical comedy and the musical play remain the two principal branches of the American musical theater today. Both forms are thriving, both have made their place in our theater secure. Protagonists of the one sometimes denounce the other. George S. Kaufman, in a Sunday feature article, once lamented the fact that the present-day musical theater was so partial to death, murder, mayhem, grim realism, and sordid backgrounds; that it had lost so much of its one-time light heart, gaiety, and insouciance. He remarked wryly that the musical play should more aptly be designated as "musical serious." And then there are serious critics of the theater who denounce musical comedies, however good, for their subservience to cliches and stereotypes.

Such views would tend to imply that these critics believe that our musical theater should be one thing or the other—musical comedy *or* musical play. But why so? The musical play and the musical comedy are not competitors but allies, not rivals but sisters under the skin. They supplement each other. Each has its audience, each has a role to fill.

Musical comedy today is entertainment par excellence, drawing to itself the best talent our theater has to offer in every department. Continually refreshened and revitalized by new performing and creative talent, the musical

244

comedy retains both its vitality and its youth magically.

Such a musical is *Bye Bye Birdie* which, in 1960, introduced a new trio of writers—Charles Strouse, composer; Lee Adams, lyricist; and Michael Stewart, librettist. Also making their Broadway bows here were Gower Champion as stage director, and a fresh new performing face and talent, Dick Van Dyke. *Bye Bye Birdie* is a gentle, humorous spoof of a singing idol of the type of Elvis Presley and the impact his presence has on a small community and on a group of adulating teen-agers. A rare combination of motion-picture montages, rock 'n' roll sequences, exciting dance numbers, effective songs ("Kids," "A Lot of Livin' to Do," for example), satire and uproarious comedy all helped make *Bye Bye Birdie* a veritable "sleeper."

Few connected with it were known to the public when the show opened. Nevertheless the show went on to become a major success and an outstanding screen musical starring Dick Van Dyke, Janet Leigh and Bobby Rydell. As for some of the unknowns who helped make this musical as good as it was: Dick Van Dyke, of course, went on to new heights not only in television, where his brilliant show had a five-year run, but also in several motion pictures, including *Mary Poppins*. Gower Champion became one of the most highly esteemed and sought after directors of stage musicals. And librettist Lee Adams and composer Charles Strouse wrote scores for a number of subsequent musicals, the most successful of these being *Golden Boy* in 1964, starring Sammy Davis in the musical adaptation of Clifford Odets' famous stage play.

The direction of Gower Champion, and the stunning performance of Carol Channing in the title role, were two strong factors in making *Hello, Dolly!* one of the most successful musical comedies of the post World War II era. This was a big, bountiful, handsomely mounted production that made no pretense that it was anything but a source of entertainment for eye and ear. Michael Stewart drew his text from the Thornton Wilder play, *The Match-*

maker; lyrics and music were the work of Jerry Herman, who had made an impressive bow on Broadway in 1961 with *Milk and Honey,* a musical with an Israeli setting.

It was Miss Channing's boisterous and effervescent performance as Dolly that endowed this show with so much of its buoyancy and bounce. During its long Broadway run, and its extended tours, *Hello, Dolly!* had to seek replacements for the starring role and found them in Ginger Rogers and Martha Raye. Both gave lustrous and personal performances. Nevertheless, the show remained basically an unforgettable Carol Channing vehicle; it was the brass and vigor of her delivery that clings to the ear and memory whenever we hear the title number.

That title number, incidentally, is one of the most formidable song hits to come from Broadway in many a year. In writing it, Jerry Herman planned a routined production number in the 1890 style and did not consider it exceptional in any way. But a Louis Armstrong recording sold over a million disks; within a year over seventy more recordings were made in the United States, and thirty-five in Europe. The number received a "Grammy" from the National Academy of Recording Arts and Sciences as "the song of the year." It was adopted as a campaign song for Lyndon B. Johnson during the Democratic National Convention in Atlantic City, New Jersey, in 1964, where it was sung by Miss Channing with Jerry Herman at the piano.

The history of "Hello, Dolly!" does not end here, but was soon to rise toward a dramatic, unexpected climax. In 1965, Mack David and Paramount-Famous Music Company brought suit against it, maintaining that it was an infringement of the copyright of "Sunflower," a song David had written and published in 1948. Apparently there was a good deal of validity to the suit. The matter was settled out of court early in 1966 for one of the largest payments ever made in copyright infringement actions, in the neighborhood of between a quarter of a million and half a million dollars, with Herman retaining the exclusive rights to his number.

Jerry Herman had another musical-comedy block buster in *Mame,* the last new musical production of the 1965–1966 season. The subject matter had previously proved successful as a novel by Patrick Dennis, as a Broadway play by Jerome Lawrence and Robert E. Lee, and as a non-musical motion picture starring Rosalind Russell. The eccentric and lovable lady who is its principal character—who gets in her charge a nephew, Patrick, whose life she begins to shape according to her own quixotic methods—was, then, no stranger when the curtain rose on *Mame* at the Winter Garden. Nevertheless, familiarity failed to breed contempt. As played by Angela Lansbury, Mame was still as irresistible as a whirlwind. There was still another thoroughly engaging performance here, that of Frankie Michaels as the ten-year-old Patrick. The Jerry Herman score—one of his best—was another strong suit, including as it did a genuine hit number in the title song (which gave more than a passing reminder of "Hello, Dolly!") and in such other memorable tunes as "If He Walks Into My Life" and "My Best Girl."

Hello, Dolly! has the distinction of being one of the ten musicals in Broadway history to run there for more than three years. Another musical joining this elect group is *How to Succeed in Business Without Really Trying* in 1961, which in addition earned the honor of becoming the fourth musical ever to capture the Pulitzer Prize for drama. For composer-lyricist Frank Loesser, this production represented a return from musical play to musical comedy. His zestful score might be more functional than original or subtle, yet it was good enough to embrace such winning numbers as "I Believe in You" and "Brotherhood of Man." As Finch, the window cleaner who rises to the highest echelon of success in business through opportunism, maneuvering and sheer gall, Robert Morse gave an infectious performance, which he later recreated for the screen. Robert Morse—supported by an altogether winning performance by Rudy Vallee as the stuffy business tycoon, J. B. Biggley—was an ingredient in this succulent stew. Another was Abe Burrows who served both as a stage director and as a collaborator of Jack Weinstock and Willie Gilbert in adapting Shepherd Mead's novel.

Still very much in the format of traditional musical comedy is *Funny Girl* (another musical to enjoy a more than three-year Broadway run). Here Barbra Streisand was lifted to the topmost rank in the musical theater. She was, however, no newcomer, having made her Broadway debut (most effectively, it must be added, though more as a comedienne than as a singer) in *I Can Get It For You Wholesale*, a musical with lyrics and music by Harold Rome, and with text by Jerome Weidman taken from his own best-selling novel. This was in 1962, when Miss Streisand was an unknown. After that show closed, her singing career soared—in night clubs, over television, and most of all in recordings. She proved herself one of the most distinguished song stylists of our time. When a musical comedy, based on the life and career of Fanny Brice, was being discussed, Barbra Streisand appeared as the logical choice for the role, first because she physically resembled Fanny Brice, then because of Miss Streisand's unique way with a song, and finally because of her consummate gift at comedy. The part, then, was tailor-made for Miss Streisand, and in it she scored a personal triumph —and not merely for the way she delivered songs like "People" and "I'm the Greatest Star" (words by Bob Merrill, music by Jule Styne), but also for the nimble way in which she moved, and almost in a split second, from the comic to the tragic, and then back again to the comic. When *Funny Girl* passed on to the screen, Barbra Streisand was once again, inevitably, the star.

Musical comedies like *Bye Bye Birdie, Hello, Dolly!* and *How to Succeed in Business Without Really Trying* may follow a basic pattern but they follow it with imagination and innovation. This is the reason why musical comedy is by no means an outmoded stage form.

Where musical comedy is frivolity and entertainment, where musical comedy uses text as a convenience for song and dance and humor, the musical play is an art form

248

concerned mainly with important human values, characterization, and sometimes even ideas. The world famous prima donna, Mary Garden, once said that when great American opera is finally written it will resemble the musical plays of people like Rodgers and Hammerstein and not those synthetic productions put on by formal opera houses. Others have said the same thing in different ways. To Leonard Bernstein, an American opera "intelligible to all" is now emerging from "our natural musical theater which is wholly an outgrowth of our culture." Kurt Weill told an interviewer: "You hear a lot of talk about American opera. It's my opinion that we can and will develop a musical-dramatic form in this country, but it will develop from and remain a part of the American theater, the Broadway theater." We have already had ample evidence that this is so—in works ranging from Jerome Kern's *Show Boat* through *South Pacific* and *Carousel* by Rodgers and Hammerstein and *My Fair Lady* by Lerner and Loewe. Some of the best musical productions mounted since 1960 continue to prove further that this is the case.

For Richard Rodgers, the post-Hammerstein period has proved a time for excruciating readjustment. Hammerstein, like Lorenz Hart before him, had been for Rodgers —probably the greatest creative figure produced by the musical play—a stimulation and an inspiration, beyond providing him with the most remarkable lyrics heard on our stage. Now that Hammerstein was gone, Rodgers had to seek out a new lyricist, after having worked so closely for over forty years with just two men; to a theater musician of Rodgers' imagination and genius, retirement was unthinkable.

For his first musical play following Hammerstein's death, Rodgers became his own lyricist. This production was *No Strings* in 1962, the libretto by Samuel Taylor. *No Strings* provided innovation on several counts. Its plot involved a love affair between a Negro girl (played by Diahann Carroll) and a young white writer (enacted by Richard Kiley). Pairing white and black in a romance was, to be sure, nothing new, but to do so easily, naturally, and without any racial consciousness whatsoever was a fresh approach. Fresher still was the way Rodgers used his orchestra. In keeping with the title of the play, he used no strings. The wind players were seated not in the pit as is customary but in the wings of the stage. From time to time, now one player, now another, now a pair or a trio, would drift informally onto the stage, stand near a character or characters, and provide a soft musical commentary to what was happening. A long established artificial barrier between the music in the pit and the action on the stage was thus broken down. Another way in which some of the old artificial barriers were broken down came in the studied attempt to "push the walls of the theater out," in Rodgers' own words: the way in which the scenery was frequently changed with the performers themselves doing the chore in full sight of the audience.

These experiments went off well. *No Strings* was a success, both as an artistic adventure and as a financial investment. As for Rodgers' musical contribution it remained, at best, top-drawer, with songs like the title number, "The Sweetest Sounds" and "Nobody Told Me." The lyrics which Rodgers fashioned for himself were consistently graceful, slick and professional.

Despite the success of *No Strings* (which carried Rodgers to first place in a national poll of critics conducted by *Variety* for the best theater composer of the year, and which brought him a "Grammy" as the best "show-cast album" of the season) Rodgers was not altogether satisfied with working on songs without the benefit of a words collaborator. He missed the give-and-take, the provocative exchange of ideas, the artistic communication which he had once found with Lorenz Hart, and later with Oscar Hammerstein II. Rodgers now went looking for a new collaborator, and thought he had found him in Alan Jay Lerner. Together they worked on a musical play tentatively entitled *I Picked a Daisy,* touching on the subject of extrasensory communication. The partnership at first went well, but in time it bogged down as two strong-willed creators became increasingly intransigent in their respective points of view. Finally, Alan Jay Lerner took his completed script, renamed it *On a Clear Day You Can See Forever,* and had Burton Lane prepare for it a new score.

Rodgers now joined with Stephen Sondheim on *Do I Hear a Waltz?* which opened on Broadway in 1965. This was a musical version of Arthur Laurents' successful play, *The Time of the Cuckoo,* describing a romance in Venice between a plain-looking American girl and a romantic Italian. The pace of the production was slow-moving, the emotion restrained, the tone *sotte voce*—and Broadway rejected it as dull. For Rodgers, the search for the ideal words collaborator must still continue.

The musical play Rodgers had planned with Alan Jay Lerner, and which Lerner finally completed with Burton Lane's music—*On a Clear Day You Can See Forever*—had one particularly powerful asset when it opened in 1965: the performance of Barbara Harris as Daisy Gamble, a "kook" with extrasensory perception. She was the actress Rodgers originally had in mind when first he conceived this idea, and she was the one who stole the show. She laid still further claim to stardom in her next musical-play vehicle, *The Apple Tree,* in 1966. This was an unusual production in that it comprised three simple and charming musical playlets. The book was based on stories by Frank R. Stockton, Jules Feiffer, and Mark Twain, and songs were contributed by Sheldon Harnick, as lyricist, and Jerry Bock, as composer. Walter Kerr described Miss Harris in the following way in the *New York Times:* "Exquisite, appetizing, alarming, seductive, out of her mind, irresistible, and from now on unavoidable. . . . 'Whatever I am, I'm certainly a beautiful one,' is practically the first remark out of her face in the opening musical playlet . . . and whoever you are you're going to agree."

The songwriting team of Sheldon Harnick and Jerry Bock became partners in the creation of one of the freshest, most original and most exciting musical plays of all time, as well as one of the most successful. *Fiddler on the Roof*, which made its triumphant appearance on Broadway in 1964, tapped a setting, a subject matter and characters completely new to the American musical theater. The material came out of the Jewish stories of Sholom Aleichem. The main characters are Teyve, a hardworking dairyman who often talks to, questions and even argues with God in a simple, direct, peasant way; his wife, Golde, a practical and occasionally acid-tongued woman; and their five daughters, whose destiny lies in making a good marriage. The background is the small Russian village of Anatevka, in 1905. Joseph Stein made the book adaptation, and Jerome Robbins was responsible for staging and choreography.

The rich folklore character of Sholom Aleichem's stories was retained magically in the text, both in the speech inflections and old-world characterizations. At the same time, a studied effort was made by Jerome Robbins to recreate the mores, the social outlook, the homely philosophy and the indigenous religious customs of the *Shtetl*—the European society in which the religious Jews lived, worked, suffered, worshiped their God, and died. Very much in the same old-world Judaic spirit are some of the production's best songs: "Sunrise, Sunset," "To Life," "Matchmaker, Matchmaker," and "If I Were a Rich Man."

The part of Teyve was originated by Zero Mostel who here and now emerged as one of the great comic performers of our generation. This was not his first musical-stage success, however. After most of a lifetime in the theater, motion pictures, on television, in night clubs—where he always found a small but devoted following—Zero Mostel finally soared to the heights of success on Broadway in 1962 in the musical farce, *A Funny Thing Happened on the Way to the Forum*. As the wheeling-dealing slave Pseudolus in ancient Rome, Mostel earned in 1963 a "Tony" as the best musical star of the year. Teyve, in

1964, brought him new and greater accolades. "If Sholom Aleichem had known Zero Mostel," wrote Howard Taubman in the *New York Times*, "he would have chosen him, one is sure, for Teyve. . . . Mr. Mostel does not keep his acting and singing or his walking and dancing in separate compartments. His Teyve is a unified, lyrical conception. . . . The scope of this performance is summed up best in moments made eloquent through music and movement."

Still another extraordinary musical play to tap fresh subject matter in a highly provocative way is *Cabaret*, in 1966. Here the source was *I Am a Camera* by John van Druten, in turn come out of *Berlin Diary*, a series of sketches by Christopher Isherwood; the adaptation was made by Joe Masteroff, with lyrics by Fred Ebb and music by John Kander. Here the setting is the decadent, demoralized Berlin of the late 1920s—specifically a shabby honky tonk where Joel Grey serves as Master of Ceremonies and Jill Hayworth (as Sally Bowles) is the main singing attraction. In addition to these two, a topflight performance is also contributed by Lotte Lenya as a drab landlady. Her place in a production like this one is uniquely appropriate since (it will surely be remembered) she was the star in the world premiere of the Kurt Weill-Bertolt Brecht musical, *The Three-Penny Opera*, which took Germany by storm in the late 1920s and put a mirror to its social, political and moral foibles and follies.

In presenting a picture of German decadence just before the rise of Nazism, *Cabaret* made no compromise. It was strong and heady brew and not just a sip of champagne. As a critic for *Variety* remarked: "Ugliness, decadence and combination of hysteria and moral lethargy were apparently the prevailing characteristic of Berlin on the eve of the Nazi takeover, and they are luridly reflected in *Cabaret*." Or as Walter Kerr put it: "It has elected to wrap its arms around all that was troubling and all that was intolerable with a demonic grin, an insidious slink, and the painted-on charm that keeps revelers up until midnight making false faces at the hangman."

Distinguished musical plays have also come from off-

Broadway. Indeed, what up to this time is the longest run in the history of the American musical theater was enjoyed by an off-Broadway musical: *Fantasticks,* which opened at the Sullivan Street Playhouse in Greenwich Village on March 3, 1960, and stayed there for more than three thousand performances. This is a thoroughly charming though off-beat little musical based on a variation of the Pierrot and Columbine theme, the idea derived from Edmond Rostand's *Les Romanesques.* Book and lyrics were by Tom Jones, and music by Harvey Schmidt, both newcomers. Original staging, a freshness of dialogue and song (the latter yielding a standard in "Try to Remember") and an overall light and graceful touch made the *Fantasticks* an endearing production. From this, Tom Jones and Harvey Schmidt graduated into Broadway proper in 1966 with a two-character musical play, *I Do, I Do,* starring Mary Martin and Robert Preston and directed by Gower Champion; it was taken from the successful Broadway stage play by Jan de Hartog, *The Fourposter.*

If any production is likely to break the long-run record of the *Fantasticks* it will be still another off-Broadway musical play—*Man of La Mancha.* It came to the Anta Washington Square Theater quietly and unobtrusively in 1965, having been tried out at the Godspeed Opera House in Connecticut without giving much of an indication that it was something super-special. But with a cast headed by Richard Kiley in the title role, with choreography by Jack Cole, and with remarkable staging by Albert Marre, *Man of La Mancha* proved a stage masterwork that made the critics chant rhapsodies, brought capacity audiences to Washington Square for several years, and captured both the New York Drama Critics Circle Award and a "Tony" as the best musical of the season.

The Dale Wasserman text described the picaresque career of Cervantes, and his brainchild Don Quixote, with the latter turning out to be Cervantes's other self. These characterizations of author and character are drawn with

254

sensitive lines, with depth of perception, with humor and pathos. As both Cervantes and Don Quixote, Kiley gave remarkably perceptive and subtly shaded delineations. "As Cervantes," said Taubman, "he is a man of spirit with a quizzical humor and a keen flexible intelligence. Shading into Quixote, he becomes the amiable visionary, childlike in his pretensions, and oddly, touchingly gallant. His eyes take on a wild, proud, otherworldly look. His posture is preternaturally erect. His folly becomes a kind of humbling wisdom." Dance and songs are beautifully and inextricably integrated into action. The score is the work of Joe Darion, lyricist, and Mitch Leigh, composer, including several outstanding numbers, the best of which are "The Impossible Dream" and "To Each His Dulcinea."

The musical theater—whether musical comedy or musical play—is, then, in a period of efflorescence. Indeed, most of the vitality of the American theater in the past few years has sprung from musical rather than nonmusical productions.

Musical comedy? Musical play? You make your choice, you buy your ticket. In either case you are likely to get an evening of enchantment.

Index

257

266

267

268

271